Understanding Object-Oriented Programming with JAVA

Timothy Budd

Oregon State University

 ADDISON-WESLEY

An imprint of Addison Wesley Longman, Inc.

Reading, Massachusetts • Harlow, England • Menlo Park, California
Berkeley, California • Don Mills, Ontario • Sydney
Bonn • Amsterdam • Tokyo • Mexico City

Acquisitions Editor: Susan Hartman
Production Editor: Patricia A. O. Unubun
Design Editor: Alwyn R. Velásquez
Packager: Jennifer Brownlow Bagdigian
Compositor: Windfall Software, Paul C. Anagnostopoulos & Jacqui Scarlott
Manufacturing Coordinator: Judy Sullivan
Cover Illustrator: Susan Cyr

Access the latest information about Addison-Wesley titles from our World Wide Web site:
http://www.awl.com/cseng

Java is a trademark of Sun Microsystems, Inc.

Many of the designations used by manufacturers and sellers to distinguish their products are claimed as trademarks. Where those designations appear in this book, and the publisher was aware of a trademark claim, the designations have been printed in initial caps or in all caps.

The programs and the applications presented in this book have been included for their instructional value. They have been tested with care but are not guaranteed for any particular purpose. Neither the publisher or the author offers any warranties or representations, nor do they accept any liabilities with respect to the programs or applications.

This book was typeset in ZzTEX on a PC. The fonts used were Sabon, Univers, MathTime, and Bell Centennial. It was printed on New Era Matte.

Library of Congress Cataloging-in-Publication Data

Budd, Timothy.
   Understanding object-oriented programming with Java / Timothy A.
Budd.
      p.   cm.
   Includes index.
   ISBN 0-201-30881-9
      1. Object-oriented programming (Computer science)   2. Java
(Computer program language)   I. Title.
   QA76.64.B835   1998
   005.13′3—dc21   97-46728
                                                             CIP
                                                             AC

ISBN 0-201-30881-9

1 2 3 4 5 6 7 8 9 10   MA   0201009998

Preface

There are many books on Java that teach you *how* to use the language, but few books that teach you *why* the language works in the way that it does.

Many books help you learn the mechanics of Java programming; few books teach you the deeper issues that lie behind the programming syntax. The goal of this book is to give the reader a fuller, more complete understanding of the philosophy behind Java, not just the mechanics of the language.

Throughout the book these principles and practices are illustrated with extensive examples from the Java standard library. Here you can learn, for example, the many design patterns that are found in the AWT, the multitude of purposes for which inheritance is used in the standard classes, and why there are 22 different types of input/output file streams. Here you can discover why the lack of an ordered container class in the standard library is not a simple omission, but is instead a reflection of a fundamental and deep property of the Java language.

In short, this book should not be considered a reference manual for the Java language, but rather a tool for understanding the Java philosophy.

STRUCTURE OF THE BOOK

The book is structured in five major sections:

Part 1 is a general, language-independent introduction to the ideas that lie at the heart of the Java world. The first major object-oriented concepts, those of classes, encapsulation, behavior, and responsibilities, will be introduced in this part and reinforced in Part 2. Here the student will be introduced to the idea that the solution to a problem can be structured as interactions among a community of agents. The second chapter of Part 1 presents a brief history of the development of Java, and can be omitted at the instructor's discretion. However, Chapter 3, on design, should in no way be avoided. In fact, I strongly encourage students to conduct at least one, if not several, design exercises using CRC cards, similar to the one presented here, even before they start to learn aspects of the Java programming language.

Part 2 introduces Java through several graduated example programs (paradigms, in the original sense of the word). These examples lead the reader through successively more of the Java language, introducing new features as they are required for specific applications. This is not a systematic introduction to all of the Java language, but rather provides examples designed to motivate the need for mechanisms discussed in other parts of the text.

Part 3 discusses inheritance, the next major object-oriented concept that the student must master after learning about classes and objects. Inheritance is a technique that is superficially obvious, but that possesses many subtle aspects that can trap the unwary programmer. The introduction of inheritance into a programming language has an impact on almost every other aspect of the language. For this reason, students familiar with conventional non-object-oriented languages should pay careful attention to this part of the book.

Part 4 discusses polymorphism, which is often an even subtler concept for the student to understand than inheritance. Polymorphism is the mechanism through which much of the power and applicability of object-oriented techniques is manifest. Polymorphism is found in Java in many ways, as shown by the extensive examples studied in this part of the book.

Part 5 discusses features of the Java world that are important for the student to understand, but not particularly notable for their object-oriented features. These items are separated from the remainder of the text so that they do not interrupt the flow of the narrative developed earlier in the book. However, the features discussed are not as difficult as their late placement in the book might indicate. At the instructor's discretion these features can be omitted altogether, or introduced in parallel with earlier material.

Obtaining the Source

Source code for the case studies presented in the book can be accessed via the mechanism of anonymous ftp from the machine `ftp.cs.orst.edu`, in the directory `/pub/budd/java`. This directory is also used to maintain a number of other items, such as an errata list. This information can also be accessed via the World Wide Web, from my personal home pages at `http://www.cs.orst.edu/~budd/`. Requests for further information can be forwarded to the electronic mail address `budd@cs.orst.edu`, or to Professor Timothy A. Budd, Department of Computer Science, Oregon State University, Corvallis, Oregon, 97331.

Acknowledgments

Invaluable advice was provided by the reviewers who examined an early draft of the book. These included Richard Anderson, University of Washington; Richard Carver, George Mason University; Deborah Frincke, University of Idaho; Matt Greenwood, Bell Laboratories; David Riley, University of Wisconsin–La Crosse; J. Richard Rinewalt, Texas Christian University.

I would like to thank my editors at Addison-Wesley, Susan Hartman and Deborah Lafferty, who patiently and quietly suffered through countless delays and postponements. It is my sincere hope that they, as well as the reader, will find the result to have been worth the wait.

Contents

II   UNDERSTANDING PARADIGMS   51

V UNDERSTANDING THE JAVA WORLD   257

16 Exception Handling   259

17 Utility Classes   267

I

Understanding the Object-Oriented Worldview

1 Object-Oriented Thinking

This is a book about object-oriented programming. In particular, this is a book that explores the principal ideas of object-oriented programming in the context of the Java programming language. Object-oriented programming has been a hot topic for over a decade, and more recently Java has become the commonly perceived embodiment of object-oriented ideas. This book will help you *understand* Java. It makes no pretensions to being a language reference manual; there are many other books that fall into that category. But knowing the syntax for a language should not be confused with understanding why the language has been developed in the way it has, why certain things are done the way they are, or why Java programs look the way they do. This book explores the *why*'s.

Object-oriented programming is frequently referred to as a new programming *paradigm*. The word "paradigm" originally meant example, or model. For example, a paradigm sentence would help you remember how to conjugate a verb in a foreign language. More generally, a model is an example that helps you understand how the world works. For example, the Newtonian model of physics explains why apples fall to the ground. In computer science, a paradigm explains how the elements that go into making a computer program are organized and how they interact with one another. For this reason the first step in understanding Java is appreciating the object-oriented worldview.

1.1 A Way of Viewing the World

To illustrate the major ideas in object-oriented programming, let us consider how we might go about handling a real-world situation and then ask how we could make the computer more closely model the techniques employed. Suppose I wish to send flowers to a friend who lives in a city many miles away. Let me call my friend Sally. Because of the distance, there is no possibility of my picking

3

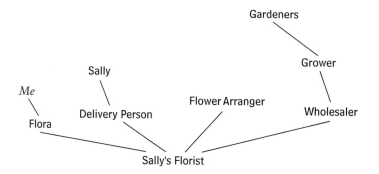

Figure 1.1   The community of agents helping me.

the flowers and carrying them to Sally's door myself. Nevertheless, sending her the flowers is an easy enough task; I merely go down to Flora, my local florist, tell her the variety and quantity of flowers I wish to send and Sally's address, and I can be assured the flowers will be delivered expediently and automatically.

1.1.1   *Agents and Communities*

At the risk of belaboring a point, let me emphasize that the mechanism I used to solve my problem was to find an appropriate *agent* (namely, Flora) and to pass to her a *message* containing my request. It is the *responsibility* of Flora to satisfy my request. There is some *method*—some algorithm or set of operations—used by Flora to do this. I do not need to know the particular method she will use to satisfy my request; indeed, often I do not want to know the details. This information is usually *hidden* from my inspection.

If I investigated, however, I might discover that Flora delivers a slightly different message to another florist in my friend's city. That florist, in turn, perhaps has a subordinate who makes the floral arrangement. The florist then passes the flowers, along with yet another message, to a delivery person, and so on. Earlier, the florist in Sally's city had obtained her flowers from a flower wholesaler who, in turn, had interactions with the flower growers, each of whom had to manage a team of gardeners.

So, our first observation of object-oriented problem solving is that the solution to my problem required the help of many other individuals (Figure 1.1). Without their help, my problem could not be easily solved. We phrase this in a general fashion as the following:

> An object-oriented program is structured as a *community* of interacting agents, called *objects*. Each object has a role to play. Each object provides a service, or performs an action, that is used by other members of the community.

1.1.2   *Messages and Methods*

The chain reaction that ultimately resulted in the solution to my program began with my request to Flora. This request led to other requests, which led to still more requests, until my flowers ultimately reached my friend. We see, therefore, that members of this community interact with one another by making requests. So, our next principle of object-oriented problem solving is the vehicle by which activities are initiated:

> Action is initiated in object-oriented programming by the transmission of a *message* to an agent (an *object*) responsible for the action. The message encodes the request for an action and is accompanied by any additional information (arguments) needed to carry out the request. The *receiver* is the object to whom the message is sent. If the receiver accepts the message, it accepts the responsibility to carry out the indicated action. In response to a message, the receiver will perform some *method* to satisfy the request.

We have noted the important principle of *information hiding* in regard to message passing—that is, the client sending the request need not know the actual means by which the request will be honored. Another all too human principle is implicit in message passing. If there is a task to perform, the first thought of the client is to find somebody else he or she can ask to do the work. This second reaction often becomes atrophied in many programmers with extensive experience in conventional techniques. Frequently, a difficult hurdle to overcome is the programmer's belief that he or she must write everything and not use the services of others. An important part of object-oriented programming is the development of reusable components, and an important first step in the use of reusable components is a willingness to trust software written by others.

Information hiding is also an important aspect of programming in conventional languages. In what sense is a message different from, say, a procedure call? In both cases, there is a set of well-defined steps that will be initiated following the request. But, there are two important distinctions.

The first is that a message has a designated *receiver*; the receiver is some object to which the message is sent. In a procedure call, there is no designated receiver.

The second is that the *interpretation* of the message (that is, the method used to respond to the message) is dependent on the receiver and can vary with different receivers. I can give a message to my wife Elizabeth, for example, and she will understand it and a satisfactory outcome will be produced (that is, flowers will be delivered to my friend). However, the method Elizabeth uses to satisfy the request (in all likelihood, simply passing the request on to Flora) will be different from that used by Flora in response to the same request. If I ask Kenneth, my dentist, to send flowers to my friend, he may not have a method for solving that problem. If he understands the request at all, he will probably issue an appropriate error diagnostic.

Let us move our discussion back to the level of computers and programs. There, the distinction between message passing and procedure calling is that message passing has a designated receiver, and the interpretation—the selection of a method to execute in response to the message—may vary with different receivers. Usually, the specific receiver for any given message will not be known until run time, so the determination of which method to invoke cannot be made until then. Thus, we say there is late *binding* between the message (function or procedure name) and the code fragment (method) used to respond to the message. This situation is in contrast to the very early (compile-time or link-time) binding of name to code fragment in conventional procedure calls.

1.1.3 *Responsibilities*

A fundamental concept in object-oriented programming is to describe behavior in terms of *responsibilities*. My request for action indicates only the desired outcome (flowers for my friend). Flora is free to pursue any technique that achieves the desired objective and is not hampered by interference on my part.

By discussing a problem in terms of responsibilities, we increase the level of abstraction. This permits greater *independence* between objects, a critical factor in solving complex problems. The entire collection of responsibilities associated with an object is often termed the *protocol*.

A traditional program often operates by acting *on* data structures, for example changing fields in an array or record. In contrast, an object-oriented program *requests* data structures (that is, objects) to perform a service. This difference between viewing software in traditional, structured terms and viewing it from an object-oriented perspective can be summarized by a twist on a well-known quote:

> Ask not what you can do *to* your data structures, but what your data structures can do *for* you.

1.1.4 *Classes and Instances*

Although I have only dealt with Flora a few times, I have a rough idea of the behavior I can expect when I walk into her shop and present my request. I am able to make certain assumptions because I have information about florists in general, and I expect that Flora, being an instance of this category, will fit the general pattern. We can use the term Florist to represent the category (or *class*) of all florists. Let us incorporate these notions into our next principle of object-oriented programming:

> All objects are *instances* of a *class*. The method invoked by an object in response to a message is determined by the class of the receiver. All objects of a given class use the same method in response to similar messages.

1.1.5   *Class Hierarchies—Inheritance*

I have more information about Flora—not necessarily because she is a florist but because she is a shopkeeper. I know, for example, that I probably will be asked for money as part of the transaction, and that in return for payment I will be given a receipt. These actions are true of grocers, stationers, and other shopkeepers. Since the category Florist is a more specialized form of the category Shopkeeper, any knowledge I have of Shopkeepers is also true of Florists and hence of Flora.

One way to think about how I have organized my knowledge of Flora is in terms of a hierarchy of categories (see Figure 1.2). Flora is a Florist, but Florist is a specialized form of Shopkeeper. Furthermore, a Shopkeeper is also a Human; so I know, for example, that Flora is probably bipedal. A Human is a Mammal (therefore they nurse their young and have hair), and a Mammal is an Animal (therefore it breathes oxygen), and an Animal is a Material Object (therefore it has mass and weight). Thus, quite a lot of knowledge that I have that is applicable to Flora is not directly associated with her, or even with her category Florist.

The principle that knowledge of a more general category is also applicable to a more specific category is called *inheritance*. We say that the class Florist will inherit attributes of the class (or category) Shopkeeper.

Another graphical technique is often used to illustrate this relationship, particularly when there are many individuals with differing lineages. This technique

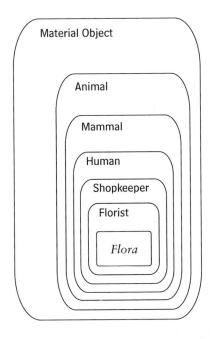

Figure 1.2   The categories surrounding Flora.

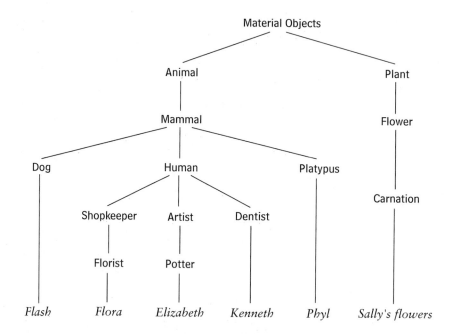

Figure 1.3   A class hierarchy for various material objects.

shows classes listed in a hierarchical treelike structure, with more abstract classes (such as Material Object or Animal) listed near the top of the tree, and more specific classes, and finally individuals, listed near the bottom. Figure 1.3 shows this class hierarchy for Flora. This same hierarchy also includes Elizabeth, my dog Flash, Phyl the platypus who lives at the zoo, and the flowers I am sending to my friend.

Information that I possess about Flora because she is an instance of class Human is also applicable to my wife Elizabeth. Information that I have about her because she is a Mammal is applicable to Flash as well. Information about all members of Material Object is equally applicable to Flora and to her flowers. We capture this in the idea of inheritance:

> Classes can be organized into a hierarchical *inheritance* structure. A *child class* (or *subclass*) will inherit attributes from a *parent class* higher in the tree. An *abstract parent class* is a class (such as Mammal) for which there are no direct instances; it is used only to create subclasses.

1.1.6   *Method Binding, Overriding, and Exceptions*

Phyl the platypus presents a problem for our simple organizing structure. I know that mammals give birth to live offspring, and Phyl is certainly a Mammal, yet

Phyl (or rather his mate Phyllis) lays eggs. To accommodate this variation, we need to find a technique to encode *exceptions* to a general rule.

We do this by decreeing that information contained in a subclass can *override* information inherited from a parent class. Most often, implementations of this approach take the form of a method in a subclass having the same name as a method in the parent class, combined with a rule stating how to conduct the search for a method to match a specific message:

> The search for a method to invoke in response to a given message begins with the *class* of the receiver. If no appropriate method is found, the search is conducted in the *parent class* of this class. The search continues up the parent class chain until either a method is found or the parent class chain is exhausted. In the former case the method is executed; in the latter case, an error message is issued. If methods with the same name can be found higher in the class hierarchy, the method executed is said to *override* the inherited behavior.

Even if the compiler cannot determine which method will be invoked at run time, in many object-oriented languages, such as Java, it can determine whether there will be an appropriate method and issue an error message as a compile-time error diagnostic rather than as a run-time message.

That my wife Elizabeth and my florist Flora will respond to my message by different methods is an example of one form of *polymorphism*, an important aspect of object-oriented programming discussed in Chapter 12. As explained, that I do not, and need not, know exactly what method Flora will use to honor my message is an example of *information hiding*.

1.1.7   *Summary of Object-Oriented Concepts*

Alan Kay, considered by some to be the father of object-oriented programming (OOP), identified the following characteristics as fundamental to OOP [Kay 1993]:

1. Everything is an *object*.

2. Computation is performed by objects communicating with each other, requesting that other objects perform actions. Objects communicate by sending and receiving *messages*. A message is a request for action bundled with whatever arguments may be necessary to complete the task.

3. Each object has its own *memory*, which consists of other objects.

4. Every object is an *instance* of a *class*. A class simply represents a grouping of similar objects, such as integers or lists.

5. The class is the repository for *behavior* associated with an object. That is, all objects that are instances of the same class can perform the same actions.

6. Classes are organized into a singly rooted tree structure, called the *inheritance hierarchy*. Memory and behavior associated with instances of a class are automatically available to any class associated with a descendant in this tree structure.

1.2   COMPUTATION AS SIMULATION

The view of programming represented by the example of sending flowers to my friend is very different from the conventional conception of a computer. The traditional model describing the behavior of a computer executing a program is a *process-state* or *pigeonhole* model. In this view, the computer is a data manager, following some pattern of instructions, wandering through memory, pulling values out of various slots (memory addresses), transforming them in some manner, and pushing the results back into other slots (see Figure 1.4). By examining the values in the slots, we can determine the state of the machine or the results produced by a computation. Although this model may be a more or less accurate picture of what takes place inside a computer, it does little to help us understand how to solve problems using the computer, and it is certainly not the way most people (pigeon handlers and postal workers excepted) go about solving problems.

In contrast, in the object-oriented framework we never mention memory addresses, variables, assignments, or any of the conventional programming terms. Instead, we speak of objects, messages, and responsibility for some action. In Dan Ingalls's memorable phrase:

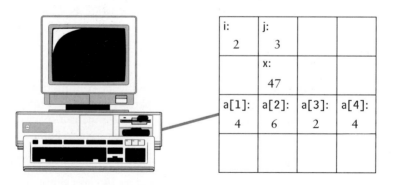

Figure 1.4   Visualization of imperative programming.

> Instead of a bit-grinding processor . . . plundering data structures, we have a universe of well-behaved objects that courteously ask each other to carry out their various desires. [Ingalls 1981]

Another author has described object-oriented programming as "animistic": a process of creating a host of helpers that form a community and assist the programmer in the solution of a problem (see the *Actor Language Manual*) [Actor 1987].

This view of programming as creating a "universe" is in many ways similar to a style of computer simulation called "discrete event-driven simulation." In brief, in a discrete event-driven simulation the user creates computer models of the various elements of the simulation, describes how they will interact with one another, and sets them moving. This is almost identical to the average object-oriented program, in which the user describes what the various entities in the universe for the program are, and how they will interact, and finally sets them in motion. Thus, in object-oriented programming, we have the view that *computation is simulation* [Kay 1977].

1.2.1   *The Power of Metaphor*

An easily overlooked benefit to the use of object-oriented techniques is the power of *metaphor*. When programmers think about problems in terms of behaviors and responsibilities of objects, they bring with them a wealth of intuition, ideas, and understanding from their everyday experience. When solutions to problems are envisioned as pigeonholes, mailboxes, or slots containing values, there is little in the programmer's background to provide insight into how problems should be structured.

Although anthropomorphic descriptions such as the quote by Ingalls may strike some people as odd, in fact they reflect the great expositive power of metaphor. Journalists make use of metaphor every day, as in the following description of object-oriented programming from *Newsweek*:

> Unlike the usual programming method—writing software one line at a time—NeXT's "object-oriented" system offers larger building blocks that developers can quickly assemble the way a kid builds faces on Mr. Potato Head.

Possibly it is this power of metaphor, more than any other feature, that is responsible for the frequent observation that it is often easier to teach object-oriented programming concepts to computer novices than to computer professionals. Novice users quickly adapt the metaphors with which they are already comfortable from their everyday life, whereas seasoned computer professionals are blinded by an adherence to more traditional ways of viewing computation.

As you start to examine the Java programs presented in the book, as well as create your own Java programs, you may find it useful to envision the process of programming as like the task of "training" a universe of agents to interact smoothly with each other, each providing a certain small and well-defined service to the others, each contributing to the effective execution of the whole. Think about how you have organized communities of individuals, such as a club or committee. Each member of the group is given certain responsibilities, and the achievement of the goals for the organization depends upon each member fulfilling his or her role.

1.3 CHAPTER SUMMARY

- Object-oriented programming is not simply a few new features added to programming languages. Rather, it is a new way of *thinking* about the process of decomposing problems and developing programming solutions.

- Object-oriented programming views a program as a collection of loosely connected agents, termed *objects*. Each object is responsible for specific tasks. It is by the interaction of objects that computation proceeds. In a certain sense, therefore, programming is nothing more or less than the simulation of a model universe.

- An object is an encapsulation of *state* (data values) and *behavior* (operations). Thus, an object is in many ways similar to a module or an abstract data type.

- The behavior of objects is dictated by the object *class*. Every object is an instance of some class. All instances of the same class will behave in a similar fashion (that is, invoke the same method) in response to a similar request.

- An object will exhibit its behavior by invoking a method (similar to executing a procedure) in response to a message. The interpretation of the message (that is, the specific method used) is decided by the object and may differ from one class of objects to another.

- Objects and classes extend the concept of abstract data types by adding the notion of *inheritance*. Classes can be organized into a hierarchical inheritance tree. Data and behavior associated with classes higher in the tree can also be accessed and used by classes lower in the tree. Such classes are said to inherit their behavior from the parent classes.

- Designing an object-oriented program is like organizing a community of individuals. Each member of the community is given certain responsibilities. The achievement of the goals for the community as a whole comes about through the work of each member, and the interactions of members with each other.

- By reducing the interdependency among software components, object-oriented programming permits the development of reusable software systems. Such components can be created and tested as independent units, in isolation from other portions of a software application.

- Reusable software components permit the programmer to deal with problems on a higher level of abstraction. We can define and manipulate objects simply in terms of the messages they understand and a description of the tasks they perform, ignoring implementation details.

Further Reading

I said at the beginning of the chapter that this is not a reference manual. The reference manual written by the developers of the language, James Gosling, Billy Joy, and Guy Steele is [Gosling, Joy, and Steele 1996]. But perhaps even more useful for most programmers is the annotated description of the Java class library presented by Patrick Chan and Rosanna Lee [Chan 1996]. Information on the internal workings of the Java system is presented by Tim Lindholm and Frank Yellin [Lindholm and Yellin 1997].

I noted earlier that many consider Alan Kay to be the father of object-oriented programming. Like most simple assertions, this one is only somewhat supportable. Kay himself [Kay 1993] traces much of the influence on his development of Smalltalk to the earlier computer programming language Simula, developed in Scandinavia in the early 1960s by Ole-Johan Dahl and Kristen Nygaard [Dahl and Nygaard 1966]. A more accurate history would be that most of the principles of object-oriented programming were fully worked out by the developers of Simula, but that these would have been largely ignored by the profession had they not been rediscovered by Kay in the creation of the Smalltalk programming language. I will discuss the history of OOP in more detail in the next chapter.

Like most terms that have found their way into the popular jargon, *object-oriented* is used more often than it is defined. Thus, the question What is object-oriented programming? is surprisingly difficult to answer. Bjarne Stroustrup has quipped that many arguments appear to boil down to the following syllogism:

- X is good.
- Object-oriented is good.
- *Ergo,* X is object-oriented [Stroustrup 1988].

Roger King argued [Kim and Lochovsky 1989], that his cat is object-oriented. After all, a cat exhibits characteristic behavior, responds to messages, is heir to a long tradition of inherited responses, and manages its own quite independent internal state.

Many authors have tried to provide a precise description of the properties a programming language must possess to be called *object-oriented*. I myself have written an earlier book [Budd 1997] that tries to explain object-oriented concepts in a language-independent fashion. See also, for example, the analysis by Josephine Micallef [1998], or Peter Wegner [1986]. Wegner, distinguishes *object-based* languages, which support only abstraction (such as Ada), from *object-oriented* languages, which must also support inheritance.

Other authors—notably Brad Cox [1990]—define the term much more broadly. To Cox, object-oriented programming represents the *objective* of programming by assembling solutions from collections of off-the-shelf subcomponents, rather than any particular *technology* we may use to achieve this objective. Rather than drawing lines that are divisive, we should embrace any and all means that show promise in leading to a new software industrial revolution. Cox's book on OOP [Cox 1986], although written early in the development of object-oriented programming and now somewhat dated in details, is nevertheless one of the most readable manifestos of the object-oriented movement.

Study Questions

1. What is the original meaning of the word *paradigm*?

2. How do objects interact with one another?

3. How are messages different from procedure calls?

4. What is the name applied to an algorithm an object uses to respond to a request?

5. Why does the object-oriented approach naturally imply a high degree of information hiding?

6. What is a class? How are classes linked to behavior?

7. What is a class inheritance hierarchy? How is it linked to classes and behavior?

8. What does it mean for one method to override another method from a parent class?

9. What are the basic elements of the process-state model of computation?

10. How does the object-oriented model of computation differ from the process-state model?

11. In what way is an object-oriented program like a simulation?

Exercises

1. In an object-oriented inheritance hierarchy, each level is a more specialized form of the preceding level. Give an example of a hierarchy found in everyday life that has this property. Some types of hierarchy found in everyday

life are not inheritance hierarchies. Give an example of a hierarchy that is not an inheritance hierarchy.

2. Look up the definition of *paradigm* in at least three dictionaries. Relate these definitions to computer programming languages.

3. Take a real-world problem, like the task of sending flowers described earlier, and describe its solution in terms of agents (objects) and responsibilities.

4. Consider an object in the real world, such as a pet. Describe some of the classes, or categories, to which the object belongs. Can you organize these categories into an inheritance hierarchy? What knowledge concerning the object is represented in each category?

5. If you are familiar with two or more distinct computer programming languages, give an example of a problem showing how one language would direct the programmer to one type of solution, and a different language would encourage an alternative solution.

6. Argue either for or against the position that computing is basically simulation. (You may want to read the article by Alan Kay in *Scientific American* [Kay 1977].)

2. A Brief History of Object-Oriented Programming

It is commonly thought that object-oriented programming (OOP) is a relatively recent phenomenon in computer science. To the contrary in fact, almost all the major concepts we now associate with object-oriented programs, such as objects, classes, and inheritance hierarchies, were developed in the 1960s as part of a language called Simula, designed by researchers at the Norwegian Computing Center. Simula, as the name suggests, was a language inspired by problems involving the simulation of real-life systems. However the importance of these constructs, even to the developers of Simula, was only slowly recognized [Nygaard and Dahl 1981].

In the 1970s Alan Kay organized a research group at Xerox PARC (the Palo Alto Research Center). With great prescience, Kay predicated the coming revolution in personal computing that was to develop nearly a decade later (see, for example, his 1977 article in *Scientific American* [Kay 1977]). Kay was concerned with discovering a programming language that would be understandable to people who were not computer professionals, to ordinary people with no prior training in computer use.[1] He found in the notion of classes and computing as simulation a metaphor that could easily be understood by novice users, as he then demonstrated by a series of experiments conducted at PARC using children as programmers. The programming language developed by his group was named Smalltalk. This language evolved through several revisions during

---

[1] I have always found it ironic that Kay missed an important point. He thought that to *use* a computer one would be required to *program* a computer. Although he correctly predicated in 1977 the coming trend in hardware, few could have predicated at that time the rapid development of general purpose computer applications that was to accompany, perhaps even drive, the introduction of personal computers. Nowadays the vast majority of people who use personal computers have no idea how to program.

the decade. A widely read 1981 issue of *Byte* magazine, in which the remark by Ingalls quoted in the first chapter appears, did much to popularize the concepts developed by Kay and his team at Xerox.

Roughly contemporaneous with Kay's work was another project being conducted on the other side of the country. Bjarne Stroustrup, a researcher at Bell Laboratories who had learned Simula while completing his doctorate at Cambridge University in England, was developing an extension to the C language that would facilitate the creation of objects and classes [Stroustrup 1982]. This was eventually to evolve into the language C++ [Stroustrup 1994].

With the dissemination of information on these and similar projects, an explosion of research in object-oriented programming techniques began. By the time of the first major conference on object-oriented programming, in 1986, there were literally dozens of new programming languages vieing for acceptance. These included Eiffel [Meyer 1988], Objective-C [Cox 1986], Actor, Object Pascal, and various Lisp dialects.

In the decade since the 1986 OOPSLA conference, object-oriented programming has moved from being revolutionary to being mainstream, and in the process has transformed a major portion of the field of computer science as a whole.

2.1   THE HISTORY OF JAVA

The language we now call Java was originally named Oak, and was developed in 1991 by a computer scientist at Sun Microsystems named James Gosling. Oak's intended purpose was as a language for use in embedded consumer electronic applications, such as VCRs. Although this intended use might at first seem to be only a bit of historical computer trivia, in fact it was important in determining the characteristics of the language we see today.

In designing Oak, Gosling envisioned a world where many electronic devices, such as your telephone, your VCR, your television, your computer, would all be connected together over a vast computer network. Such applications would generally possess embedded computer processors, which would control the essential running of the component. (Although we have not yet reached the point where telephones are routinely connected to the Internet, the part about electronic devices having embedded processors is now almost universally true.)

Several characteristics of embedded systems make them different from the average general purpose computer. Two of the most important features are size and reliability. Generally, the processors that run in embedded systems are very small, possessing only meager amounts of memory. Thus, a programming language designed for an embedded system must be able to be translated into a very concise encoding. An even more important aspect is reliability. When a program fails on a typical general purpose computer, the user is annoyed, but even in the worst case the user can generally recover and continue the program by rebooting the computer. The annoyance is greater if, for example, the software controlling a telephone fails. For this reason embedded systems should almost never fail, and should respond as gracefully as possible to exceptional and erroneous conditions.

Many features of Java reflect this original mindset. The language itself is small and simple, and can be translated into a very compact internal representation. Programming constructs, such as pointers or the goto statement, which experience had shown to be a source of many programming errors, were simply eliminated from the language. A powerful concept called exception handling was borrowed from earlier languages but greatly extended and intimately tied into the other aspects of the language. This *exception-handling* facility meant that any programmer writing in Java would be forced to deal with the possibilities of how programs could fail in unpredictable ways, and create code to handle the unexpected in a (hopefully) graceful fashion.

For a number of reasons, Java (or Oak) as a language for embedded consumer electronics did not materialize. But as interest in embedded systems at Sun was starting to wane, the phenomenon known as the World Wide Web was just beginning. The Web was originally developed in the early 1990s by a small group of scientists at a research lab in Switzerland as a means of quickly communicating research results to a physically far-flung set of colleagues. It was quickly realized, however, that the framework provided by the Web was applicable to a wide range of information. First, scientists in all disciplines started using the Web, and eventually the ideas found their way into the mainstream. Now, almost every organization, large or small, must have a Web page. Similarly, almost every advertisement in print or television contains an obligatory Web address (the universal resource locator, or URL).

To understand how Java fits into the World Wide Web, and to grasp the importance of Internet computing, one must first understand a little about the concept of clients and servers, and the difference between server-side computing and client-side computing.

2.2 CLIENT-SIDE COMPUTING

Although Java is a general purpose programming language that can be used to create almost any type of computer program, much of the excitement surrounding Java has been generated by its employment as a language for creating programs intended for execution across the Internet. To understand the process of programming for the Web, one must first understand a few basic characteristics of the Internet in general. The Internet is a classic example of a *client/server* system. A person using the Internet works at his or her own computer, which runs an Internet-aware application, such as a Web browser (Figure 2.1). This is

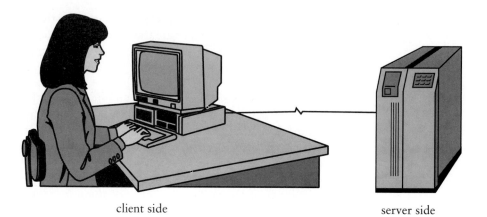

client side   server side

Figure 2.1   Client and server-side computing.

called the *client* system. The client application communicates over the Internet with another computer, perhaps one physically very far away. For example, a Web browser might request the information on a Web page stored on a distant computer. The second computer, the *server* computer, transmits the contents of the Web page to the client application. The client computer then determines how to display this information to the user.

From the beginning of the Web, it has been possible to add dynamic behavior to Web pages by executing programs. However, in the past these programs executed on the server computer. The client transmitted a request, and the server responded by executing a program, and transmitting the result. Many Web-based forms are still implemented in this fashion. Such an arrangement is sometimes termed *CGI–bin* processing, after the directory where executable programs are conventionally located on the server computer.

Several problems occur with this arrangement. For one, transmission times are often slow, causing a noticeable delay between the moment when the client asks that a program be executed and the time the results are returned. In addition, server programs often deal with many clients at once (perhaps hundreds or thousands), further reducing performance. In contrast, the client machines are often lightly loaded personal machines. Frequently the client machine is executing little more than the single Internet application.

The key idea of *client-side* computing is that rather than executing the program on the server side and transmitting the result, the server will transmit the *program* to the client. The client will then execute the program locally. Not only is the program then run on a less heavily loaded system, but the only delay is the time to transmit the program. Once the program starts executing, any interactions between the user and the program take place locally, and do not need to cross the Internet.

2.2.1 *Bytecode Interpreters and Just In Time Compilers*

Of course, many difficulties must be overcome for this process to succeed. The first is that the client computer must be able to execute the program. Often the server and client machines will be different types of computers. Indeed, the client may not even know what type of machine the server is using. Thus, the traditional concept of computer programs being translated into machine code for a specific machine will not work in this environment; machine code that executes well on the server computer may not work at all for the client computer.

Instead, Java is translated into a device-independent *bytecode*. This bytecode (so-called because most instructions are one or two bytes long), is like a machine language for an imaginary machine, a Java-specific machine, or *virtual machine*. Each computer that runs Java programs then processes these bytecodes into a form that works correctly on the current system.

There are several ways this can be done. The easiest scheme is to have an *interpreter* that reads and executes bytecodes one by one as they are needed. Better performance can be obtained by using a *just-in-time (JIT) compiler*. This system takes the Java bytecodes and translates them into the machine code native to the client system. These programs then run as fast as any compiled program created specifically for the client computer.

2.2.2 *Security Issues*

Another problem that must be overcome for client-side computing to be widely accepted is the issue of security. A program running on a server machine can do very little damage to a client machine; the server simply does not have access to memory or to files to which damage could be done. But a program running on the client side could, in theory, have full access to the client computer resources. There is great potential for such a program to do significant damage, such as erasing files from a hard drive.

Java programs get around this problem by using a *security manager*. The security manager is provided by the client, and limits the actions that can be performed by the Java program provided by the server. For example, most security managers will not allow a Java program to access the file system or to transmit information across the Internet to machines other than the client or server processors. Thus, the potential damage that a Java program can cause is very limited.

Despite the use of a security manager, the issue of security remains one of the more controversial aspects of Java programming. In fact, the security manager is only part of a multilayer approach to providing security for client machines that run Java programs. Despite these, the short history of experiences with computer viruses and other attacks should caution us that a truly malicious programmer can probably still find weaknesses to exploit. However, the use of techniques such as the security manager has made the task of the malicious programmer greatly more difficult.

2.2.3   *Specialization of Interfaces*

Yet another issue arises due to the fact that the client and server systems can be entirely different types of computers. As anybody who has tried to write a graphical program in another language for multiple platforms has discovered, the sequences of commands needed to perform graphical operations, such as placing a window on the display, varies greatly from one machine to another. As will be explained in Section 15.11, the solution to this problem requires a careful coordination between the client and server computers, with portions of a Java program originating on one machine, and other parts coming from the second.

The server program is structured in terms of generic classes, such as Window and Button. These classes are the same regardless of the type of system on which the Java program is run. But when executed, the first task these components perform is to create a *peer* component. The peer component originates on the client system and is not part of the server program. Thus, a button running on a PC will create a PC-Button peer, while the same program running on a Macintosh will create a Mac-Button peer. All the device-specific aspects of drawing the image on the local computer system are held in the peer class, and not in the generic button class.

2.3   THE WHITE PAPER DESCRIPTION

In one of the first papers published by Sun Microsystems that dealt with Java, the language was described in the following fashion:

> Java: A simple, object-oriented, network-savvy, interpreted, robust, secure, architecture neutral, portable, high-performance, multithreaded, dynamic language.

The tongue-in-cheek description is intentionally reminiscent of the hyperbole-laden and buzzword-heavy descriptions characteristic of advertising copy. Nevertheless, each phrase had been carefully selected, and in total they accurately sum up the language.

2.3.1   *Java Is Simple*

Although much of the syntax of Java is based on the earlier object-oriented language C++, the Java language is considerably simpler than C++. Many keywords have been eliminated, there is no preprocessor, there are far fewer special cases, and the language is augmented with a much larger library of high-level development tools. Confusing features such as operator overloading have been eliminated, as have independent functions, global variables, the goto statement, structures and pointers.

One of the more notable omissions from Java is the latter, the concept of the pointer. In many other languages there is a distinction between a *value* and a *pointer to a value*. Values are static, fixed-size entities. Pointers are dynamic quantities that are filled at run time. As explained in Chapter 11, there are important reasons why an object-oriented language should make heavy use of pointers. Java does so, but hides this fact from the programmer. As far as the programmer is concerned, there are no pointers, although in truth this illusion is only possible because almost everything is internally a pointer. However, the elimination of this construct removes an entire class of common programming errors, making it greatly easier to construct reliable and correct programs.

2.3.2 *Java Is Object-Oriented*

The language Java is founded upon the object-oriented principles described in Chapter 1. The only unit of programming is the class description. Unlike other languages, Java has no functions and no variables that can exist outside of class boundaries. Thus, all Java programs must be built out of objects. Other languages, notably C++ and Object Pascal, have tried to combine object-oriented features on top of an existing, non–object-oriented language. The unfortunate consequence of such a design is that programmers can continue working in their old, non–object-oriented fashion. By forcing all programs into an object-oriented structure, the many benefits of object-oriented design (an emphasis on encapsulation, an orientation toward reusability) are much more easily realized.

2.3.3 *Java Is Network Savvy*

From the start, Java was designed with the Internet in mind. Although it is possible to construct Java programs that do not deal with the Internet (indeed, most of the programs in this book will not), the language provides a rich set of tools for programming across a network. The Java standard library provides a plethora of classes for describing universal resource locators (URLs), for making connections between client and server computers (see Chapter 21), and for execution in controlled environments such as a World Wide Web browser.

2.3.4 *Java Is Interpreted*

Java was designed for a multicomputer execution environment. From the first, it was intended that the computer a program was developed on might not be the same as the computer on which it is stored, which might again be different from the computer on which it is finally executed. Thus, the traditional model where a program is translated by a *compiler* into the machine language for a particular machine will not work for Java; the machine language for the system on which the program is developed will probably not work for the machine on which the program is eventually executed.

Java systems initially got around this problem by using an *interpreter*. Java programs were compiled into an assembly language for an imaginary machine, called the *virtual machine*. These assembly language instructions, called *bytecodes*, could be stored on any type of machine. Any machine that supported Java programs would provide a simulator, an *interpreter*, that would read the bytecode values and execute them. In this fashion, any type of computer could be used as a Java virtual machine.

However, interpreters have one serious disadvantage over conventional systems. They are generally much slower in execution. Recent innovations in the Java world have advanced upon this idea of interpreters, and largely eliminated this performance penalty. A *just-in-time (JIT) compiler* is a system that reads the machine-independent bytecode representation of a Java program, and immediately prior to execution translates the bytecode representation into actual machine instructions for the system on which the Java program is being run. Because Java programs then execute as machine instructions, they can be almost as fast as programs compiled in more conventional languages for the specific hardware platform, and still retain the portability of the virtual machine.

2.3.5 *Java Is Robust*

The Java language and associated libraries are designed to be graceful in the presence of hardware and software errors. An example of this is the extensive use of *exception handling*. Statements that can potentially receive an error, such as a file operation that could attempt to read from a nonexistent source, will generate an exception instead of performing an erroneous operation. The semantics of the language insist that the programmer *must* deal with this possibility any time a file operation is intended. Thus, programmers are forced into thinking about potential sources of error, and their programs are therefore much more robust in the presence of error-producing conditions.

Another feature that makes Java programs more robust is automatic memory management, or garbage collection. Programmers writing in languages that use manual memory management, for example C++, frequently forget to release memory resources once they are finished with them. Long-running programs therefore slowly increase their memory requirements, until they catastrophically fail. The Java run-time system instead automatically detects and recovers memory that is no longer being used by the currently running program. This both simplifies the programmer's task and makes programs more reliable.

2.3.6 *Java Is Secure*

By eliminating pointers, the Java language removes what is perhaps the most common source of programming errors, inadvertently overwriting memory locations that are being addressed by pointers with improperly set values. The Java language also insists that array index values are checked for validity before they are referenced and that all variables must be assigned a value before being used.

But the Java language is just the first layer in a multilevel security system. Bytecodes themselves (which may or may not have been produced by a Java compiler) are examined before they are executed by the Java interpreter. This check determines that bytecodes are free of a number of common errors, for example that they do not access classes incorrectly, overflow or underflow the operand stack, or use illegal data conversions.

Finally, as we will discuss in Chapter 21, many of the applications envisioned for Java involve programs that are stored on one computer but executed on another. Typically, the computer on which the Java program will execute is a user's personal computer. Few users would trust Java if it were possible that programs brought over a network could possibly cause damage, such as erasing a hard drive or removing a file. For this reason, the designers of Java purposely created a programming environment where programs are severely restricted in the type of operations they can perform. Because of these restrictions, users can be largely assured that when they execute a program brought over the network, their local computer is safe from tampering.

2.3.7 *Java Is Architecture Neutral*

Because Java bytecodes do not correspond to any particular machine, they work with all machines. A Java program is the same whether it runs on a PC, a Macintosh, or a Unix system. This is very different from conventional languages. Although C++ is a standard language, and therefore should be the same on all machines, the libraries needed to perform activities such as placing a window on a display, or responding to a button press, differ considerably from one platform to another. This is why it is very difficult to, for example, move programs designed for the PC onto a Macintosh, or vice versa. But Java hides these application-specific details under a layer of abstraction in the standard Java library. Thus, from the programmer's point of view, all machines look the same.

2.3.8 *Java Is Portable*

Because the Java library hides architecture-specific concepts, and because bytecodes are the same regardless of the machine on which they are generated, Java programs possess an unparalleled degree of portability. Indeed, the exact same program can be compiled on one system, then executed on many different types of systems.

2.3.9 *Java Is High-performance*

Although the initial implementations of Java bytecode interpreters exacted a heavy performance penalty, the technology of Java execution has rapidly evolved since the language was introduced. Systems such as just-in-time compilers now allow platform-independent Java programs to be executed with nearly the same run-time performance as conventional compiled languages.

2.3.10 *Java Is Multithreaded*

Java is one of the first languages to be designed explicitly for the possibility of multiple threads of execution running in one program. As shown in Chapter 20, not only is it easy to set up such multitasking, but the coordination of these parallel processes is also relatively simple.

2.3.11 *Java Is Dynamic*

Finally, because Java programs move across the Internet and execute on the user's local computer, they permit a degree of dynamic behavior impossible in older style systems.

2.4 CHAPTER SUMMARY

Although much of the excitement of Java stems from its use in developing Web-based application programs, or *applets*, the Java language itself is a general purpose programming language suitable for any task that can be solved using a computer. For most of this book we will deal with more general application programs. We will return to a discussion of Web-based programming and applets in Chapter 21.

The intent of this book is to discuss the principles of object-oriented programming, and in particular the way that object-oriented concepts are manifest in the Java programming language. Nevertheless, an understanding of Java is not possible without an appreciation of the history and intent of the language. In this chapter we have examined how the Java language was developed and the original purpose for the language. The characteristics required for this original purpose, namely a small language with a high degree of reliability, turn out also to be desirable characteristics for any programming language. Thus, the Java language has potential uses that far exceed the original designers' intent.

STUDY QUESTIONS

1. What was the name of the first object-oriented language? In what country was it developed?

2. What problem was the research group founded by Alan Kay concerned with when they developed the language Smalltalk?

3. What was the original name given to the Java language?

4. What was the original intended use of Java programs?

5. What are some characteristics of embedded systems?

6. What is the difference between server-side computing (also known as CGI-bin processing) and client-side computing?

7. What is a bytecode interpreter?

8. What is a just-in-time compiler?

EXERCISES

1. Read Alan Kay's 1977 paper in *Scientific American*. List the issues that Kay thought would be important when truly personal computers attained widespread use. In hindsight, in what ways were his predictions correct, and in what ways did his predictions miss the mark?

2. Try to identify all the embedded computer processors found in a typical home.

3 Object-Oriented Design

A superficial description of the distinction between an object-oriented language, such as Java, and a conventional programming language, such as Pascal, might concentrate on syntactic differences. In this area discussion would center on topics such as classes, inheritance, message passing, and methods. But such an analysis would miss the most important point of object-oriented programming, which has nothing to do with syntax.

Working in an object-oriented language (that is, one that supports inheritance, message passing, and classes) is neither a necessary nor sufficient condition for doing object-oriented programming. As emphasized in Chapter 1, an object-oriented program is like a community of interacting individuals, each having assigned responsibilities, working together toward the attainment of a common goal. As in real life, a major aspect in the design of such a community is determining the specific responsibilities for each member. To this end, practitioners of object-oriented design have developed a design technique driven by the specification and delegation of responsibilities. Rebecca Wirfs-Brock and Brian Wilkerson have called this technique *responsibility-driven design* [Wirfs-Brock 1989, 1990].

3.1 RESPONSIBILITY IMPLIES NONINTERFERENCE

As anyone can attest who can remember being a child, or who has raised children, responsibility is a sword that cuts both ways. When you make an object (be it a child or a software system) responsible for specific actions, you expect a certain behavior, at least when the rules are observed. But just as important, responsibility implies a degree of independence or noninterference. If you tell a child that she is responsible for cleaning her room, you do not normally stand over her and watch while that task is being performed—that is not the nature of

29

responsibility. Instead, you expect that, having issued a directive in the correct fashion, the desired outcome will be produced.

Similarly, in the floral delivery example from Chapter 1, I give the request to deliver flowers to my florist without stopping to think about how my request will be serviced. Flora, having taken on the responsibility for this service, is free to operate without interference on my part.

The difference between conventional programming and object-oriented programming is in many ways the difference between actively supervising a child while she performs a task, and delegating to the child responsibility for that performance. Conventional programming proceeds largely by doing something *to* something else—modifying a record or updating an array, for example. Thus, one portion of code in a software system is often intimately tied, by control and data connections, to many other sections of the system. Such dependencies can come about through the use of global variables, through use of pointer values, or simply through inappropriate use of and dependence on implementation details of other portions of code. A responsibility-driven design attempts to cut these links, or at least make them as unobtrusive as possible.

This notion might at first seem no more subtle than the notions of information hiding and modularity, which are important to programming even in conventional languages. But responsibility-driven design elevates information hiding from a technique to an art. The principle of information hiding becomes vitally important when one moves from programming in the small to programming in the large.

One of the major benefits of object-oriented programming is reaped when software subsystems are reused from one project to the next. For example, a simulation system might work for both a simulation of balls on a billiards table and a simulation of fish in a fish tank. This ability to reuse code implies that the software can have almost no domain-specific components; it must totally delegate responsibility for domain-specific behavior to application-specific portions of the system. The ability to create such reusable code is not one that is easily learned—it requires experience, careful examination of case studies (paradigms, in the original sense of the word), and use of a programming language in which such delegation is natural and easy to express. In subsequent chapters, we will look at several such examples.

3.2   PROGRAMMING IN THE SMALL AND IN THE LARGE

The difference between the development of individual projects and of more sizable software systems is often described as programming in the small versus programming in the large. *Programming in the small* characterizes projects with the following attributes:

- Code is developed by a single programmer, or perhaps by a very small collection of programmers. A single individual can understand all aspects of a project, from top to bottom, beginning to end.

- The major problem in the software development process is the design and development of algorithms for dealing with the problem at hand.

Programming in the large, on the other hand, characterizes software projects with features such as the following:

- The software system is developed by a large team of programmers. Individuals involved in the specification or design of the system may differ from those involved in the coding of individual components, who may differ as well from those involved in the integration of various components in the final product. No single individual can be considered responsible for the entire project or even necessarily understand all aspects of the project.

- The major problem in the software development process is the management of details and the communication of information between diverse portions of the project.

While the beginning student will usually be acquainted with programming in the small, aspects of many object-oriented languages are best understood as responses to the problems encountered while programming in the large. Thus, some appreciation of the difficulties involved in developing large systems is a helpful prerequisite to understanding OOP.

3.3   WHY BEGIN WITH BEHAVIOR?

Why begin the design process with an analysis of behavior? The simple answer is that the behavior of a system is usually understood long before any other aspect.

Earlier software development techniques concentrated on ideas such as characterizing the basic data structures or the overall sequence of function calls, often within the creation of a formal specification of the desired application. But structural elements of the application can be identified only after a considerable amount of problem analysis. Similarly, a formal specification often ended up as a document understood by neither programmer nor client. But *behavior* is something that can be described almost from the moment an idea is conceived, and (often unlike a formal specification) can be described in terms meaningful to both the programmers and the client.

The following case study illustrates the application of responsibility-driven design (RDD).

3.4 A Case Study in RDD

Imagine you are the chief software architect in a major computer firm. One day your boss walks into your office with an idea that, it is hoped, will be the next major success in your product line. Your assignment is to develop the Interactive Intelligent Kitchen Helper (IIKH) (Figure 3.1). The task given to your software team is stated in very few words, written on what appears to be the back of a slightly used paper napkin, in handwriting that appears to be your boss's.

3.4.1 *The Interactive Intelligent Kitchen Helper*

Briefly, the Interactive Intelligent Kitchen Helper is a PC-based application that will replace the index-card system of recipes found in the average kitchen. But more than simply maintaining a database of recipes, the kitchen helper assists in the planning of meals for an extended period, say a week. The user of the IIKH can sit down at a terminal, browse the database of recipes, and interactively create a series of menus. The IIKH will automatically scale the recipes to any number of servings and will print out menus for the entire week, for a particular day, or for a particular meal. And it will print an integrated grocery list of all the items needed for the recipes for the entire period.

As is usually true with the initial descriptions of most software systems, the specification for the IIKH is highly ambiguous on a number of important

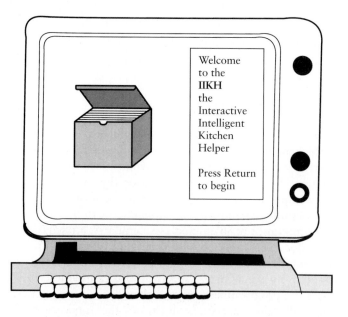

Figure 3.1 View of the Interactive Intelligent Kitchen Helper.

points. It is also true that, in all likelihood, the eventual design and development of the software system to support the IIKH will require the efforts of several programmers working together. Thus, the initial goal of the software team must be to clarify the ambiguities in the description and to outline how the project can be divided into components to be assigned for development to individual team members.

The cornerstone of object-oriented programming is to characterize software in terms of *behavior*, that is, actions to be performed. We will see this repeated on many levels in the development of the IIKH. Initially, the team will try to characterize, at a very high level of abstraction, the behavior of the entire application. This then leads to a description of the behavior of various software subsystems. Only when all behavior has been identified and described will the software design team proceed to the coding step. In the next several sections we will trace the tasks the software design team will perform in producing this application.

3.4.2   *Working Through Scenarios*

The first task is to refine the specification. As already noted, initial specifications are almost always ambiguous and unclear on anything except the most general points. There are several goals for this step. One objective is to get a better handle on the "look and feel" of the eventual product. This information can then be carried back to the client (in this case, your boss) to see if it is in agreement with the original conception. It is likely, perhaps inevitable, that the specifications for the final application will change during the creation of the software system, and it is important that the design be developed to easily accommodate change and that potential changes be noted as early as possible. (See Section 3.6.2, "Preparing for Change.") Equally important, at this point very high-level decisions can be made concerning the structure of the eventual software system. In particular, the activities to be performed can be mapped onto components.

3.4.3   *Identification of Components*

The engineering of a complex physical system, such as a building or an auto-mobile engine, is simplified by dividing the design into smaller units. So, too, the engineering of software is simplified by the identification and development of software components. A *component* is simply an abstract entity that can per-form tasks—that is, fulfill some responsibilities. At this point, it is not necessary to know exactly the eventual representation for a component or how a compo-nent will perform a task. A component may ultimately be turned into a function, a structure or class, or a collection of other components (a *pattern*). At this level of development, just two characteristics are important:

- A component must have a small, well-defined set of responsibilities.
- A component should interact with other components as little as possible.

We will shortly discuss the reasoning behind the second characteristic. For the moment we are simply concerned with the identification of component responsibilities.

3.5   CRC Cards—Recording Responsibility

In order to discover components and their responsibilities, the programming team walks through scenarios. That is, the team acts out the running of the application just as if it already possessed a working system. Every activity that must take place is identified and assigned to some component as a responsibility. (See Figure 3.2.)

As part of this process, it is often useful to represent components using small index cards. On the face of the card the programming team writes the name of the software component, the responsibilities of the component, and the names of other components with which the component must interact. Such cards are sometimes known as CRC (component, responsibility, collaborator) cards [Beck and Cunningham 1989], [Bellin and Simone 1997], and are associated with each software component. As responsibilities for the component are discovered, they are recorded on the face of the CRC card.

3.5.1   *Giving Components a Physical Representation*

While working through scenarios, it is useful to assign CRC cards to different members of the design team. The member holding the card representing a component records the responsibilities of the associated software component, and

```
┌─────────────────────────────────────────────────┐
│                                                   │
│   Component Name                                  │
│                                   Collaborators   │
│   Description of the responsibilities             │
│   assigned to this component      List of         │
│                                   other           │
│                                   components       │
│                                                   │
│                                                   │
│                                                   │
└─────────────────────────────────────────────────┘
```

Figure 3.2   A component, responsibility, collaborator (CRC) card.

acts as the "surrogate" for the software during the scenario simulation. He or she describes the activities of the software system, passing "control" to another member when the software system requires the services of another component.

An advantage of CRC cards is that index cards are widely available, inexpensive, and erasable. This encourages experimentation, since alternative designs can be tried, explored, or abandoned with little investment. The physical separation of the cards encourages an intuitive understanding of the importance of the logical separation of the various components, helping to emphasize the cohesion and coupling (described shortly). The constraints of an index card are also a good measure of approximate complexity–a component that is expected to perform more tasks than can fit easily in the space of a card is probably too complex, and the team should find a simpler solution, perhaps by moving some responsibilities elsewhere to divide a task between two or more new components.

3.5.2   *The What/Who Cycle*

As noted at the beginning of this discussion, the identification of components takes place during the process of imagining the execution of a working system. Often this proceeds as a cycle of what/who questions. First, the programming team identifies *what* activity needs to be performed next. This is immediately followed by answering the question of *who* performs the action. In this manner, designing a software system is much like organizing a collection of people, such as a club. Any activity that is to be performed must be assigned as a responsibility to some component.

We know, from real life, that if any action is to take place, there must be an agent assigned to perform it. Just as in the running of a club any action to be performed must be assigned to some individual, in organizing an object-oriented program all actions must be the responsibility of some component. The secret to good object-oriented design is to first establish an agent for each action.

3.5.3   *Documentation*

At this point the development of documentation should begin. Two documents should be essential parts of any software system: the user manual and the system design documentation. Work on both of these can commence even before the first line of code has been written.

The user manual describes the interaction with the system from the user's point of view; it is an excellent means of verifying that the development team's conception of the application matches the client's. Since the decisions made in creating the scenarios will closely match the decisions the user will be required to make in the eventual application, the development of the user manual naturally dovetails with the process of walking through scenarios.

Before any actual code has been written, the mindset of the software team is most similar to that of the eventual users. Thus, it is at this point that the developers can most easily anticipate the sort of questions to which a novice user will need answers.

The second essential document is the design documentation. Because the design documentation records the major decisions made during software design, it should thus be produced when these decisions are fresh in the minds of the creators, and not after the fact when many of the relevant details will have been forgotten. It is often far easier to write a general global description of the software system early in the development. Too soon, the focus will move to the level of individual components or modules. And although it is also important to document the module level, too much concern with the details of each module will make it difficult for subsequent software maintainers to form an initial picture of the larger structure.

CRC cards are one aspect of the design documentation, but they do not reflect *all* important decisions. Arguments for and against any major design alternatives should be recorded, as well as factors that influenced the final decisions. A log or diary of the project schedule should be maintained. Both the user manual and the design documents are refined and evolve over time in exactly the same way the software is refined and evolves.

3.6 COMPONENTS AND BEHAVIOR

To return to the Interactive Kitchen Helper application, the IIKH, the team decides that when the system begins, the user will be presented with an attractive informative window (shown in Figure 3.1). The responsibility for displaying this window is assigned to a component called the Greeter. In some as yet unspecified manner (perhaps by pull-down menus, button or key presses, or use of a pressure-sensitive screen), the user can select one of several actions. Initially, the team identifies just five actions:

1. Casually browse the database of existing recipes, but without reference to any particular meal plan.

2. Add a new recipe to the database.

3. Edit or annotate an existing recipe.

4. Review an existing plan for several meals.

5. Create a new plan of meals.

These activities seem to divide themselves naturally into two groups. The first three are associated with the recipe database; the latter two are associated with menu plans. As a result, the team next decides to create components corresponding to these two responsibilities. Continuing with the scenario, the

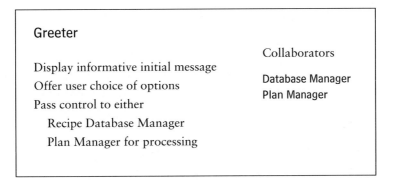

Greeter

Display informative initial message
Offer user choice of options
Pass control to either
    Recipe Database Manager
    Plan Manager for processing

Collaborators

Database Manager
Plan Manager

Figure 3.3 CRC card for the Greeter.

team elects to ignore the meal plan management for the moment and move on to refine the activities of the Recipe Database component. Figure 3.3 shows the initial CRC card representation of the Greeter.

Broadly speaking, the responsibility of the recipe database component is simply to maintain a collection of recipes. We have already identified three elements of this task: The recipe component database must facilitate browsing the library of existing recipes, editing the recipes, and including new recipes in the database.

3.6.1 *Postponing Decisions*

A number of decisions must eventually be made concerning how best to let the user browse the database. For example, should the user first be presented with a list of categories, such as "Soups," "Salads," "Main Courses," and "Desserts"? Alternatively, should the user be able to describe keywords to narrow a search, perhaps by providing a list of ingredients, and then see all the recipes that contain those items ("Almonds, Strawberries, Cheese"), or a list of previously inserted keywords ("Bob's favorite cake")? Should scroll bars be used or simulated thumbholes in a virtual book? These choices are fun to think about, but the important point is that such decisions do not need to be made at this point (see next section). Since they affect only a single component and do not affect the functioning of any other system, all that is necessary to continue the scenario is to assert that by some means the user can select a specific recipe.

3.6.2 *Preparing for Change*

It has been said that all that is constant in life is the inevitability of change. The same is true of software. No matter how carefully one tries to develop the initial specification and design of a software system, it is almost certain that changes in the user's needs or requirements will, sometime during the life of the system, force changes to be made in the software. Programmers and software designers need to anticipate this and plan accordingly.

- The primary objective is that changes should affect as few components as possible. Even major changes in the appearance or functioning of an application should be possible with alterations to only one or two sections of code.

- Try to predict the most likely sources of change and isolate the effects of such changes to as few software components as possible. The most likely sources of change are interfaces, communication formats, and output formats.

- Try to isolate and reduce the dependency of software on hardware. For example, the interface for recipe browsing in our application may depend in part on the hardware on which the system is running. Future releases may be ported to different platforms. A good design will anticipate this change.

- Reducing coupling between software components will reduce the dependence of one upon another and increase the likelihood that one can be changed with minimal effect on the other.

- In the design documentation maintain careful records of the design process and the discussions surrounding all major decisions. It is almost certain that the team responsible for maintaining the software and designing future releases will be at least partially different from the team producing the initial release. The design documentation will allow future teams to know the important factors behind a decision and help them avoid spending time discussing issues that have already been resolved.

3.6.3   *Continuing the Scenario*

Each recipe will be identified with a specific recipe component. Once a recipe is selected, control is passed to the associated recipe object. A recipe must contain certain information. Basically, it consists of a list of ingredients and the steps needed to transform the ingredients into the final product. In our scenario, the recipe component must also perform other activities. For example, it will display the recipe interactively on the terminal screen. The user may be given the ability to annotate or change either the list of ingredients or the instruction portion. Alternatively, the user may request a printed copy of the recipe. All of these actions are the responsibility of the Recipe component. (For the moment, we will continue to describe the Recipe in singular form. During design we can think of this as a prototypical recipe that stands in place of a multitude of actual recipes. We will later return to a discussion of singular versus multiple components.)

Having outlined the actions that must take place to permit the user to browse the database, we return to the recipe database manager and pretend the user has indicated a desire to add a new recipe. The Database Manager somehow decides in which category to place the new recipe (again, the details of how this is done are unimportant for our development at this point), requests the name of the new recipe, and then creates a new recipe component, permitting the user to edit this new blank entry. Thus, the responsibilities of performing this new task are a subset of those we already identified in permitting users to edit existing recipes.

Having explored the browsing and creation of new recipes, we return to the Greeter and investigate the development of daily menu plans, which is the Plan Manager's task. In some way (again, the details are unimportant here) the user can save existing plans. Thus, the Plan Manager can either be started by retrieving an already developed plan or by creating a new plan. In the latter case, the user is prompted for a list of dates for the plan. Each date is associated with a separate Date component. The user can select a specific date for further investigation, in which case control is passed to the corresponding Date component. Another activity of the Plan Manager is printing out the recipes for the planning period. Finally, the user can instruct the Plan Manager to produce a grocery list for the period.

The Date component maintains a collection of meals as well as any other annotations provided by the user (birthdays, anniversaries, and other reminders). It prints information on the display concerning the specified date. By some means (again unspecified), the user can indicate a desire to print all the information concerning a specific date or choose to explore in more detail a specific meal. In the latter case, control is passed to a Meal component.

The Meal component maintains a collection of augmented recipes, where the augmentation refers to the user's desire to double, triple, or otherwise increase a recipe. The Meal component displays information about the meal. The user can add or remove recipes from the meal, or can instruct that information about the meal be printed. In order to discover new recipes, the user must be permitted at this point to browse the recipe database. Thus, the Meal component must interact with the recipe database component. The design team will continue in this fashion, investigating every possible scenario.

The major category of scenarios we have not developed here is exceptional cases. For example, what happens if a user selects a number of keywords for a recipe and no matching recipe is found? How can the user cancel an activity, such as entering a new recipe, if he or she decides not to continue? Each possibility must be explored, and the responsibilities for handling the situation assigned to one or more components.

Having walked through the various scenarios, the software design team eventually decides that all activities can be adequately handled by six components (Figure 3.4). The Greeter needs to communicate only with the Plan Manager and the Recipe Database components. The Plan Manager needs to communicate only

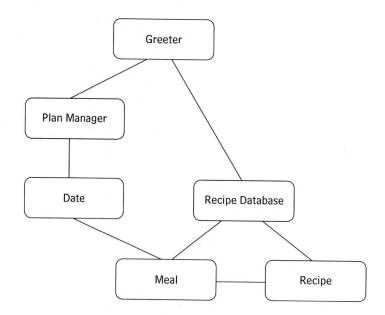

Figure 3.4 Communication among the six components in the IIKH.

with the Date component; and the Date agent, only with the Meal component. The Meal component communicates with the Recipe Database and, through this agent, with individual recipes.

3.6.4 *Interaction Diagrams*

While a description such as that shown in Figure 3.4 may describe the static relationships between components, it is not very good for describing their dynamic interactions during the execution of a scenario. A better tool for this purpose is an *interaction diagram*. Figure 3.5 shows the beginning of an interaction diagram for the Interactive Kitchen Helper. In the diagram, time moves forward from the top to the bottom. Each component is represented by a labeled vertical line. A component sending a message to another component is represented by a horizontal arrow from one line to another. Similarly, a component returning control and perhaps a result value back to the caller is represented by an arrow. (Some authors use two different arrow forms, such as a solid line to represent message passing and a dashed line to represent returning control.) The commentary on the right-hand side of the figure explains more fully the interaction taking place.

With a time axis, the interaction diagram is able to describe better the sequencing of events during a scenario. For this reason, interaction diagrams can be a useful documentation tool for complex software systems.

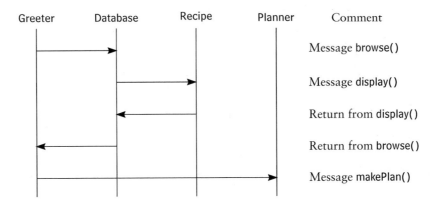

Figure 3.5   An example interaction diagram.

3.7   SOFTWARE COMPONENTS

In this section we will explore a software component in more detail. As is true of all but the most trivial ideas, there are many aspects to this seemingly simple concept.

3.7.1   *Behavior and State*

We have already seen how components are characterized by their behavior, that is, by what they can do. But components may also hold certain information. Let us take as our prototypical component a Recipe structure from the IIKH. One way to view such a component is as a pair consisting of *behavior* and *state*.

- The *behavior* of a component is the set of actions it can perform. The complete description of all the behavior for a component is sometimes called the *protocol*. For the Recipe component this includes activities such as editing the preparation instructions, displaying the recipe on a terminal screen, or printing a copy of the recipe.

- The *state* of a component represents all the information held within it. For our Recipe component the state includes the ingredients and preparation instructions. Notice that the state is not static and can change over time. For example, by editing a recipe (a behavior) the user can make changes to the preparation instructions (part of the state).

It is not necessary that all components maintain state information. For example, it is possible that the Greeter component will not have any state since it does not need to remember any information during the course of execution. However, most components will consist of a combination of behavior and state.

3.7.2   *Instances and Classes*

The separation of state and behavior permits us to clarify a point we avoided in our earlier discussion. Note that in the real application there will probably be many different recipes. However, all of these recipes will *perform* in the same manner. That is, the behavior of each recipe is the same; it is only the state—the individual lists of ingredients and instructions for preparation—that differs between individual recipes. In the early stages of development our interest is in characterizing the behavior common to all recipes; the details particular to any one recipe are unimportant.

The term *class* is used to describe a set of objects with similar behavior. We will see in later chapters that a class is also used as a syntactic mechanism in Java. An individual representative of a class is known as an *instance*. Note that behavior is associated with a class, not with an individual. That is, all instances of a class will respond to the same instructions and perform in a similar manner. On the other hand, state is a property of an individual. We see this in the various instances of the class Recipe. They can all perform the same actions (editing, displaying, printing) but use different data values.

3.7.3   *Coupling and Cohesion*

Two important concepts in the design of software components are coupling and cohesion. *Cohesion* is the degree to which the responsibilities of a single component form a meaningful unit. High cohesion is achieved by associating in a single component tasks that are related in some manner. Probably the most frequent way in which tasks are related is through the necessity to access a common data area. This is the overriding theme that joins, for example, the various responsibilities of the Recipe component.

Coupling, on the other hand, describes the relationship between software components. In general, it is desirable to reduce the amount of coupling as much as possible, since connections between software components inhibit ease of development, modification, or reuse.

In particular, coupling is increased when one software component must access data values—the state—held by another component. Such situations should almost always be avoided in favor of moving a task into the list of responsibilities of the component that holds the necessary data. For example, one might conceivably first assign responsibility for editing a recipe to the Recipe Database component, since it is while performing tasks associated with this component that the need to edit a recipe first occurs. But if we did so, the Recipe Database agent would need the ability to directly manipulate the state (the internal data values representing the list of ingredients and the preparation instructions) of an individual recipe. It is better to avoid this tight connection by moving the responsibility for editing to the recipe itself.

3.7.4   *Interface and Implementation: Parnas's Principles*

The emphasis on characterizing a software component by its behavior has one extremely important consequence. It is possible for one programmer to know how to *use* a component developed by another programmer, without needing to know how the component is *implemented*. For example, suppose each of the six components in the IIKH is assigned to a different programmer. The programmer developing the Meal component needs to allow the IIKH user to browse the database of recipes and select a single recipe for inclusion in the meal. To do this, the Meal component can simply invoke the browse behavior associated with the Recipe Database component, which is defined to return an individual Recipe. This description is valid regardless of the particular implementation used by the Recipe Database component to perform the actual browsing action.

The purposeful omission of implementation details behind a simple interface is known as *information hiding*. We say the component *encapsulates* the behavior, showing only how the component can be used, not the detailed actions it performs. This naturally leads to two different views of a software system. The interface view is the face seen by other programmers. It describes *what* a software component can perform. The implementation view is the face seen by the programmer working on a particular component. It describes *how* a component goes about completing a task.

The separation of interface and implementation is perhaps *the* most important concept in software engineering. Yet it is difficult for students to understand, or to motivate. Information hiding is largely meaningful only in the context of multiperson programming projects. In such efforts, the limiting factor is often not the amount of coding involved, but the amount of communication required among the various programmers and among their respective software systems. As will be described shortly, software components are often developed in parallel by different programmers, and in isolation from one another.

There is also an increasing emphasis on the reuse of general purpose software components in multiple projects. For this to be successful, there must be minimal and well-understood interconnections between the various portions of the system. These ideas were captured by computer scientist David Parnas in a pair of rules, known as *Parnas's principles:*

- The developer of a software component must provide the intended user with all the information needed to make effective use of the services provided by the component, and should provide *no* other information.

- The developer of a software component must be provided with all the information necessary to carry out the given responsibilities assigned to the component, and should be provided with *no* other information.

A consequence of the separation of interface from implementation is that a programmer can experiment with several different implementations of the same structure without affecting other software components.

3.8 FORMALIZING THE INTERFACE

We continue with the description of the IIKH development. In the next several steps the descriptions of the components will be refined. The first step in this process is to formalize the patterns and channels of communication.

A decision should be made as to the general structure that will be used to implement each component. A component with only one behavior and no internal state may be made into a function—for example, a component that simply takes a string of text and translates all capital letters to lowercase. Components with many tasks are probably more easily implemented as classes. Names are given to each of the responsibilities identified on the CRC card for each component, and these will eventually be mapped onto function or procedure names. Along with the names, the types of any arguments to be passed to the function are identified. Next, the information maintained within the component itself should be described. All information must be accounted for. If a component requires some data to perform a specific task, the source of the data, either through argument or global value, or maintained internally by the component, must be clearly identified.

3.8.1 *Coming Up with Names*

Careful thought should be given to the names associated with various activities. Shakespeare has Juliet claiming that a name change does not alter the object being described, but certainly not all names will conjure up the same mental images in the listener.[1] As government bureaucrats have long known, obscure and idiomatic names can make even the simplest operation sound intimidating. The selection of useful names is extremely important, as names create the vocabulary with which the eventual design will be formulated. Names should be internally consistent, meaningful, preferably short, and evocative in the context of the problem. Often a considerable amount of time is spent finding just the right set of terms to describe the tasks performed and the objects manipulated. Far from being a barren and useless exercise, proper naming early in the design process greatly simplifies and facilitates later steps.

The following general guidelines have been suggested [Keller 1990]:

---

[1] "What's in a name? That which we call a rose, by any other name would smell as sweet; So Romeo would, were he not Romeo call'd, retain that dear perfection which he owes without that title." *Romeo and Juliet*, Act II, Scene 2.

- Use pronounceable names. As a rule of thumb, if you cannot read a name out loud, it is not a good one.

- Use capitalization (or underscores) to mark the beginning of a new word within a name, such as "CardReader" or "Card_reader," rather than the less readable "cardreader."

- Examine abbreviations carefully. An abbreviation that is clear to one person may be confusing to the next. Is a "TermProcess" a terminal process, something that terminates processes, or a process associated with a terminal?

- Avoid names with several interpretations. Does the empty function tell whether something is empty, or empty the values from the object?

- Avoid digits within a name. They are easy to misread as letters (0 as O, 1 as l, 2 as Z, 5 as S).

- Name functions and variables that yield Boolean values so they describe clearly the interpretation of a true or false value. For example, "Printer-IsReady" clearly indicates that a true value means the printer is working, whereas "PrinterStatus" is much less precise.

- Take extra care in the selection of names for operations that are costly and infrequently used. Doing so can avoid errors caused by using the wrong function.

Once names have been developed for each activity, the CRC cards for each component are redrawn, with the name and formal arguments of the function used to elicit each behavior identified. An example of a CRC card for the Date is shown in Figure 3.6. What is not yet specified is how each component will perform the associated tasks.

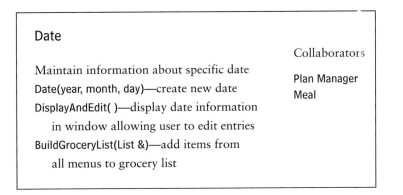

Figure 3.6   Revised CRC card for the Date component.

Once more, scenarios or role playing should be carried out at a more detailed level to ensure that all activities are accounted for and that all necessary information is maintained and made available to the responsible components.

3.9   DESIGNING THE REPRESENTATION

At this point, if not before, the design team can be divided into groups, each responsible for one or more software components. The task now is to transform the description of a component into a software system implementation. The major portion of this process is designing the data structures that will be used by each subsystem to maintain the state information required to fulfill the assigned responsibilities.

It is here that the classic data structures of computer science come into play. The selection of data structures is an important task, central to the software design process. Once they have been chosen, the code used by a component in the fulfillment of a responsibility is often almost self-evident. But data structures must be carefully matched to the task at hand. A wrong choice can result in complex and inefficient programs, while an intelligent choice can result in just the opposite.

It is also at this point that descriptions of behavior must be transformed into algorithms. These descriptions should then be matched against the expectations of each component listed as a collaborator, to ensure that expectations are fulfilled and necessary data items are available to carry out each process.

3.10   IMPLEMENTING COMPONENTS

Once the design of each software subsystem is laid out, the next step is to implement each component's desired behavior. If the previous steps were correctly addressed, each responsibility or behavior will be characterized by a short description. The task at this step is to implement the desired activities in a computer language. In a later section we will describe some of the more common heuristics used in this process.

If they were not determined earlier (say, as part of the specification of the system), then decisions can now be made on issues that are entirely self-contained within a single component. A decision we saw in our example problem was how best to let the user browse the database of recipes.

As multiperson programming projects become the norm, it becomes increasingly rare that any one programmer will work on all aspects of a system. More often, the skills a programmer will need to master are understanding how one section of code fits into a larger framework and working well with other members of a team. Often, in the implementation of one component it will

become clear that certain information or actions might be assigned to yet another component that will act "behind the scene," with little or no visibility
to users of the software abstraction. Such components are sometimes known
as *facilitators*. We will see examples of facilitators in some of the later case
studies.

An important part of analysis and coding at this point is characterizing and
documenting the necessary preconditions a software component requires to
complete a task, and verifying that the software component will perform correctly when presented with legal input values. This is establishing the correctness
aspect of the algorithms used in the implementation of a component.

3.11   INTEGRATION OF COMPONENTS

Once software subsystems have been individually designed and tested, they can
be integrated into the final product. This is often not a single step, but part of
a larger process. Starting from a simple base, elements are slowly added to the
system and tested, using *stubs*—simple dummy routines with no behavior or
with very limited behavior—for the as yet unimplemented parts.

For example, in the development of the IIKH, it would be reasonable to start
integration with the Greeter component. To test the Greeter in isolation, stubs
are written for the Recipe Database manager and the daily Plan manager. These
stubs need not do any more than print an informative message and return. With
these, the component development team can test various aspects of the Greeter
system (for example, that button presses elicit the correct response). Testing of
an individual component is often referred to as *unit testing*.

Next, one or the other of the stubs can be replaced by more complete code.
For example, the team might decide to replace the stub for the Recipe Database
component with the actual system, maintaining the stub for the other portion.
Further testing can be performed until it appears that the system is working as
desired. (This is sometimes referred to as *integration testing*.)

The application is finally complete when all stubs have been replaced with
working components. The ability to test components in isolation is greatly facili-
tated by the conscious design goal of reducing connections between components,
since this reduces the need for extensive stubbing.

During integration it is not uncommon for an error to be manifested in one
software system, and yet to be caused by a coding mistake in another system.
Thus, testing during integration can involve the discovery of errors, which
then results in changes to some of the components. Following these changes
the components should once again be tested in isolation before an attempt
to reintegrate the software, once more, into the larger system. Reexecuting
previously developed test cases following a change to a software component is
sometimes referred to as *regression testing*.

3.12   MAINTENANCE AND EVOLUTION

It is tempting to think that once a working version of an application has been delivered the task of the software development team is finished. Unfortunately, that is almost never true. The term *software maintenance* describes activities subsequent to the delivery of the initial working version of a software system. A wide variety of activities fall into this category.

- Errors, or *bugs*, can be discovered in the delivered product. These must be corrected, either in *patches* to existing releases or in subsequent releases.

- Requirements may change, perhaps as a result of government regulations or standardization among similar products.

- Hardware may change. For example, the system may be moved to different platforms, or input devices, such as a pen-based system or a pressure-sensitive touch screen, may become available. Output technology may change—for example, from a text-based system to a graphical window-based arrangement.

- User expectations may change. Users may expect greater functionality, lower cost, and easier use. This can occur as a result of competition with similar products.

- Better documentation may be requested by users.

A good design recognizes the inevitability of changes and plans an accommodation for them from the very beginning.

3.13   CHAPTER SUMMARY

Object-oriented programming begins with object-oriented design. Object-oriented design is characterized by an emphasis on responsibility, rather than on structure. Responsibility and behavior are attributes that can be discovered for a software system well before any other features can be identified. By systematically tracing the behavior of a system, the design of the software elements flows naturally from the general specification.

A key tool in the characterization of behavior is the idea of scenarios. Developers trace through the execution of an imaginary system, identifying actions that need to be performed, and more importantly assigning the responsibilities for these actions to individual software components. A useful tool in this activity is the CRC card, which is an index card that records the responsibilities of a software system. As design evolves, the descriptions of the actions of each component can be rewritten in more precise formats.

Developing a working software system involves many steps, frequently termed the software life cycle. Design and implementation are the first major steps. Implementation can be broken into the identification of components, development and testing of components in isolation, integration of components into larger units, and finally testing of the completed application. The life of a software system does not, however, halt with the first completed applications. Errors are uncovered, requirements change, and hardware modifications can all cause changes in the software system. The management of these changes that come after the first release is known as software maintenance.

STUDY QUESTIONS

1. What is the key idea driving object-oriented design?

2. How is the idea of responsibility tied to information hiding?

3. What are some of the characteristics of programming in the small?

4. How does programming in the large differ from programming in the small?

5. Why is information hiding an important aspect of programming in the large?

6. Why should the design of a software system begin with the characterization of behavior?

7. What is a scenario? How does a scenario help the identification of behaviors?

8. What do the three fields of a CRC card represent?

9. What are some of the advantages of using a physical index card to represent a CRC card?

10. What is the what/who cycle?

11. Why should the user manual be written before actual coding of an application is begun?

12. What are the most common sources of change in the requirements for an application over time? How can some of the difficulties inherent in change be mitigated?

13. What information is being conveyed by an interaction diagram?

14. Describe in your own words the following aspects of software components:
    (a) Behavior and state
    (b) Instances and classes
    (c) Coupling and cohesion
    (d) Interface and implementation

15. What are Parnas's principles of information hiding?

16. What are some guidelines to follow in the selection of names for components, arguments, behaviors, and so on?

17. After design, what are the later stages of the software life cycle?

18. What is software maintenance?

EXERCISES

1. Finish the development of CRC cards for the IIKH.

2. Having done Exercise 1, give a complete interaction diagram for one scenario use of the IIKH.

3. Describe the responsibilities of an organization that includes at least six types of members. Examples of such organizations are a school (students, teachers, principal, janitor), a business (secretary, president, worker), and a club (president, vice-president, member). For each member type, describe the responsibilities and the collaborators.

4. Create a scenario for the organization you described in Exercise 1 using an interaction diagram.

5. For a common game such as solitaire or twenty-one, describe a software system that will interact with the user as an opposing player. Example components include the deck and the discard pile.

6. Describe the software system to control an automated teller machine (ATM). Give interaction diagrams for various scenarios that describe the most common uses of the machine.

7. Consider a large program with which you are familiar (not necessarily object-oriented), and examine the names of variables and functions. Which names do you think are particularly apt? Why? Which names do you think might have been badly selected?

II

Understanding Paradigms

4. A Paradigm

As we noted in Chapter 1, to a medieval scholar a *paradigm* was an example sentence, one that could be used as a model or as an aid in learning a language. You are learning a new language, the programming language Java. This book will introduce Java by means of many small paradigms, or example code fragments. You as the reader should examine these programs carefully, paying close attention to those features that are new or different in comparison to earlier programs. Learning to view programs as a form of literature, that is, learning how to read programs as well as to write them, is a skill well worth an investment in time.

Our first paradigm is shown in Figure 4.1. Line numbers have been provided in comments along the right side. Like all comments, these are mainly intended to help the human reader, and are not actually part of the program. While exceedingly short and largely lacking in interesting functionality (the program prints one line of output and exits), this program nevertheless exhibits characteristics found in all Java programs, and is therefore a good place to begin our explorations. In the remainder of this chapter we will analyze the features of this program from several different perspectives.

```
import java.io.*;                                          // 1

public class FirstProgram {                               // 2

    public static void main ( String [ ] args ) {         // 3
        System.out.println( "Your first Java program!" );  // 4
    }                                                      // 5
}                                                          // 6
```

Figure 4.1 A simple Java program.

4.1 PROGRAM STRUCTURE

The first step is to understand the structure of a Java program. As noted in Chapter 1, the Java universe is a community populated by *objects*, and by little else (for more on the types of values found in the Java world, see the next section). Objects are all instances of *classes*, and thus the overall structure of a Java program is simply a series of class descriptions. In our example program there is a single class, named FirstProgram. The name of the class (given on line number 2) is important in several respects. First, it will be the handle we use to create instances of the class. Of more pragmatic concern in running your first program, it is also the name used to create the file in which the executable version of the class will be stored. On most systems this file will be named FirstProgram.class. To execute the program, this would be the file you hand to the Java interpreter.

Figure 4.2 shows the commands used to compile and execute this first program on a computer running the Unix operating system. The text of the program is stored in a file named FirstProgram.java. The command javac, the Java compiler, analyzes this program, creating the file FirstProgram.class to hold the executable version of the program. The command ls lists the contents of the directory, showing these two files. The command java, the Java bytecode interpeter, is used to execute the program. The output of the program is shown immediately after this command.

The names of the applications used to compile and execute a Java program, the steps needed to invoke these applications, and the location of the output are all features that differ greatly between platforms. We will not discuss these

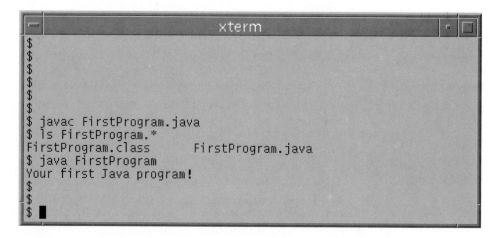

Figure 4.2 Compiling and executing a Java program.

further here, concentrating instead on the features of the Java programming language, which will be the same on all platforms.

A class consists of a class *header* and a class *body*. The header is found on line 2, and provides the name of the class. The keyword class indicates (both to the compiler, and to you as a program reader) that this is a new class description, and that the text following the class keyword should be taken to be the class name.

```
public class FirstProgram {                                    // 2
    .
    .
    .
}                                                              // 6
```

The class body begins with the curly brace at the end of line 2 and terminates with the matching curly brace on line 6. The Java language places few restrictions on the use of spaces in programs, and the placement of elements such as curly braces relative to the rest of the line is largely a matter of personal taste—and consequently the subject of a great deal of heated debate. I personally like to place the starting brace on the same line as the unit it is grouping, with the closing brace on a line all by itself. I deviate from this only when an entire statement group can be placed on a line by itself. Others prefer to place both braces on separate lines, as in the following:

```
public class FirstProgram
{
    public static void main ( String [ ] args )
    {
        System.out.println( "Your first Java program!");
    }
}
```

Find a style that seems comfortable to you personally, and use it consistently.

Within the body of a class are found a series of *members*. A member can be either a *data field*, or a *method*. The former characterize the internal data being held by an object, while the latter define the behaviors an instance of the class can perform.

In our initial program there are no data fields, and only one method. This method is named main, which *must* be the name used in describing the first method that will be invoked when execution commences.

A method is a function. Like a class, a function consists of two parts; a function *header* and a function *body*. All function headers have the same form, which can be described as a sequence of zero or more modifiers, a return type, a name, and a list of arguments. Thus, a prototypical function has the following form:

```
modifiers return-type function-name ( arguments ) {
    sequence-of-statements
}
```

The function header for main is given on line number 3 of the example program. It includes two modifiers, public and static. The first, as indicated earlier, will be subsequently discussed in Section 4.4, while the latter is described in Section 4.5. The return type for this procedure is void, which will be introduced in Section 4.3. The remaining parts are the name of the function (main) and the list of arguments to the function. The initial function for execution always takes a single argument, which is an array of string values. More will be said about Java types, such as the types shown in the argument declaration, in Section 4.3.

```
public static void main ( String [ ] args ) {          // 3
    .
    .
    .
}                                                        // 5
```

The function body begins with the curly brace on line 3, and ends with the corresponding curly brace on line 5. Function bodies must always be properly nested within a class description.

Within a function body are a series of statements that indicate the actions to be executed when an instance of the given class is asked to perform the indicated method. In our sample program, there is one action, which is to print a single line of output. We will discuss this statement in more detail in the next section.

4.2   THE CONNECTION TO THE JAVA WORLD

A Java program is never entirely self-contained but must instead execute in the "universe" provided by the Java run-time system. We see this characteristic exhibited in two ways in our sample program. The first connection to the Java world is created by the import statement in line 1.

```
import java.io.*;                                        // 1
```

This statement makes a portion of the Java library visible to the following class description. The Java run-time library is both powerful and exceedingly large. Because of the size, portions of the Java universe are only made available when the user explicitly requests them. The import statement requests that a portion of the Java run-time system related to input and output should be treated as part of this program.

This particular section of the Java run-time system has been selected because it is where the object System is defined.[1] Among the data fields held by System is one named out, that holds various features associated with output. Among the behaviors provided by out is the function println, which takes as argument a text string, and uses the argument to print a single line of output on a standard output area (often called the *output console*).

```
System.out.println( "Your first Java program!" );                // 4
```

System is one of many useful objects that already populate the Java universe when a program begins execution. Another example is Math, which is an object that can perform many common mathematical operations. We will encounter several other system objects in later case studies.

4.3   TYPES

In addition to a variety of useful objects, the initial Java world contains the descriptions for a large collection of useful *types* that programmers can employ in their own code. The most basic types are integers and real (or floating-point) values. Integer variables are declared using the keyword int, as in the following, which both declares a new integer variable and initializes it with a value.

```
int newVar = 42;
```

Such variables could be declared either as data fields within a class or as local variables within a function. Floating-point values are declared using either the type float or the type double. Another basic type is boolean. A Boolean value is either true or false. Boolean values are produced by the relational operators (less-than, written <; less-than-or-equal, written <=; and so on) as well as the logical operators (and, written &; or, written |; and the like). The most common use for Boolean values is in the test portion of an if or a while statement.

The keyword void is used as a type mainly to describe procedures that do not, in fact, return any value. We see this in our example program, as the return type for the procedure main:

```
public static void main ( String [ ] args ) {                    // 3
```

The argument list for this procedure also illustrates another useful data type provided by the Java language, the type String. A literal value, for example, has the type String.

```
String name = "Fred Smith";
```

---

[1] Actually, System is a class, but classes can be considered to be objects in certain respects. The distinction is not important here.

Notice that the types int, float, double, and boolean all begin with lowercase letters, while the type String, as well as the majority of other types provided by the Java library, begin with an uppercase letter. The reason for this is that the more primitive types (int and the like) are technically not objects, while all other values are objects. That is, there is no class definition that corresponds to int, while there *is* a class description that defines the characteristics of the String data type. This is a minor distinction that in rare situations is important, and one we will return to in a later chapter.

An *array* in Java is rather different from arrays in many other languages. One difference is that the array type declaration does not specify the number of elements, or extent, of the array. We see this in our sample program in line 3:

```
public static void main ( String [ ] args ) {                        // 3
```

The parameter value for this procedure is named args, and is an array of string values. The square brackets in the declaration give us the clue that the value is an array; however, they do not specify the size of the array. Instead, methods provided by the class Array can be used to access information about the array. For example, consider the following program, which is only slightly more complicated than the first example:

```
import java.io.*;

public class SecondProgram {

    public static void main ( String [ ] args ) {
        if (args.length > 0)
            System.out.println("Hello " + args[0]);
        else
            System.out.println( "Hello  everybody!");
    }
}
```

Here the data field length is being used to determine the number of values held by the array named args. If the user entered a command line argument, such as the string "Fred", the output would be "hello Fred".[2]

If the size of the array args is larger than zero (that is, if there are array elements) then the subscript operator is used to access the first element. The set of legal index values for an array in Java begins with zero, and extends to the value one smaller than the number of elements in the array.

Finally, this example shows the use of the + operator with a string value. When at least one argument to the "addition" operator is a String, the other

---

[2] Exactly how command-line arguments are entered differs depending upon which platform you are executing your Java programs. Consult a reference manual for further information.

argument is automatically converted into a string, and the operation of string catenation is performed. The result will be a new string value in which the left argument is immediately followed by the right argument. This feature is often used to format output. For example, suppose x is an integer variable, we could display the value of x by means of the following statement:

```
System.out.println("The value of x is " + x);
```

There are other interesting features of both strings and the array data type in Java that we will discuss in subsequent chapters.

4.4 ACCESS MODIFIERS

The modifier public appears twice in our example program, first in line 2 and then again in line 3.

```
public class FirstProgram {                                    // 2
    public static void main ( String [ ] args ) {              // 3
```

This modifier is one of a trio that are used to control the *accessibility* of names. The other possibilities are protected and private. By controlling access we mean that these modifiers control which objects in a program can make use of a name, and in which portions of a program that name can appear.

Recall once again our intuitive description of an object-oriented program as a community populated by many agents, or objects, that interact with one another in order to achieve some desired objective. Each object has a role to play, and that role is defined by the data values it holds and the services it can provide to the other objects in the universe.

Those features that are public are the aspects of an object that another object can see; the outward appearance of the object. Any feature that another object might want to use should be declared as public.

The use of the public modifier in front of the class keyword in our first program indicates that the entire class description is public; is visible to the program loader that gets an application ready for execution.

```
public class FirstProgram {                                    // 2
```

Similarly, the keyword used in front of the function named main indicates that the function is visible outside of the class. This means that the program loader not only can see the class FirstProgram, but also can see the function inside of the class. This is important; otherwise the program loader would not be able to execute the function.

```
public static void main ( String [ ] args ) {                  // 3
```

```
class BankAccount {

    private int accountBalance = 0;

    public void deposit (int amount) {
        accountBalance = accountBalance + amount;
        }

    public void withdrawal (int amount) {
        accountBalance = accountBalance - amount;
        }
}
```

Figure 4.3   A data field being hidden using the keyword private.

Frequently a programmer desires that features of a class, or entire classes themselves, be "hidden" from other classes. This means that other objects in the program universe cannot "see" these features, and since they cannot be seen, they cannot be manipulated.

Data fields are most commonly hidden. An object might want to hold a data value and not let the value be seen by other objects. It can do this by using the keyword private. For example, the class description shown in Figure 4.3 is a simple model of a bank account. The bank account object holds an "internal" piece of information, which represents the account balance. Because the variable holding this value is declared private, other objects in the program universe are not allowed to directly examine or modify the account balance. There are, however, two functions that are declared public. These allow deposits or withdrawals to be made from the bank account object. Thus, other objects in the simulation can indirectly modify the value of the balance (by performing a deposit or a withdrawal) even though they cannot directly set the account balance.

Private features (both data fields and functions) can only be accessed within the bounds of a class description. A third possibility, termed protected, comes into play when inheritance is used as a technique to create new types of objects out of an existing, older class description. A protected field is one that is still inaccessible to other objects but that *is* accessible within the bounds of any subclass (or derived class). We will see examples of this in subsequent chapters.

4.5   LIFETIME MODIFIERS

Another important keyword in our first program is the term static, which appears preceding the function main. Like the accessibility keywords, the keyword static can be applied both to data fields and to functions.

```
public static void main ( String [ ] args ) {              // 3
```

There are two ways to envision the meaning of the attributes described using this term. One way is to imagine that static fields are shared by all instances of a class. That is, no matter how many similar objects are created, only one manifestation of a static field will be created. This one field will be shared by all the instances of the class.

Because a static field is shared by all instances, it is not *part* of any one instance. In this sense it can be imagined to be outside of all instances. (Although accessibility modifiers can still be applied, a private but static data field is outside of all objects but can only be accessed from inside the class definition). Since a static data field is outside of the object definitions, it also exists no matter how many instances of a class have been created. In particular, a static field exists even if *no instances of a class have yet been created*!

It is for this reason that the main function in any program must be declared to be static. The main function must exist, even before any instances of the class have been created. The program loader selects this static function (which must also be public) and runs it. If it were not declared static, it would be necessary to first create an instance of the class before executing the function.

4.6   CHAPTER SUMMARY

The first *paradigm*, or example program, we have examined will print a single line of output and halt. Although trivial in purpose, the structure of this program is similar to every Java program we will subsequently encounter. Thus, a good appreciation of this simple example is a necessary prerequisite to understanding the remainder of this book:

```
import java.io.*;

public class FirstProgram {

   public static void main (String [ ] args ) {
      System.out.println ( "Your first Java program!" );
   }
}
```

- The import statement connects *this* Java program to the initial Java universe; it indicates which portions of the Java run-time system will be used by this program.

- A Java program is a sequence of class descriptions.

- Each class description consists of a class heading and a class body.

- The class heading consists of modifiers, the keyword class, and a class name.

- A class body is a sequence of members.

- A member is either a data member or a method.

- A method is a function, and it consists of a function heading and a function body.

- A function heading consists of modifiers, the function name, and the argument list.

- A function body is a sequence of statements.

- The modifier public indicates attributes (entire classes, or members within a class) that can be accessed and used by other objects.

- The modifier static indicates attributes (data members of methods) that are shared by all instances of a class. Such fields exist even when no instances of the class have yet been created.

- The function main must be declared as both public and static, since it must be visible to the program loader and must exist even before instances of the class have been created.

CROSS REFERENCES

Other, more extensive paradigms will be introduced in the remaining chapters in this part of the book. The keyword protected, discussed briefly in Section 4.4, becomes important when *inheritance* is used to create new classes. Inheritance will be investigated more fully beginning in Chapter 8. The class String and related facilities will be explored in Chapter 17.

STUDY QUESTIONS

1. What is the original meaning of the word *paradigm*?

2. What is the overall structure of a Java program?

3. What are the two major parts of a class description?

4. What are the two types of members that can be found within a class body?

5. What are the parts of a function header?

6. What operation is performed by System.out.println?

7. What is the type void mainly used for?

8. What does the difference in case in the initial letter of the types int and String indicate?

9. How in Java does one determine the number of elements held by an array?

10. What is the meaning of the + operator when one of the arguments is a String?

11. What are the three access modifier keywords? What does each of them signify?

12. When applied to a data field, what does the modifier static signify?

EXERCISES

1. Add a member function named display to the class description shown in Figure 4.3. When invoked, this function should print the current account balance.

2. The looping statement in Java uses the for keyword, and consists of three parts. The first part is an initialization statement, which can also be used to declare the loop variable. The second part is a test for termination; the loop will execute as long as the expression returns true. The final part is the increment, which is a statement that is evaluated to update the loop variable.

    Consider the following main program. Describe the effect produced by the program when it is executed with three command-line arguments.

    ```java
    public static void main ( String [ ] args ) {
        for (int i = 0; i < args.length; i = i + 1)
            System.out.println(args[i]);
    }
    ```

3. Now consider the following, slightly more complex program:

    ```java
    public static void main ( String [ ] args ) {
        for (int i = 0; i < args.length; i = i + 1)
            for (int j = 0; j <= i; j = j + 1)
                System.out.println(args[i]);
    }
    ```

    Describe the pattern of the output when the program is executed with three command-line arguments.

4. Consider the following main program:

    ```java
    public static void main ( String [ ] args ) {
        String result = "";
    ```

```
      for (int i = args.length - 1; i >= 0; i = i - 1)
          result = result + " " + args[i];
      System.out.println(result);
  }
```

What does this function do? What will be the result printed given the arguments Sam saw Sarah said Sally ?

5. Another useful function provided by the class String is the substr operation. This takes an integer argument, and returns the portion of the string that remains following the given index position. For example, if word is a variable containing the string "unhappy", then word.substr(2) is the string "happy".

   This operation is used in the following program. What will the output be given the command-line argument Sally?

```
static public void main ( String [ ] args ) {
    String name = args[0];
    String shortName = name.substr(1);
    System.out.println(name + "," + name + ", bo-B" + shortName);
    System.out.println("Banana-fana Fo-F" + shortName);
    System.out.println("Fee, Fie, mo-M" + shortName);
    System.out.println(name + "!");
}
```

6. By placing the code shown in the previous question inside a loop, write a program that will take any number of command-line arguments, and write one verse of the name game for each.

5 Ball Worlds

In the intuitive description of object-oriented programming presented in Chapter 1, an object-oriented program was described as a universe of interacting agents. However, in our first example Java program, in Chapter 4, we did not actually create any new objects, but only used the static procedure named main in the program class.

Our second program is slightly more complex in structure, although hardly more complicated in functionality. It places a graphical window on the user's screen, draws a ball that bounces around the window for a few moments, and then halts. The result is the screen shown as Figure 5.1.

Our second example program, or paradigm, is constructed out of two classes. The first of these appears in Figure 5.2. Again, we have added line numbers for the purposes of reference; however, these are not part of the actual program.[1] The reader should compare this program to the example program described in the previous chapter, noting both the similarities and differences. Like the previous program, this program imports (on line 1) information from the Java library. Like the earlier program, execution will begin in the procedure named main (lines 3–6), which is declared as static, void, and public. Like all main programs, this procedure must take as argument an array of string values, which are, in this case, being ignored.

---

[1] In order to draw more attention to the Java code itself, the programs presented in this text have purposely been written using very few comments. In practice, comments would usually be used to describe each function in a class.

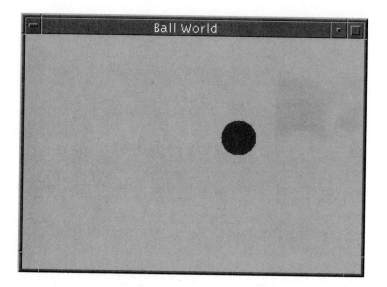

Figure 5.1   Ball World screen.

This program also incorporates a number of new features. These are summarized by the following list, and will be the subject of more detailed discussion in subsequent sections.

- The class defines a number of private internal variable fields, some of which are constant, some of which are initialized but not constant, and some of which are not initialized. These data fields will be described in detail in Section 5.1.

- The main program creates an instance of the class BallWorld. This object is initialized by means of a constructor. A *constructor* is a function that automatically ties together the actions of object *creation* and object *initialization*. Constructors will be introduced in Section 5.2.

- The class is declared as an *extension* of an existing Java class named Frame. This technique is called *inheritance*, and is the principal means in object-oriented languages for constructing new software abstractions that are variations on existing data types. Inheritance will be introduced in Section 5.3 and will be more extensively studied beginning in Chapter 8.

- The output displayed in a window by this program is created using some of the graphics primitives provided by the Java run-time library. These graphics operators are explained in Section 5.4.

```
import java.awt.*;                                            // 1

public class BallWorld extends Frame {                       // 2

    public static void main (String [ ] args) {              // 3
        BallWorld world = new BallWorld (Color.red);         // 4
        world.show ( );                                      // 5
    }                                                        // 6

    public static final int FrameWidth = 600;                // 7
    public static final int FrameHeight = 400;               // 8
    private Ball aBall;                                       // 9
    private int counter = 0;                                 // 10

    private BallWorld (Color ballColor) {// constructor for new window // 11
            // resize our frame, initialize title            // 12
        setSize (FrameWidth, FrameHeight);                   // 13
        setTitle ("Ball World");                             // 14

            // initialize aBall data field                   // 15
        aBall = new Ball (10, 15, 5);                        // 16
        aBall.setColor (ballColor);                          // 17
        aBall.setMotion (3.0, 6.0);                          // 18
    }                                                        // 19

    public void paint (Graphics g) {                         // 20
            // first, draw the ball                          // 21
        aBall.paint (g);                                     // 22
            // then move it slightly                         // 23
        aBall.move( );                                       // 24
        if ((aBall.x( ) < 0) || (aBall.x( ) > FrameWidth))   // 25
            aBall.setMotion (-aBall.xMotion( ), aBall.yMotion( )); // 26
        if ((aBall.y( ) < 0) || (aBall.y( ) > FrameHeight))  // 27
            aBall.setMotion (aBall.xMotion( ), -aBall.yMotion( )); // 28
            // finally, redraw the frame                     // 29
        counter = counter + 1;                               // 30
        if (counter < 2000) repaint( );                      // 31
        else System.exit(0);                                 // 32
    }                                                        // 33
}                                                            // 34
```

Figure 5.2   Class description for Ball World.

5.1   DATA FIELDS

We have seen in the previous chapter (Section 4.4) how data fields can be declared within a class and how they can be initialized. The example program here includes features we have not seen in our previous programs in the four data fields declared on lines 7–10:

```
public static final int FrameWidth = 600;          // 7
public static final int FrameHeight = 400;         // 8
private Ball aBall;                                 // 9
private int counter = 0;                            // 10
```

Recall that the keyword public means that the variables being declared can be accessed (that is, used directly) anywhere in a Java program, while those that are declared as private can be used only within the bounds of the class description in which the declaration appears. Recall also that the keyword static means that there is one instance of the data field, shared by all instances of the class. The modifier keyword final means that this is the last time when an object is changed. It is here applied to a variable declaration; we will in later chapters see how the modifier can also be applied to a function definition. When used with a variable declaration, the declaration must also include an initialization, as shown here.

Variables that are static and final are used to create symbolic names for constants, as they are variables that are guaranteed to exist only in one place and not change values. Because they cannot be modified, there is less reason to encapsulate a static final variable by declaring it private. Thus, such values are often made public, as shown here. The particular symbolic values being defined in this program represent the height and width of the window in which the application will eventually produce its output. Symbolic constants are useful in programs for a number of different reasons:

- By being defined in only one place, they make it easy to change subsequently, should circumstances require. For example, changing the height and or width of the window merely requires editing the file to change the values being used to initialize these symbolic constants, rather than hunting down all locations in the code where the quantities are used.

- When subsequently used elsewhere in the program, the symbolic name helps document the purpose of the constant values.

The counter data field is an integer value, initialized to zero:

```
private int counter = 0;                            // 10
```

Because the field is declared private, we know it can be used only within the bounds of the class definition. Because it was not declared static, we know that each instance of the class will hold its own different value. Because it was not declared final we know that the value being assigned is simply the initial value the variable will hold, but that it could subsequently be reassigned. We will see how this variable is used in the discussion of the graphical aspects of the current program.

```
private Ball aBall;                                              // 9
```

The final data field is declared as an instance of class Ball, which is the second class used in the creation of our example program. A ball is an abstraction that represents a bouncing ball. It is represented by a colored circle that can move around the display surface. The class Ball will be described in Section 5.5. How this field is initialized is described in the next section.

5.2   CONSTRUCTORS

As noted at the beginning of the chapter, one of the major topics of this chapter is the creation of new objects. This occurs in two places in the program shown in Figure 5.2. The first is in the main program, which creates an instance of the class BallWorld.

```
BallWorld world = new BallWorld (Color.red);                    // 4
```

The new operator is always used to create a new object. In this case, it is being used to create an instance of BallWorld, which (the next section shows) is the name given to the window in which the program will display its output. The new operator is followed by a class name, indicating the type of object being created. A parenthesized list then gives any arguments needed in the *initialization* of the object.

Object *creation* and object *initialization* are intimately tied in concept, and it is important that a programming language also bring these concepts together. Without support from the programming language, two types of errors can easily occur:

- An object is created, but it is used before it is initialized.

- An object is created and is initialized several times before it is used.

The language Java uses a concept called a *constructor* to guarantee that objects are placed into a proper initial state the moment they are created. A constructor bears a strong resemblance to a function; however, the name of the function matches the name of the class in which it appears, the function does not specify a return type, and the user will never directly execute the constructor. Like a function, though, a constructor can have arguments, and the body of the constructor consists of a sequence of statements. In our example program the constructor occurs in lines 11–19:

```
      private BallWorld (Color ballColor) {// constructor for new window 11
          // resize our frame, initialize title                    // 12
      setSize (FrameWidth, FrameHeight);                           // 13
      setTitle ("Ball World");                                     // 14

          // initialize aBall data field                           // 15
      aBall = new Ball (10, 15, 5);                                // 16
      aBall.setColor (ballColor);                                  // 17
      aBall.setMotion (3.0, 6.0);                                  // 18
      }                                                            // 19
```

When an object is created (via the new operator), the first function invoked using the newly created object is the constructor function. The arguments passed to the constructor are the arguments supplied in the new expression.

In this particular case, the argument represents a color. The class Color is part of the Java run-time library. The value red is simply a constant (a value declared both as static and final) in the class description of Color.

```
      BallWorld world = new BallWorld (Color.red);                 // 4
```

The corresponding parameter value in the constructor function is named ballColor (see line 11). The constructor function must ensure that the instance of the class BallWorld is properly initialized. As noted earlier, the BallWorld represents the window in which the output will be displayed. The first two statements in the constructor set some of the attributes for this window; namely, the size and the title.

Line 17 of the constructor again uses the new operator to create and initialize a new object. In this case the object is an instance of the class Ball. Not only will memory for this object be created by the new statement, but also the arguments will be matched by a corresponding constructor in the class Ball, which will then be invoked to initialize the newly created ball:

```
      public class Ball { // a generic round colored object that moves
         .
         .
         .
         public Ball (int x, int y, int r) { // ball with given center
                                             // and radius
            .
            .
            .
         }
      }
```

The complete class description for Ball will be shown in Figure 5.3. Not all aspects of a Ball are set by the constructor. The final two statements in the

```
public class Ball { // a generic round colored object that moves
   protected Rectangle location; // position on graphic surface
   protected double dx, dy; // x and y components of motion vector
   protected Color color;   // color of ball

   public Ball (int x, int y, int r) { // ball with given center and radius
      location = new Rectangle(x-r, y-r, 2*r, 2*r);
      dx = 0; dy = 0; // initially no motion
      color = Color.blue;
   }

      // functions that set attributes
   public void setColor (Color newColor) { color = newColor; }

   public void setMotion (double ndx, double ndy) { dx = ndx; dy = ndy; }

      // functions that access attributes of ball
   public int radius () { return location.width / 2; }

   public int x () { return location.x + radius(); }

   public int y () { return location.y + radius(); }

   public double xMotion () { return dx; }

   public double yMotion () { return dy; }

   public Rectangle region () { return location; }

      // functions that change attributes of ball
   public void moveTo (int x, int y) { location.setLocation (x, y); }

   public void move () { location.translate ((int) dx, (int) dy); }

   public void paint (Graphics g) {
      g.setColor (color);
      g.fillOval
         (location.x, location.y, location.width, location.height);
   }
}
```

Figure 5.3 Implementation of the class Ball.

constructor for **BallWorld** set the color of the ball, and set the direction of motion for the ball. These attributes will be discussed in more detail in Section 5.5.

5.3   INHERITANCE

The most important feature of this program is the use of *inheritance* (sometimes also called *extension*). As noted earlier, the ball world is a rectangular window in which the action of the program (the bouncing ball) is displayed. The code needed to display and manipulate a window in a modern graphical user interface is exceedingly complex, in part because of the fact that the user can indicate actions such as moving, resizing, or iconifying the window. As a consequence, recent languages attempt to provide a means of reusing existing code so that the programmer need only be concerned with those features of the application that distinguish the program from other window applications.

The programming language Java uses the class **Frame** to represent a generic window. By saying that the class **BallWorld** extends the class **Frame**, we indicate that our new class, **BallWorld**, is a type of frame, but a more specialized type with a single purpose. The class **Frame** defines code to perform actions such as resizing the window, arranging for the window to be displayed on the workstation screen, and so on. By extending the class **Frame**, our new class *inherits* this functionality, which means the abilities are made available to the new class, and do not need to be rewritten anew.

```
public class BallWorld extends Frame {                          // 2
```

By executing the example program, the reader can verify that the window exhibits the functionality we expect of graphical windows—the ability to move, resize, and iconify, even though the program does not explicitly define any code to support these behaviors. (The reader might also note some expected behaviors that are not provided. For example, the handling of menu items and the close or quit box. A later chapter will describe how these features can be provided.)

We can observe the use of inheritance in the variety of methods that are invoked in our example program, but are not defined by the class **BallWorld**. These functions are instead inherited from the *parent class* **Frame**. Two examples are the functions **setSize** and **setTitle** invoked in the **BallWorld** constructor. These functions set the dimensions (in pixels) and title value for the window, respectively.

```
private BallWorld (Color ballColor) {// constructor for new window 11
        // resize our frame, initialize title                  // 12
    setSize (FrameWidth, FrameHeight);                          // 13
    setTitle ("Ball World");                                    // 14
        .
        .
        .
    }                                                           // 19
```

Another example is the function show, which is invoked in the static procedure main after the instance of BallWorld has been created. The show function arranges for the window to appear on the display surface, and then for the surface of the window to be drawn.

```
public static void main (String [ ] args) {          // 3
    BallWorld world = new BallWorld (Color.red);     // 4
    world.show ();                                   // 5
}                                                    // 6
```

5.4   THE JAVA GRAPHICS MODEL

Graphics in Java is provided as part of the Abstract Windowing Toolkit (AWT). The Java AWT is an example of a software *framework*. The idea of a framework is to provide the structure of a program but no application-specific details. The overall control, the flow of execution, is provided by the framework and therefore does not need to be rewritten for each new program. Thus, the programmer does not "see" the majority of the program code.

This is illustrated by the actions that occur subsequent to the program issuing the show method that is inherited from the class Frame. The window in which the action will take place is created, and the image of the window must be rendered. To do so, the show method invokes a function named paint, passing as argument a *graphics object*.

The programmer defines the appearance of the window by providing an implementation of the function paint. The graphics object passed as argument provides the ability to draw a host of items, such as lines and polygons as well as text. In our example program we use the paint procedure for two purposes. The only image in the window itself is the bouncing ball. The image of the ball is produced by invoking the paint method in the class Ball (see Figure 5.3). The second purpose of the paint method is to provide a simple means of updating the location for the ball. The ball is moved slightly, checking to see if the resulting new location is outside the bounds of the window. If it is outside the window the direction of the ball is reversed. Finally, invoking the repaint method (also inherited from Frame) indicates to the framework that the window should be redrawn, and the cycle continues.[2] A counter is used to prevent the program from running indefinitely, invoking the function System.exit after a certain number of iterations. (Later programs will use other techniques to halt the program.)

---

[2] Some readers might object that the control of the animation has little to do with the rendering of the image on the window and thus does not belong in the paint routine. While there is merit to this argument, this is also the simplest way to make primitive animations. Later chapters present more robust ways to control animations.

```
public void paint (Graphics g) {                                // 20
    // first, draw the ball                                      // 21
  aBall.paint (g);                                               // 22
    // then move it slightly                                     // 23
  aBall.move( );                                                 // 24
  if ((aBall.x( ) < 0) || (aBall.x( ) > FrameWidth))            // 25
    aBall.setMotion (-aBall.xMotion( ), aBall.yMotion( ));      // 26
  if ((aBall.y( ) < 0) || (aBall.y( ) > FrameHeight))          // 27
    aBall.setMotion (aBall.xMotion( ), -aBall.yMotion( ));      // 28
    // finally, redraw the frame                                 // 29
  counter = counter + 1;                                         // 30
  if (counter < 2000) repaint( );                                // 31
  else System.exit(0);                                           // 32
}                                                                // 33
```

Note that the programmer calls the inherited method named repaint, which in turn will eventually result in the paint method being invoked. The programmer does not directly call the paint method for the class.

In later examples we will investigate more of the abilities of the graphics objects provided by the Java library.

5.5   THE CLASS Ball

We will use a ball, that is, round colored object that moves, in a number of our subsequent example programs. It is therefore useful to define the behavior of a Ball in a general fashion so that it can be used in a variety of ways. The description of class Ball is placed in its own file (Ball.java) and is linked together with the BallWorld class to create the executable program.

A Ball (Figure 5.3) maintains four data fields. The location of the ball is represented by a Rectangle, a general purpose class provided in the Java runtime library. Two floating-point values represent the horizontal and vertical components of the direction of motion for the ball. Finally, the color of the ball is represented by an instance of class Color, a Java library class we have previously encountered.

These four data fields are declared as protected. This allows any subsequent child classes we might create to have access to the data fields, without exposing the data to modification by other objects. It is good practice to declare data fields protected, rather than private, even if you do not anticipate extending the class to make new classes.

The constructor for the class Ball records the location by creating a new instance of class Rectangle. Note that the three integer arguments passed as arguments to the constructor represent the center location of the ball and the radius: A simple calculation is used to convert these to the corner of the rectangle and the extent. The constructor also provides default values for color (blue) and motion. As we have seen in our example program, these can be redefined by invoking the functions setColor and setMotion.

A number of functions are used to access some of the attributes of a ball. Attributes that can be obtained in this fashion include the radius, the *x* and *y* coordinate of the center of the ball, the horizontal and vertical directions of motion, and the region occupied by the ball. Functions that allow access to a data field in a class are termed *accessor functions*. The use of accessor functions is strongly encouraged in preference to making the data fields themselves public, as an accessor function only permits the value to be *read*, and not modified. This ensures that any modification to a data field will be mediated by the proper function, such as through the function setMotion or moveTo.

Some of the functions use operations provided by the class Rectangle. A rectangle can provide a width (used in function radius), the location of the upper corner (used in functions x and y), can move to a new position (used in function moveTo), and can transliterate on the two-dimensional surface (used in the function move).

Finally, the function paint uses two operations that are provided by the class Graphics in the Java library. These are the ability to set the current color for rendering graphics (setColor) and to display a painted oval at a given location on the window (fillOval).

5.6 MULTIPLE OBJECTS OF THE SAME CLASS

Every instance of a class maintains its own internal data fields. We can illustrate this by making variations on our sample program. The simplest change is to modify the main routine to create two independent windows. Each window will have a different ball, each window can be independently moved or resized.

```
public static void main (String [ ] args) {
        // create first window with red ball
    BallWorld world = new BallWorld (Color.red);
    world.show( );
        // now create a second window with yellow ball
    BallWorld world2 = new BallWorld (Color.yellow);
    world2.show( );
}
```

The reader should try making this change, and observe the result. Note how one window is bouncing a red ball and the second is bouncing a yellow ball. This indicates that each instance of class BallWorld must be maintaining its own Ball value, given that a ball cannot be both red and yellow at the same time.

A second variation illustrates even more dramatically the independence of different objects, even when they derive from the same class. The class MultiBallWorld

```
public class MultiBallWorld extends Frame {

    .
    .
    .
  private Ball [ ] ballArray;
  private static final int BallArraySize = 10;

  private MultiBallWorld (Color ballColor) {
      .
      .
      .
      // initialize object data field
    ballArray = new Ball [ BallArraySize ];
    for (int i = 0; i < BallArraySize; i++) {
       ballArray[i] = new Ball(10, 15, 5);
       ballArray[i].setColor (ballColor);
       ballArray[i].setMotion (3.0+i, 6.0-i);
       }
    }

  public void paint (Graphics g) {
     for (int i = 0; i < BallArraySize; i++) {
        ballArray[i].paint (g);
          // then move it slightly
        ballArray[i].move();
        if ((ballArray[i].x() < 0) ||
             (ballArray[i].x() > FrameWidth))
           ballArray[i].setMotion
              (-ballArray[i].xMotion(), ballArray[i].yMotion());
        if ((ballArray[i].y() < 0) ||
             (ballArray[i].y() > FrameHeight))
           ballArray[i].setMotion
              (ballArray[i].xMotion(), -ballArray[i].yMotion());
        .
        .
        .
        }
     }
}
```

Figure 5.4   Class description for Multiple Ball World.

(Figure 5.4) is similar to our initial program except that it creates a collection of balls rather than just a single ball. Only the lines that have changed are included, and those that are elided are the same as the earlier program. The new program declares an array of Balls, rather than just a single ball. Note the syntax used to declare an array. As noted in the previous chapter, arrays in Java are different from arrays in most other languages. Even though the array is declared, space is still not set aside for the array elements. Instead, the array itself must be created (again with a new command):

```
ballArray = new Ball [ BallArraySize ];
```

Note how the size of the array is specified by a symbolic constant, defined earlier in the program. Even then, however, the array elements cannot be accessed. Instead, each array element must be individually created, once more using a new operation:

```
for (int i = 0; i < BallArraySize; i++) {
    ballArray[i] = new Ball(10, 15, 5);
    ballArray[i].setColor (ballColor);
    ballArray[i].setMotion (3.0+i, 6.0-i);
    }
```

Each ball is created, then initialized with the given color, and set in motion. We have used the loop index variable to change the direction of motion slightly, so that each ball will initially move in a different direction.

When the program is executed, ten different balls will be created. Each ball will maintain its own location and direction. As each ball is asked to paint, it will display its value on the window. Each ball will then move, independently of all other balls.

5.7 CHAPTER SUMMARY

The two major themes introduced in this chapter have been the creation of new objects using the operator new, and the definition of new classes using *inheritance* to extend an existing class. Topics discussed in this chapter include the following:

- Data fields that are declared final cannot be subsequently redefined. A static and final value is the technique normally used to create a symbolic constant.

- New objects are always created using the operator new.

- When a new object is created, the *constructor* for the class of the object is automatically invoked as part of the creation process. The constructor should guarantee the object is properly initialized.

- A constructor is a function that has the same name as the class in which it is defined.

- Any arguments used by the constructor must appear in the new statement that creates the corresponding object.

- Classes can be defined using *inheritance*. Such classes extend the functionality of an existing class. Any public or protected data fields or functions defined in the parent class become part of the new class.

- The class Frame can be used to create simple Java windows. This class can be extended to define application-specific windows.

- The *framework* provided by the Java AWT displays a frame (a window) when the frame object is given the message show. To create the image shown in the window the message paint is used. The programmer can define this method to produce application-specific pictures.

- The paint method is given as argument an instance of the library class Graphics. This object can be used to create a variety of graphical images.

- The class Rectangle (used in our class Ball) is a library class that represents a rectangular region on the two-dimensional window surface. The class provides a large amount of useful functionality.

- Multiple instances of the same class each maintain their own separate data fields. This was illustrated by creating multiple independent Ball objects, which move independently of each other.

Cross References

We will use the Ball class in case studies in Chapters 6–8 and 20. The topic of inheritance is simple to explain but has many subtle points that can easily trap the unwary. We will examine inheritance in detail in Chapters 8 through 11. The AWT will be examined in more detail in Chapter 13.

Study Questions

1. How would you change the color of the ball in our example application to yellow?

2. How would you change the size of the application window to 500 by 300 pixels?

3. What does the modifier keyword final mean when applied in a data field declaration?

4. Why do symbolic constants make it easier to read and maintain programs?

5. What two actions are tied together by the concept of a constructor?

6. What types of errors does the use of constructors prevent?

7. What does it mean to say that a new class inherits from an existing class?

8. What methods inherited from class Frame are used in our example application?

9. What methods provided by our example program are invoked by the code inherited from class Frame?

10. What abstraction does the Java library class Rectangle represent?

11. What are some reasons that data fields should be declared as private or protected, and access provided only through member functions?

12. In Java, what are the steps involved in creating an array of objects?

EXERCISES

1. The function Math.random returns a random floating-point value between 0 and 1.0. Using this function, modify the example program shown in Figure 5.2 so that the ball will initially move in a random direction.

2. Modify the MultiBallWorld so that the colors of the various balls created are selected randomly from the values red, blue and yellow. (*Hint*: Call Math.random( ) and test the resulting value for various ranges, selecting red if the value is in one range, blue if it is in another, and so on.)

3. Modify the MultiBallWorld so that it will produce balls of different radiuses, as well as different colors.

4. Rather than testing whether or not a ball has hit the wall in our main program, we could have used inheritance to provide a specialized form of Ball. Create a class BoundedBall that inherits from class Ball. The constructor for this class should provide the height and width of the window, which should subsequently be maintained as data fields in the class. Rewrite the move function so that if the ball moves outside the bounds, it automatically reverses direction. Finally, rewrite the BallWorld class to use an instance of BoundedBall, rather than an ordinary Ball, and eliminate the bounds test in the main program.

5. Our Ball abstraction is not as simple as it could have been. Separate the Ball class into two separate classes. The first, the new class Ball, knows only a location, its size, and how to paint itself. The second class, MovableBall, extends the class Ball and adds all behavior related to motion, such as the data fields dx and dy, the functions setMotion and move, and so on. Rewrite the MultiBallWorld to use instances of class MovableBall.

A Cannon Game

In this chapter we will examine an implementation of a classic "shooting cannon" game. In this simple game there is a cannon on the left portion of the user's window, and a target on the right portion, as shown in Figure 6.1. The user can control the angle of elevation for the cannon and fire a cannonball. The objective of the game is, of course, to hit the target.

As with all the case studies, our objective is not so much the cannon application itself, which is only moderately interesting, but the use of a simple program to illustrate a number of different features of the Java language. In particular, in this chapter we will examine the features of the Java library that simplify the creation of a graphical user interface (GUI). We will develop two variations on this game:

- The first version is the simplest. The user enters the angle of the cannon from the command argument line, the cannon fires once, and the program halts.

Figure 6.1   A window of the Cannon Game.

■ In the second version, we improve user interaction, by providing both a slider with which the angle of the cannon can be changed, and a button to fire the cannon. Thus, multiple attempts to hit the target can be made during one execution of the program.

6.1   THE SIMPLE CANNON GAME

The principal class for our cannon application is shown in Figure 6.2. The main method is similar to those described in the previous chapters. The universe for our application is termed CannonGame. An instance of this class is created, then passed the message show. The message show causes the window in which the application is played to be displayed.

In our first version of the Cannon Game, the angle for the cannon is read from the command-line argument. The first string in the command-line argument list is assumed to be an integer value, representing the angle (in degrees) for the cannon to be set prior to launch of the cannonball. This value is parsed by a method from the Java library class Integer, and passed as argument to the constructor for the cannon world. There, the method intValue) is used to convert an Integer into an int. We will return to a discussion of the relationship between these two data types in Section 6.1.2.

The cannon world is declared to be a type of Frame, which you will recall from the preceding chapter is how Java declares a new type of window. The class description defines two public constant values (declared as static final, see Section 5.1) that describe the height and width of the window that represents the cannon application. In addition, three new data fields are declared. These are the angle of the cannon, a message that will be displayed in the middle of the playing window, and a cannonball. The latter is an instance of class CannonBall, which will be described shortly.

The constructor for the class CannonGame resizes the window frame to the declared bounds, and sets the window title. The argument value is converted from the type Integer to the built-in type int using the method intValue. The string representing the message is set to a value that will, when printed, indicate the current angle of the cannon. Finally, the cannonball is created using the angle to determine the initial direction of movement. There are two other methods defined in this class. The method dy is used in the display function and will be described shortly. The remaining method paints the window area.

Rendering pictures is complicated by the fact that Java, like almost all windowing systems, uses a coordinate system that is "upside down." As shown in Figure 6.3, the upper left corner of a window is the 0,0 coordinate, with x values increasing as they move right, and y values increasing as they move *down*. However, most people prefer to think in a coordinate system where the 0,0 location is the bottom left corner, and y values increase as they move *up* as depicted in Figure 6.4.

```
class CannonGame extends Frame {

    public static void main (String [ ] args) {
        CannonGame world = new CannonGame (Integer.valueOf(args[0]));
        world.show ( );
    }

    public static final int FrameWidth = 600;
    public static final int FrameHeight = 400;

        // data fields
    private int angle = 45;
    private String message = "";
    private CannonBall cannonBall = null;
    private static final int barrelLength = 30;
    private static final int barrelWidth = 10;

        // constructor
    public CannonGame (Integer theta) {

        setSize (FrameWidth, FrameHeight);
        setTitle ("Cannon Game");

            // set the local variables
        angle = theta.intValue( );
        message = "Angle = " + angle;

            // create the cannon ball
        double radianAngle = angle * Math.PI / 180.0;
        double sinAngle = Math.sin(radianAngle);
        double cosAngle = Math.cos(radianAngle);
        double initialVelocity = 12;
        cannonBall = new CannonBall (   // calculations determine end of cannon
            20 + (int) (barrelLength * cosAngle),
            dy(5+(int) (barrelLength * sinAngle)),
            5, initialVelocity * cosAngle, -initialVelocity * sinAngle);
    }

    public int dy (int y) { return FrameHeight - y; }

    public void paint (Graphics g) { ... }
}
```

Figure 6.2 Description of the principal class for the Cannon Game.

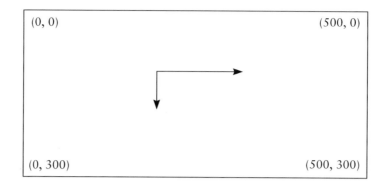

Figure 6.3   The "upside down" coordinate system of Java and other windowing software.

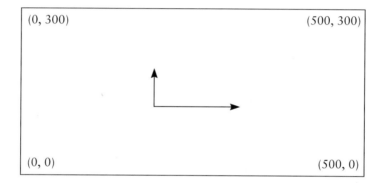

Figure 6.4   Coordinate system as most people think of it.

One way to handle this is to perform a coordinate transformation as the very last operation before any drawing command. This is the task of the function dy, shown in Figure 6.2. By subtracting a value from the maximum window size, we can take a value in the more natural coordinate system, and convert it into a value in the upside-down coordinate system. An advantage of the function dy is that it is self-inverting; applying the function twice returns the original value. We will use this observation by expressing all our drawing operations in the zero-centered form while allowing the ball itself to work in the Java window coordinates.

The method to draw the elements in the Cannon Game world is shown in Figure 6.5. Recall from the previous chapter that drawing is performed by the method paint, which will be invoked implicitly when the application is shown, and can be requested explicitly by invoking the method repaint. Also recall that

```
class CannonGame {
    public void paint (Graphics g) {
        int x = 20;  // location of cannon
        int y = 5;
        double radianAngle = angle * Math.PI / 180.0;
        int lv = (int) (barrelLength * Math.sin(radianAngle));
        int lh = (int) (barrelLength * Math.cos(radianAngle));
        int sv = (int) (barrelWidth * Math.sin(radianAngle + Math.PI/2));
        int sh = (int) (barrelWidth * Math.cos(radianAngle + Math.PI/2));
            // draw cannon
        g.setColor(Color.green);
        g.drawLine(x, dy(y), x+lh, dy(y+lv));
        g.drawLine(x+ln, dy(y+lv), x+lh+sh, dy(y+lv+sv));
        g.drawLine(x+lh+sh, dy(y+lv+sv), x+sh, dy(y+sv));
        g.drawLine(x+sh, dy(y+sv), x, dy(y));
        g.drawOval(x-8, dy(y+10), 12, 12);
            // draw target
        g.setColor(Color.red);
        g.fillRoundRect(FrameWidth-100, dy(12), 50, 10, 6, 6);
            // draw cannon ball
        if (cannonBall != null) {
            cannonBall.move();
            cannonBall.paint(g);
            if (dy(cannonBall.y()) > 0)
                repaint();
            else {
                int targetX = FrameWidth - 100;
                if ((cannonBall.x() > targetX) &&
                        (cannonBall.x() < (targetX + 50)))
                    message = "You Hit It!";
                else
                    message = "Missed!";
                cannonBall = null;
            }
        }
            // draw message
        g.drawString(message, FrameWidth/2, FrameHeight/2);
    }
}
```

Figure 6.5 Class description for the Cannon Game application.

drawing commands are provided by the library class Graphics, an instance of which is supplied to the paint method. The cannon itself is represented by a rectangle, 10 pixels by 30, with a circular wheel. A bit of simple math is used to tilt the cannon to the appropriate angle. One complicating factor is that the application is representing angles in degrees using an integer value, while the sine and cosine functions in the Math library require a double-precision floating-point value in radians. A simple algorithm is used to convert between the two. The target is represented by a red rectangle. If a cannonball exists, it is asked to move itself, paint itself at the transformed location, and if not at the final target, schedule the picture for another repainting.[1] Finally, the message is printed in the middle of the playing area.

6.1.1   *Balls That Respond to Gravity*

The class Ball was introduced in Chapter 5. A Ball, you will recall, possessed a radius, a location, a color, and a direction. The latter was represented by a pair of values, representing the extent of motion in the *x* coordinate and the extent of motion in the *y* coordinate.

A CannonBall is built using inheritance as an extension of class Ball. This means that a CannonBall has all the properties of a Ball and also includes new properties or alters existing properties. In this case, a CannonBall changes the move method, simulating the effect of gravity by reducing the change in the vertical direction by a small amount each update cycle.

```
public class CannonBall extends Ball {

    public CannonBall (int sx, int sy, int r, double dx, double dy)
    {
        super (sx, sy, r);
        setMotion (dx, dy);
    }

    public int GravityEffect = 0.3;

    public void move () {
        dy = dy + GravityEffect;
        super.move( ); // update the ball position
    }
}
```

---

[1] Please remember that we are using the paint procedure in this manner merely as a simple means of animation. Later chapters will demonstrate how to move the control over the animation out of the paint routine.

We have not yet encountered the pseudovariable super, shown here in both functions. When a method *overrides* (that is, replaces) a similarly named function in the parent class, a technique must be provided to indicate that the function should invoke the procedure inherited from the parent class. The function cannot simply be named, as the name in the child class and the parent class are the same. Thus, for example, if one was to try to invoke the move function in class Ball by simply executing the function move, the result would be an infinite series of recursive function calls; which is not the outcome we wish.

The pseudovariable super is used to represent the receiver but is viewed as an instance of the parent class, not the current class. Thus, by invoking super.move( ), the procedure move is asking that the move function from the parent class be executed, and not the version overridden by the class CannonBall.

Similarly, the use of the name super as a function in a constructor is used to indicate that the constructor for the parent class should be invoked, using the arguments shown. Note how the class CannonBall is invoked with a slightly different set of arguments than were used for the class Ball.

6.1.2 *Integers and* ints

As noted in Section 4.3 of Chapter 4, integer values are not actually *objects*, in the technical sense of the world. Thus, integers do not have classes, there are no methods associated with integers, and so on. For each of the nonclass primitive types, the Java library defines a "wrapper" class that can be used as an object. For integers this wrapper class is named Integer. The class Integer provides a number of useful operations. The one we utilize in our example program is the ability to take a String (the command-line argument), and convert it into a numeric value. To do this, a string is passed as argument to the message valueOf:

```
CannonGame world = new CannonGame (Integer.valueOf(args[0]));
```

The result produced by the message valueOf is a new instance of class Integer, initialized to the indicated value. The conversion from Integer to int is performed using the message intValue:

```
angle = theta.intValue( );
```

6.2 ADDING USER INTERACTION

The user interaction in our first application was very primitive. The user could select one angle, run the program, and see the result. In our second variation, we improve user interaction by providing the ability to dynamically set the angle of the cannon, and fire several times during one execution.

The conventional way to set a varying quantity, such as the angle of the cannon, is with a scroll bar. The normal way to indicate that an action should

Figure 6.6   A screen of the revised game, renamed CannonWorld.

commence, such as the cannon should be fired, is with a button. In our revised game we will incorporate both these items, placing the button on the top of the screen, and the scroll bar to the right of the playing area, as shown in Figure 6.6.

The program for the revised game, now named CannonWorld, is shown in Figure 6.7. One feature to note is that we must now import the Java library java.awt.Event.*, in order to include the definitions of the event-handling routines for the Java system. This is in addition to the java.awt.* library we have been including from the start. Although in code length the amount of change from the first version of our program is relatively small, a number of important features distinguish this program. We will explore these in the following sections.

6.2.1   *Inner Classes*

One of the more notable features of the program in Figure 6.7 is the declaration of two new classes *within* the application class itself. A class declared in such a fashion is known as an *inner class*. Modifiers used in declaring an inner class match the meanings we have previously described for data fields and methods; thus, an inner class that is declared as private (such as shown here) can only be used within the outer class in which it is defined.

```
class CannonWorld extends Frame {
    .
    .
    .

    private class FireButtonListener implements ActionListener {
        .
        .
        .
    }
```

```java
import java.awt.Event.*; // import the event interface

class CannonWorld extends Frame {
   .
   .
   .
   private String message = "Angle: " + angle;
   private CannonBall cannonBall = null;
   private Scrollbar slider;

   private class FireButtonListener implements ActionListener {
      public void actionPerformed (ActionEvent e) {
         double radianAngle = angle * Math.PI / 180.0;
         double sinAngle = Math.sin(radianAngle);
         double cosAngle = Math.cos(radianAngle);
         // create the cannon ball
         cannonBall = new CannonBall (
            20 + (int) (barrelLength * cosAngle),
            dy(5+(int) (barrelLength * sinAngle)),
            5, 12 * cosAngle, -12 * sinAngle);
         repaint( );
         }
   }

   private class ScrollBarListener implements AdjustmentListener {
      public void adjustmentValueChanged (AdjustmentEvent e) {
         angle = slider.getValue( );
         message = "Angle: " + angle;
         repaint( );
         }
   }

   public CannonWorld ( ) {
      setSize (FrameWidth, FrameHeight);
      setTitle ("Cannon Game");
         // add the scroll bar and button
      Button fire = new Button("fire");
      fire.addActionListener(new FireButtonListener( ));
      add ("North", fire);
      slider = new Scrollbar(Scrollbar.VERTICAL, angle, 5, 0, 90);
      slider.addAdjustmentListener(new ScrollBarListener( ));
      add ("East", slider);
   }
}
```

Figure 6.7   Revised program renamed CannonWorld with button and slider.

```
                private class ScrollBarListener implements AdjustmentListener {
                    .
                    .
                    .
                }

            .
            .
            .

        }
```

Inner classes are allowed to access their surrounding environment. That is, methods in an inner class can use data fields declared in the surrounding outer class, as well as invoke methods from the surrounding context. We see this in the method defined in class ScrollBarListener, which modifies both the data fields angle and message.

6.2.2   *Interfaces*

Both the inner classes created in this example use the keyword implements in their header. The *implementation* of an *interface* is yet another program-structuring mechanism, one that can be understood by comparison to the technique of *inheritance* we have been using previously.

An interface in Java is a description of *behavior*. It is written in a fashion that appears similar to a class definition; however, there are no implementations (function bodies) associated with methods, and the only data fields permitted must be declared static. An interface for ActionListener, used in our sample program, might be written as follows:

```
interface ActionListener {
    public void actionPerformed (ActionEvent);
}
```

The Java library, particularly in those sections that relate to the handling of events (such as pressing buttons or moving sliders), makes extensive use of interfaces. When a class is declared as implementing an interface, it is a guarantee (one that is checked by the compiler) that the class must provide a certain behavior. In this case, an assertion that a class is an ActionListener means that the class must provide a function named actionPerformed.

The reader should consider carefully the difference between this and inheritance. Using inheritance, functions and data fields that are declared in the parent class may be used in the child class. Thus, the child class inherits the *structure* of the parent, as well as being able to mimic the parent behavior. Using an interface, on the other hand, there is no implementation of the functions in the "parent interface" at all. Instead, the parent simply defines the names of the functions, which *must* then be defined in the child class. In this manner a child class inherits a specification of methods from an interface, but no structure, no data fields, and no member functions.

Despite the fact that functions of an interface have no implementation, an interface can be used as a type name in an argument declared in a function header. The matching parameter value must then be an instance of a class that implements the interface. In our example program, the addActionListener method in class Button expects an argument that implements the ActionListener interface, and the addAdjustmentListener method in class ScrollBar expects an argument that implements the AdjustmentListener interface.

6.2.3 *The Java Event Model*

Modern graphical user interfaces are structured around the concept of events. An *event* is an action, such as the user clicking the mouse on a button, selecting a menu item, pressing a key, or inserting a disk into a drive. The program responds to an event by performing certain actions. Thus, such interfaces are said to be *event-driven*.

The Java event model is based on the concept of listeners. A *listener* is an object whose sole purpose is to sit and wait for an event to occur. When the event does occur, the listener goes into action and performs the appropriate behavior.

Our sample program uses two listeners. The first is waiting for the button to be pressed. The class Button is one of many graphical elements provided by the Java library. The string argument passed to the constructor for the class is the text that will appear on the face of the button. A listener for a button must implement the interface ActionListener. The listener in our sample program is declared as an instance of the inner class FireButtonListener, and is attached to a newly created button by the following code:

```
Button fire = new Button("Fire");
fire.addActionListener(new FireButtonListener());
```

When the button is pressed, the message actionPerformed will be passed to the listener. In this case, this message will be handled by the one method in the class body:

```
private class FireButtonListener implements ActionListener {
    public void actionPerformed (ActionEvent e) {
        // convert angle in degrees to radians
        double radianAngle = angle * Math.PI / 180.0;
        double sinAngle = Math.sin(radianAngle);
        double cosAngle = Math.cos(radianAngle);
        // create the cannon ball
        cannonBall = new CannonBall ( // calculations to find end of
                                      // cannon
            20 + (int) (barrelLength * cosAngle),
```

```
            dy(5+(int) (barrelLength * sinAngle)),
            5, 12 * cosAngle, -12 * sinAngle);
        repaint( );
        }
    }
```

The argument of type ActionEvent which is passed to the procedure actionPer-formed describes details of the event with more precision. However, the value is ignored, since in this case there is only one event a button can perform that is of any interest, namely the event that occurs when it is pressed. The action when this occurs is to convert the angle of elevation for the cannon into radians, create a new cannonball for firing, and schedule the window for repainting.

The slider that is used to control the elevation of the cannon is created in a similar fashion. The constructor for class ScrollBar takes as argument an indication whether the slidebar is horizontal or vertical, an initial value, and the range of accepted values. The constructor for our application creates both a new slider and a new listener:

```
    // create a vertical scroll bar, limits zero and 90, step size 5
    // initial value set by value in variable angle
slider = new Scrollbar(Scrollbar.VERTICAL, angle, 5, 0, 90);
slider.addAdjustmentListener(new ScrollBarListener( ));
```

The listener must implement the AdjustmentListener interface. When the slider is moved, the listener is given the message adjustmentValueChanged. Note that, unlike the situation involving the button, the slide bar must be made available to the listener, so that the current value of the slide bar can be determined (using the message getValue). It is for this reason that the slide bar is saved in a data field, but the button need not be. Once the value of the slide bar has been determined, the angle and message can be changed, and the window scheduled for repainting.

```
    private class ScrollBarListener implements AdjustmentListener {
        public void adjustmentValueChanged (AdjustmentEvent e) {
            angle = slider.getValue( );
            message = "Angle: " + angle;
            repaint( );
            }
        }
```

6.2.4   Window Layout

Part of every Java program is a *layout manager*. The layout manager controls the placement of graphical items in a Java program. By using sophisticated layout managers the programmer can have a great deal of control over the appearance of a Java window. For simple programs, however, we can use the default layout manager, which permits values to be placed on the four sides of the screen. These four portions of the screen are identified as North (the top), East (the right), West (the left), and South (the bottom). The constructor for our application places the button on the top of the window, and the slider on the right hand side.

```
public CannonWorld () {
     .
     .
     .
     // add the scroll bar
     Button fire = new Button("fire");
     fire.addActionListener(new FireButtonListener());
  add ("North", fire);
     slider = new ScrollBar(Scrollbar.VERTICAL, angle, 5, 0, 90);
     slider.addAdjustmentListener(new ScrollBarListener());
  add ("East", slider);
}
```

In later chapters we will explore a variety of other layout managers.

6.3   CHAPTER SUMMARY

This chapter has once again made use of a relatively simple application as a vehicle to introduce a number of new concepts. The following list summarizes some of the ideas introduced in this chapter:

- The class Integer, which is a wrapper class that can hold an integer value. Instances of this class are objects, unlike normal integer values, which are not objects. The class Integer provides some useful functionality, such as the ability to parse a string value that holds the textual representation of an integer quantity.

- The use of inheritance in the construction of the class CannonBall, so that the majority of the behavior for the ball is inherited from the parent class Ball.

- The pseudovariable super, which when used as a value inside a method refers to the parent class from which the current class inherits.

- The idea of an *inner class*, which is a class definition nested within another class definition. Inner classes are allowed full access to the data values and functions provided by surrounding classes.

- The idea of an *interface*, which is a means to ensure that classes satisfy certain behavior. An interface defines the names and arguments for member functions but does not provide an implementation. A class that declares itself as implementing an interface must then provide an implementation for these operations. A function can insist that an argument implement certain functionality, by declaring the argument using the interface as a type.

- The Java event model, in which *listener* objects are attached to event producing objects, such as buttons. When an event occurs, the listener is notified and then performs whatever action is appropriate.

- The graphical component classes Button and Slider, which simplify the creation of graphical features in a user interface.

- The idea of a window layout manager. In our application program we used the default layout manager, which is an instance of the class BorderLayout.

Note that as our application has become more complex, we have moved closer to the idea that an object-oriented programming is a "community" of agents that interact to produce the desired behavior. Instances of following categories of objects are all used in this example program:

- The class CannonWorld, which inherits from the class Frame provided by the Java library.

- The class CannonBall, built as an extension of the earlier class Ball developed in Chapter 5.

- The class Integer, used here for its ability to translate a number in text into a numeric quantity.

- The graphical component classes Button and ScrollBar, and their listener classes FireButtonListener and ScrollBarListener, the latter two constructed as inner classes within our application class.

- Instances of the class ActionEvent and AdjustmentEvent, which are created when an event occurs and carry information to the event listener.

- The layout manager, an instance of class BorderLayout.

6.4 CROSS REFERENCES

Wrapper classes, such as Integer and Double, will be explained in more detail in Chapter 19. The distinction between inheritance and implementation, and the uses of each, will be a topic addressed in Chapter 10. Window layouts, layout managers, graphical components, and other features of the AWT will be examined in more detail in Chapter 13.

STUDY QUESTIONS

1. What is the parent class for class CannonGame?

2. In the first cannon game, how is the angle of the cannon determined?

3. What transformation is performed by the member function dy?

4. What is the difference in behavior between a Ball and a CannonBall?

5. How is the pseudovariable super used in a method? What effect does it have in a message expression?

6. What is the difference between the types Integer and int?

7. What is an inner class?

8. What is an interface?

9. What would an interface for the class CannonBall look like?

10. What does it mean to say that a class implements an interface?

11. What does it mean to say that a program is event-driven?

12. What is an event listener?

13. What is a window layout manager?

EXERCISES

1. Change the CannonGame so that the message being displayed provides not only the angle of the cannon, but also the current position of the cannon-ball. This value should change as the cannonball moves through the air.

2. Modify the class CannonBall so that the ball is colored blue when the ball is moving upward, and colored red when the ball is descending. Will this change have any impact on the rest of the program?

3. Modify the CannonWorld program so that it maintains both a count of the number of balls fired and the number of times the target was hit. Display both of these values in the message area, as well as the angle of the cannon.

4. On some platforms it may be difficult to halt the cannon application once it has finished. Add a button labeled "Quit" to the bottom (south) part of the application window. When pressed, this button should execute the method System.exit(0).

5. Create a simple program that draws a window with a colored ball in the center. Place a button at the top of the window. When the user presses the

button, the color of the ball will change from red to yellow, or from yellow to green, or from green to red.

6. Create a simple program that draws a window with a colored ball in the center. Place a slider on the right side of the window. As the user moves the slider, move the ball up and down the window.

7. The constructor for class Color can also take three integer arguments, which represent the saturation values for red, blue, and green. The arguments must be integers between 0 and 255. Create a simple program that draws a window with a colored ball in the center. Place sliders on three sides. As the user moves the sliders, the saturation values change for one of these arguments, and the ball changes color.

7

Pinball Game Construction Kit

In this chapter we will expand on the techniques introduced in the Cannon Game of Chapter 6, creating an entirely different type of interactive application. Along the way, we will use the development of this program to discuss standard data structures, event handling, inheritance, exceptions, interfaces, and multiple threads of control.

The application we will develop, the Pinball Construction Kit, simulates a pinball game. Users can fire a ball from the small square in the right corner of the bottom of the screen. (See Figure 7.1.) Balls rise, then encounter a variety of different types of targets as they fall back to the ground. The user scores points that depend upon the type and number of targets encountered as the ball descends. The objective of the game is to score as many points as possible.

As we did with the cannonball application in Chapter 6, we will develop this program in a sequence of stages, each stage emphasizing a small number of new programming concepts. The intent is simply to introduce these concepts in the context of a relatively simple and easy to understand program. Many of the major ideas introduced here will be discussed in more detail in later chapters.

7.1 FIRST VERSION OF GAME

Our first version (Figure 7.2) is in many ways the same as the cannonball application from Chapter 6, but with a number of new features. Because we will later be creating objects that will need to communicate with the window object, the variable world is declared as a public static value, rather than as a local variable to the main procedure. The "cannon" has been moved to the bottom right corner of the window and hidden behind a square box labeled with a red circle. A notable difference between this version and the cannonball application of Chapter 6 is the mechanism for placing a new ball into motion. Whereas in

Figure 7.1   The Pinball Application

the earlier program firing was tied to a button, in this version we will trap mouse activities in a more general routine. Two other notable changes are that the pinball game allows several balls to be in the air at once (the Cannon Game fired only a single ball), and we will finally move the control over the animation out of the paint routine, by introducing the concept of multiple threads of execution. Each of these ideas will be explored in more detail in the following sections.

7.1.1   Collection Classes

Unlike the Cannon Game described in the previous chapter, the pinball game allows several balls to be moving at one time. Every time the user clicks on the "fire" button, a new ball is placed in motion, even if earlier balls have not yet ceased moving.

To manage this, we need a data structure that can hold a collection of values. The one collection data structure we have seen up to now is the array (see Section 5.6). However, the array is limited by the fact that when we allocate a new array object we must state the number of elements the array will hold. In the present case, we cannot make any such estimate since we do not know how many times the user will hit the "fire" button.

```java
import java.awt.*;
import java.awt.event.*;
import java.util.Vector;

public class PinBallGame extends Frame {

   public static void main (String [ ] args) {
      world = new PinBallGame( );
      world.show( );
   }

   public static final int FrameWidth = 400;
   public static final int FrameHeight = 400;
   public static PinBallGame world;
   private Vector balls;

   public PinBallGame ( ) {
      setTitle ("PinBall Construction Kit");
      setSize (FrameWidth, FrameHeight);

      balls = new Vector( );
      addMouseListener (new MouseKeeper( ));
   }

   private class MouseKeeper extends MouseAdapter { ... }

   private class PinBallThread extends Thread { ... }

   public void paint (Graphics g) { // fire button is 30 by 30
      g.setColor (Color.white); // white rectangle
      g.fillRect (FrameWidth-40, FrameHeight-40, 30, 30);
      g.setColor (Color.red); // with red button
      g.fillOval (FrameWidth-40, FrameHeight-40, 30, 30);
         // draw balls
      for (int i = 0; i < balls.size( ); i++) {
         Ball aBall = (Ball) balls.elementAt(i);
         aBall.paint(g);
         }
      }
}
```

Figure 7.2   First version of PinBallGame class.

Fortunately, the Java library provides a number of other data structures we can employ. One of the simplest ones is a Vector. A vector is, like an array, an indexed data structure; meaning that each element has a position in the collection, and elements are accessed by requesting the value at a given position. However, unlike an array, a vector can dynamically grow as new values are inserted into the collection.

To use a vector, the programmer must first import the vector class definition from the standard library:

```
import java.util.Vector;
```

The vector is declared by simply providing a name:

```
private Vector balls;
```

Note, in particular, that unlike an array, it is not necessary to state the type of values that a Vector will hold. For technical reasons having to do with their internal structure, a vector is restricted to holding only objects. Thus, for example, one cannot create a vector of integer values (ints) but one *can* create a vector of instances of class Integer. This is one reason for the existence of "wrapper" classes, such as Integer and Float.

Just as an array in Java separates the declaration of the array name and the allocation of space for the array, the space for a Vector must be similarly created and assigned. In our example program this occurs in the constructor for the class PinBallGame. Note that no fixed limit is set for the space:

```
balls = new Vector( );
```

Although we have not seen it yet, a new element will be inserted into the vector by the method newElement:

```
balls.addElement (newBall);
```

The number of values stored in a Vector can be determined by invoking the method size.

```
for (int i = 0; i < balls.size( ); i++)
```

Finally, values are accessed in a vector using the function elementAt. Like an array, the set of legal index values ranges from zero to one less than the number of elements in the collection. The compiler only knows that the accessed element is a value of type object; it must be *cast* to the appropriate type before it can be used. Here we cast the value into the type Ball. A run-time check is performed to ensure that the conversion is actually valid:

```
Ball aBall = (Ball) balls.elementAt (i);
```

The reader should note how the paint procedure in Figure 7.2 cycles over the collection of balls, asking each to paint itself.

7.1.2 *Mouse Listeners*

As noted in Chapter 6, the Java event model is based around the concept of *listeners*; objects that wait and "listen" for an event to take place, and then respond appropriately. The earlier examples showed how to create a listener by defining a class that implements the corresponding *interface* for the event in question.

Mouse events are treated in a similar fashion; however, there are five different mouse-related events that could potentially be of interest. Thus, the interface for a MouseListener has the following structure:

```
public interface MouseListener {
    public void mouseClicked (MouseEvent e);
    public void mouseEntered (MouseEvent e);
    public void mouseExited (MouseEvent e);
    public void mousePressed (MouseEvent e);
    public void mouseReleased (MouseEvent e);
}
```

Often a programmer is interested in only one or two of these five events. However, to implement an interface the Java language insists that the programmer provide a definition for all operations. To simplify such cases, the Java library provides a simple class named MouseAdapter. The class MouseAdapter implements the MouseListener interface but uses an empty procedure for each member function. That is, a MouseAdapter does nothing in response to any mouse event. However, the programmer can write a new class that *inherits* from MouseAdapter, and overrides (or redefines) the procedures of interest.

That is what we do in the example program. An inner class defines a MouseListener by extending MouseAdapter. An instance of this class is created, and passed as argument to the method addMouseListener, which is inherited from class Frame.

```
addMouseListener (new MouseKeeper( ));
```

The class MouseKeeper inherits all five methods defined by MouseAdapter and redefines only one. The other four messages will be handled by the methods inherited from the parent class, which will do nothing.

```
private class MouseKeeper extends MouseAdapter {

    public void mousePressed (MouseEvent e) {
        int x = e.getX( ); // get coordinates where
        int y = e.getY( ); // mouse was pressed
            // only handle mouse event in the fire region
        if ((x > FrameWidth - 40) && (y > FrameHeight-40)) {
            PinBall newBall = new PinBall(x, y);
            balls.addElement (newBall);
```

```
                      Thread newThread = new PinBallThread (newBall);
                      newThread.start( );
                      }
            }
      }
```

The argument passed to each procedure in the MouseListener interface is a value of type MouseEvent. The mouse event encodes certain information relating to the type of event that occurred. In our case, the most important information is the position (or coordinate) of the mouse at the moment the button was pressed. This information can be derived from the mouse event object using the methods getX and getY. With these values, a new ball is created, added to the list of balls, and placed into motion.

7.1.3   *Multiple Threads of Execution*

The structure of the Cannon Game application (Figure 6.7) was clouded by the fact that we used the paint routine to control the animation. During each painting cycle the balls would be moved a little, and the window would be scheduled for another repainting. From a logical point of view, the animation task has little to do with repainting the screen image. Thus combining these two tasks makes the structure of the program unnecessarily difficult to understand.

In every Java program there must be one principal process that is listening for mouse clicks, repainting the window, and performing other administrative tasks. In the Cannon Game, we abused this process by slipping in control of the animation as tasks to be performed while the process was also carrying out its regular duties. A more straightforward solution is to separate these two tasks, leaving the listening for mouse clicks task to one process, and creating a separate process for the control and movement of the pinballs.

A *thread* represents a separate task being executed by the computer. One can think of a computer processor as being similar to a person reading the text of a Java program and completing the associated actions one statement at a time. With this image in mind, you can think of a program with two threads as being like two people reading the *same* program, but working independently of each other. Each may be operating in a different part of the program, executing different instructions, despite the fact that they are working at the same time. Occasionally the two may meet in the same area, or at least exchange information with each other; but in other respects, they are independent.

In our pinball program we will create a separate thread for each ball. The thread will be responsible for controlling the motion of the ball, and the interaction with other balls (and eventually, with targets). In Java a thread is created by making a class that is a subclass of the class Thread.[1] The inner class PinBallThread is shown below:

```java
public class PinBallGame {
    .
    .
    .

    private class PinBallThread extends Thread {
        private Ball theBall;

        public PinBallThread (Ball aBall)
            { theBall = aBall; }

        public void run ( ) {
            while (theBall.y( ) < FrameHeight) {
                theBall.move ( );
                    // more actions here later
                repaint ( );
                try {
                    sleep(10);
                } catch (InterruptedException e) { System.exit(0); }
            }
        }
    }
    .
    .
    .

}
```

The constructor for the thread is given the ball it will be controlling. The actions for a new thread are those provided by the method named run. In this case the actions of a pinball thread will be to move the ball slightly, schedule the window for repainting, then sleep for 10 milliseconds. The latter action is performed by the method sleep inherited from class Thread, and is designed to keep the simulation from moving too quickly. We will subsequently add more work to the loop controlling the life of a PinBall.

When the programmer hits the fire button, a new PinBall is created, and a new instance of the class PinBallThread is created to manage the new ball. The method start, inherited from class Thread, arranges the thread for execution, and begins processing.

```java
PinBall newBall = new PinBall(x, y);
balls.addElement (newBall);
Thread newThread = new PinBallThread (newBall);
newThread.start( );
```

[1] This is not the only way. In Chapter 20 we will describe an alternative way to create a thread.

Note carefully that to start a thread the programmer should execute the inherited method start. This, in turn, will eventually execute the method run that the programmer provides. You should never directly execute the run method; as there are a number of actions that the Thread manager must perform before the actions of a new thread can be initiated.

7.1.4   *Exception Handling*

The sleep command is the first occasion we have encountered where a method can potentially throw an *exception*. An exception is an error condition, which can be caught and handled so as to recover from the error in a systematic fashion. Methods that can potentially "throw" exceptions must declare so in their heading, in a manner to be described in a later chapter. Any use of such a method must either occur inside a method that itself declares that it can throw an exception, or within a try statement, as shown here:

```
try {
    sleep(10);
} catch (InterruptedException e) { System.exit(0); }
```

In this case, the potential source of exception is the fact that a thread could be interrupted while it is sleeping, for example (on some operating systems) by the user entering the "interrupt" key while the program is running. If such a condition occurs, the sleep statement will be halted before it can complete, and control will transfer to the statement in the closing block that matches the condition of the interrupt. In this case, we will terminate the program by invoking the function System.exit. In subsequent programs we will encounter many more statements that can throw a variety of different exceptional conditions.

7.2   ADDING TARGETS: INHERITANCE AND INTERFACES

To provide realism and interest to our pinball game, we need to add targets for the ball to encounter on its way down the playing surface. As in real pinball games, we will want to include a variety of different types of targets. Some targets simply add values to the score, some move the ball in a new direction, and some swallow the ball, removing it from play. In order to simplify the program, we will want to maintain all the different types of targets in a single data structure, a vector.

7.2.1   *The* Pinball Target *Interface*

Because we want to process targets uniformly, for example in a loop that asks whether a ball has hit any target, we need all the targets to have a uniform interface. However, the various different types of targets will be represented

Figure 7.3   Graphical representation of a spring.

internally by different data structures. Thus, we do not want to use *inheritance*, such as we have been doing with the different forms of Ball up to this point. Inheritance is a mechanism for sharing *structure*; a PinBall, for example, is simply a type of Ball that has the same structure and behavior as a Ball, adding a few new features (such as being able to run as a separate thread), but maintaining all the characteristics of the original. There is little in the way of common structure between a Peg (a target that when hit by a ball scores a number of points and moves the ball in a new direction) and a Wall (a target that when struck simply reflects the motion of the ball).

What is needed in this case is the ability to state that the two concepts (Peg and Wall, in this case), share the same *behavior*, although they have nothing in common in *structure*. As we saw in our earlier case study, in Java this is accomplished by describing the common behavior as an interface, and declaring that both objects implement the same interface. An interface for our pinball targets can be described as follows:

```
interface PinBallTarget {
    public boolean intersects (Ball aBall);
    public void moveTo (int x, int y);
    public void paint (Graphics g);
    public void hitBy (Ball aBall);
}
```

The interface in this case is declaring that there are four characteristics of interest in a pinball target. Each target can tell if it has been hit by a ball; that is, if it intersects the region occupied by a ball. Each target can be moved to a specific point on the playing surface, each can paint itself, and each provides some response when it has been hit by a given ball. However, the means by which each of these behaviors will be achieved is left unspecified, and different targets are free to *implement* the interface in different fashions.

An examination of a few different targets will help illustrate the point. Our first type of target will be a Spring. When hit by a falling ball, a Spring rebounds the ball back into the playing area, moving it upward where we hope it will encounter further targets. A spring is represented graphically by a small horizontal box, and a series of zigzag lines, as in Figure 7.3.

The class description for Spring is shown in Figure 7.4. Note how the class Spring must explicitly state that it implements the PinBallTarget interface, and must

```
class Spring implements PinBallTarget {
   private Rectangle pad;
   private int state = 1;

   public Spring (int x, int y)
      { pad = new Rectangle (x, y, 30, 3); }

   public void moveTo (int x, int y)
      { pad.setLocation (x, y); }

   public void paint (Graphics g) {
      int x = pad.x; int y = pad.y;
      g.setColor(Color.black);
      if (state == 1) { // draw compressed spring
         g.fillRect(x, y, pad.width, pad.height);
         g.drawLine(x, y+3, x+30, y+5);
         g.drawLine(x+30, y+5, x, y+7);
         g.drawLine(x, y+7, x+30, y+9);
         g.drawLine(x+30, y+9, x, y+11);
         }
      else {  // draw extended spring
         g.fillRect(x, y-8, pad.width, pad.height);
         g.drawLine(x, y+5, x+30, y-1);
         g.drawLine(x+30, y-1, x, y+3);
         g.drawLine(x, y+3, x+30, y+7);
         g.drawLine(x+30, y+7, x, y+11);
         state = 1;
      }
   }

   public boolean intersects (Ball aBall)
      { return pad.intersects(aBall.location); }

   public void hitBy (Ball aBall) {
      // make sure we are moving up
      if (aBall.dy > 0) aBall.dy = - aBall.dy;
         // give the ball a little boost
      aBall.dy = aBall.dy - 0.5;
      state = 2;
   }
}
```

Figure 7.4 Definition for class Spring.

provide a specific meaning for each of the four elements of that interface. In this case, we will state that a spring intersects a ball if the rectangle surrounding the ball intersects with the rectangle representing the spring platform. When the spring is hit by the ball, it reverses the vertical direction of movement for the ball. (In actual fact, it simply guarantees the ball is moving upward. In rare situations, a spring could possibly be hit from below, although we don't expect this to be the norm.) It then gives the ball a slight boost in the vertical direction.

One slight element of interest has been added to the drawing of the Spring object. We have provided two different graphical representations for the Spring object, selected by an integer variable named state. Normally, a spring will be held in state 1. When struck, the value of state is changed to 2, and the *next* time the spring is redrawn it will present an alternative image, one in which the spring has been elongated. Drawing this second image changes the state back to state 1, and a subsequent redraw will display the original. The effect is a simple form of animation, where a moving spring will appear to stretch momentarily, then return to a ready state.

A second type of target is a Wall. A Wall (Figure 7.5) is a rectangular region. A ball intersects a wall if their regions overlap, and if so the ball is simply reflected back, in effect bouncing off the wall. The bounce is either along the horizontal or along the vertical direction, depending upon which side of the wall has been hit.

The advantage of declaring these two different structures as both implementing an interface is that an interface name can be used as a *type*. That is, we can declare a variable as holding a value of type PinBallTarget. In much the same way that a variable declared as maintaining a value of type Ball could, in fact, be holding a cannonball, a pinball, or any other value derived from a class that extends the original class Ball, a variable declared as maintaining a PinBallTarget could, in fact, be holding either a Spring, a Wall, or any of the other varieties of target to be described subsequently. (This is one aspect of *polymorphism*, a topic we will return to in more detail in Chapter 12.) We will shortly make use of this property, by storing all the targets in our game in a single data structure, and testing the motion of the ball against the location of each target in turn.

Consider now a third type of target, a Hole. A Hole (Figure 7.6) consumes any ball it comes in contact with, removing the ball from the playing surface. A Hole is represented by a circular colored image, just like a ball. A Hole has a location on the playing surface, just like a Ball. In fact, because a hole is *structurally* similar to a Ball, we can use inheritance to simplify the implementation of the Hole abstraction.

This illustrates the important difference between the use of inheritance and the use of interfaces. The mechanism of inheritance should be used when two (or more) concepts have a *structural* relationship. Note that with objects, a structural relationship almost always implies at least some behavioral relationship. In contrast, the interface mechanism should be used with two (or more) concepts

```
class Wall implements PinBallTarget {
   public Rectangle location;

   public Wall (int x, int y, int width, int height)
      { location = new Rectangle(x, y, width, height); }

   public void moveTo (int x, int y)
      { location.setLocation (x, y); }

   public void paint (Graphics g) {
      g.setColor(Color.black);
      g.fillRect(location.x, location.y,
         location.width, location.height);
   }

   public boolean intersects (Ball aBall)
      { return location.intersects(aBall.location); }

   public void hitBy (Ball aBall) {
      if ((aBall.y( ) < location.y)
         || (aBall.y( ) > (location.y + location.height)))
            aBall.dy = - aBall.dy;
      else
         aBall.dx = - aBall.dx;
   }
}
```

Figure 7.5   Definition of class Wall.

having a *behavioral* relationship but no structural relationship. We will explore these ideas in more detail in Chapter 8.

Note how a Hole uses both inheritance and an interface. The hole *inherits* much of its behavior from the class Ball, including the methods paint and moveTo. The Hole declares that it implements the PinBallTarget interface, and to do so must provide a method to see if the hole has intersected with a ball, and the actions to be performed when such an event occurs. In the case of a hole, the ball is moved clear off the playing surface, and motion of the ball is halted. Eventually the ball will note that its location exceeds the window size, and the tread controlling the ball will halt.

A class that inherits from an existing class that implements an interface must of necessity also implement the interface. We will use this property in defining the next two types of targets in our pinball game. A ScorePad is, like a hole, represented by a circular region. When struck by a ball, the score pad has no

```
class Hole extends Ball implements PinBallTarget {

    public Hole (int x, int y) {
        super (x, y, 12);
        setColor (Color.black);
    }

    public boolean intersects (Ball aBall)
        { return location.intersects(aBall.location); }

    public void hitBy (Ball aBall) {
            // move ball totally off frame
        aBall.moveTo (0, PinBallGame.FrameHeight + 30);
            // stop motion of ball
        aBall.setMotion(0, 0);
    }
}
```

Figure 7.6   Definition of class Hole.

effect on the ball (the ball simply moves over it); however, the score pad adds a certain amount to the player's score. The particular amount to add is defined as part of the state for the score object.

Note how the ScorePad class (Figure 7.7) inherits the intersects behavior from class Hole and the moveTo behavior from class Ball, but overrides the paint and hitBy methods that would otherwise be inherited from class Hole. The first now draws a colored circle with the scoring amount in the middle, while the latter adds the given value to the player score.

Because a ScorePad inherits from class Hole, which implements the PinBallTarget interface, the class ScorePad is also said to implement the interface. This means, for example, that a ScorePad could be assigned to a variable that was declared to be a PinBallTarget.

7.2.2   *Adding a Label to Our Pinball Game*

In the revised version of our program we will add a new graphical element, a textual label in a banner across the top of the window. This is accomplished by declaring a new Label, and adding it in the "North" part of the window (Figure 7.8). As the user scores new points, the text of the label is updated. Note that a ScorePad refers back to the application object through the variable world.

A feature of the addScore method deserves note. In the revised form of the pinball game application class, the method addScore is declared as synchronized. Recall that balls move independently of each other, and so in theory two balls

```
class ScorePad extends Hole {
   protected int value;

   public ScorePad (int x, int y, int v) {
      super (x, y);
      value = v;
      setColor (Color.red);
   }

   public void hitBy (Ball aBall)
      { PinBallGame.world.addScore(value); }

   public void paint (Graphics g) {
      g.setColor (color);
      g.drawOval (location.x, location.y,
         location.width, location.height);
      String s = "" + value;
      g.drawString(s, location.x, y( )+2);
   }
}
```

Figure 7.7 Definition of the class ScorePad.

```
public class PinBallGame extends Frame {

   private int score;
   private Label scoreLabel;

   public PinBallGame ( ) {
         .
         .
         .
      score = 0;
      scoreLabel = new Label ("Score: 0");
      add ("North", scoreLabel);
         .
         .
         .
   }

   synchronized public void addScore (int v) {
      score = score + v;
      scoreLabel.setText ("score = " + score);
      }
   .
   .
   .
}
```

Figure 7.8 Adding labels to our pinball game.

could roll over two different score pads at much the same time. Two attempts could then be made to update the player score at once. The resulting actions could easily be unpredictable, and almost certainly wrong. By declaring the function that updates the score value as synchronized, the Java language will guarantee that two threads cannot be executing this function at once. If a thread tries to execute a synchronized method that is currently being executed by another thread, the second thread is suspended until the first thread exits the synchronized routine. Synchronization and threads will be discussed in more detail in Chapter 20.

A Peg is similar to a ScorePad, but it sticks up above the playing surface. Thus, when a Peg is struck, it deflects the ball off in a new direction, depending upon the angle of the ball and the point at which it encounters the peg. (The algorithm used in Figure 7.9 is not exactly correct as far as actual physics is concerned, but it does have the advantage of being easy to compute.) The ball is then updated

```java
class Peg extends ScorePad {
   private int state = 1;

   public Peg (int x, int y, int v)
      { super(x, y, v); }

   public void paint (Graphics g) {
      super.paint(g);
      if (state == 2) { // draw expanded circle
         g.drawOval(location.x-3, location.y-3,
            location.width+6, location.height+6);
         state = 1;
         }
      else
         g.drawOval(location.x-2, location.y-2,
            location.width+4, location.height+4);
   }

   public void hitBy (Ball aBall) {
      super.hitBy (aBall); // update the score
      aBall.setMotion (-aBall.dy, -aBall.dx); // update direction
      while (intersects(aBall)) // move out of range
         aBall.move( );
      state = 2; // next draw will expand circle
   }
}
```

Figure 7.9 Definition of the class Peg.

until it no longer intersects with the peg, thereby avoiding having the procedure executed multiple times for a single encounter. We have once again added a simple animation to the class Peg, so that the first time a peg is redrawn after it has been struck, the circle surrounding the peg will appear to enlarge and then return to a normal size.

To create the second version of our game (Figure 7.10), we simply create a Vector of targets, along with the vector of balls. We initialize the targets in the constructor for the game, including placing walls on the sides and top of the playing area, to reflect wayward balls. The user fires balls as before, which then proceed to interact with the various targets as the balls move down the playing surface. Each time a ball moves, a loop is executed to determine if the new location of the ball has struck a target. If so, the target is informed, and the location of the ball potentially updated. Finally, the entire screen is repainted, which involves repainting both the targets and the collection of balls.

7.3   PINBALL GAME CONSTRUCTION KIT: MOUSE EVENTS RECONSIDERED

Although the second version of the pinball game is certainly more interesting than the first, it is still limited by the fact that the layout of the various targets is determined by the original programmer. To create a different layout, the program must be changed and then recompiled and executed. In our final version, we will show how this limitation can be overcome, by providing a *pallet* of target elements from which the *user* can select, dynamically constructing the pinball game while the program is executing.

In appearance, our revised game will move the playing area slightly to the right, placing a sequence of potential target components along a strip in the far left. (See Figure 7.11.) The user can click the mouse down in one of these alternatives, then slide the mouse (still down) over into the playing area. When the user releases the mouse, the selected target element will be installed into the new location.

The effect is produced by overriding both the mousePressed and the mouseReleased methods inherited from the mouse adapter (Figure 7.12). The two methods communicate with each other by means of a variable named element. The mousePressed procedure creates a potential target, determined by the coordinates of the point at which the mouse goes down. Note that we have not eliminated the original use of the mouseDown procedure, simply added a new condition. The MouseReleased procedure checks the location of the release, and if it is in the playing area and if a target item was previously selected (*both* conditions must be true), then it adds a new target to the game.

Other changes needed to provide our final version of the Pinball Construction Kit simply involve repositioning the left wall, and drawing the images of the selection pallet.

```
public class PinBallGame extends Frame {

    private Vector targets;

    public PinBallGame ( ) {
        .
        .
        .
            // create the targets
        targets = new Vector( );
        targets.addElement(new Wall(30, 50, 2, 350));
        targets.addElement(new Wall(30, 50, 360, 2));
        targets.addElement(new Wall(390, 50, 2, 380));
        targets.addElement(new Hole(100, 100));
        targets.addElement(new ScorePad(150, 220, 100, this));
        targets.addElement(new Peg(300, 140, 200, this));
        targets.addElement(new Spring(120, 350));
    }

    private class PinBallThread extends Thread {
        .
        .
        .
        public void run ( ) {
            while (theBall.y( ) < FrameHeight) {
                theBall.move ( );
                    // see if we ran into anything
                for (int j = 0; j < targets.size( ); j++) {
                    PinBallTarget target =
                        (PinBallTarget) targets.elementAt(j);
                    if (target.intersects(theBall)) target.hitBy(theBall);
                }
                .
                .
                .
            }
        }
    }

    public void paint (Graphics g) {
        .
        .
        .
        for (int j = 0; j < targets.size( ); j++) { // draw targets
            PinBallTarget target = (PinBallTarget) targets.elementAt(j);
            target.paint(g);
        }
    }
}
```

Figure 7.10   Addition of targets to the class PinBallGame.

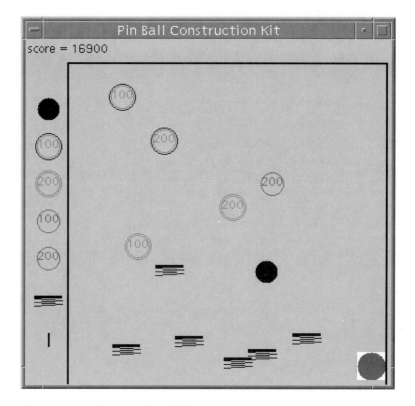

Figure 7.11   The revised Pinball Game Construction Kit.

7.4   CHAPTER SUMMARY

In this chapter the development of an example program has once again served as a vehicle to introduce a number of features of the Java programming language. Introduced in this chapter were the following features:

- The use of collection classes, in particular the collection class Vector. We will discuss collection classes in more detail in Chapter 19.

- An expanded discussion of the Java listener event model (started in Chapter 6), focusing on how to create objects that will listen for mouse events.

- The concept of a program having multiple threads of execution. While the main thread of our program listens for events and paints the windows, each ball in the simulation is being controlled by an independent routine.

```
private class MouseKeeper extends MouseAdapter {

    private PinBallTarget element;

    public void mousePressed (MouseEvent e) {
        element = null;
        int x = e.getX( );
        int y = e.getY( );
        if ((x > FrameWidth-40) && (y > FrameHeight -40)) {
            PinBall newBall = new PinBall(e.getX( ), e.getY( ));
            balls.addElement (newBall);
            Thread newThread = new PinBallThread (newBall);
            newThread.start( );
        }
        if (x < 40) { // each target occupies a 40 by 40 pixel box
            switch (y / 40) {
                case 2: element = new Hole(0, 0); break;
                case 3: element = new Peg(0, 0, 100); break;
                case 4: element = new Peg(0, 0, 200); break;
                case 5: element = new ScorePad(0, 0, 100); break;
                case 6: element = new ScorePad(0, 0, 200); break;
                case 7: element = new Spring(0, 0); break;
                case 8: element = new Wall(0, 0, 2, 15); break;
            }
        }
    }


    public void mouseReleased (MouseEvent e) {
        int x = getX( ); // only perform release action if mouse is
        int y = getY( ); // released on playing surface
        if ((element != null) && (x > 50)){
            element.moveTo(x, y);
            targets.addElement (element);
            repaint( );
        }
    }
}
```

Figure 7.12   Capturing both mouse presses and releases.

- Our first example of a statement that could potentially produce an *exception*, and the way the Java language permits the programmer to specify what actions to take when an exception occurs.

- More on interfaces, contrasting the use of the interface mechanism with the use of inheritance.

- One aspect of the important concept of *polymorphism*. A variable declared as an instance of a parent class (such as Ball) can, in fact, be holding a value derived from a child class (such as PinBall). Similarly, a variable declared as an interface value (such as PinBallTarget) can, in fact, hold any object that implements that interface (such as Peg). This property allows us to create arrays of different objects, such as an array of pinball targets, and process them in a uniform fashion.

CROSS REFERENCES

The distinction between interfaces and inheritances is explored in more detail in Chapter 8. Collection classes will be investigated in detail in Chapter 19. Chapter 13 presents a more systematic investigation of the services provided by the AWT. Chapter 20 explores the multithreading features of Java.

STUDY QUESTIONS

1. Why must the variable world be declared static?

2. In what ways is a Vector object similar to an array? In what ways is it different?

3. What command is used to determine the number of elements held in a Vector? What method is used to access the values? What method is used to insert a new value into the collection?

4. What is the relationship between MouseAdapter and MouseListener? In what ways are they different?

5. What is a *thread*? What are the tasks assigned to the different threads in our application?

6. How is a thread started? How does the programmer specify the actions a thread should perform?

7. What is an exception?

8. What action is performed by the function System.exit? Under what circumstances in our program will this function be called?

9. When should two software components be tied together through the use of inheritance rather than a common interface?

10. What type of objects can be held by a variable declared using the interface PinBallTarget?

11. In what ways does the class Hole modify the behavior inherited from class Ball?

12. What is a Label? How is a label attached to a window? What methods are used to change the text of a label?

13. What does it mean to say that a method is *synchronized*?

EXERCISES

1. The class Peg inherits from ScorePad, which in turn inherits from Hole, which in turn inherits from Ball. For each of these classes, describe all the methods defined in the class or inherited from parent classes, and for each of the latter indicate in which parent class the method definition occurs.

2. The pinball game as presented allows the user an unlimited number of balls. Change the program to fire only a fixed number of balls, disallowing firing once the supply is exhausted. Change the display at the top of the screen so that it will indicate the number of remaining balls, as well as the score.

3. Add a "reset" button to the bottom of the screen. When pressed, the reset button sets the score back to zero and, if you implemented the suggestion in the previous question, resets the number of balls in play.

4. On some platforms it may be difficult to halt the PinBall application once it has finished. Add a button labeled "Quit" to the bottom (south) part of the application window. When pressed, this button should execute the method System.exit(0).

5. In the final program, the items in the pallet are still stored on the targets vector, so that they will be redrawn, even though they can never be hit by a ball. A better solution would have been to create a new vector pallet that will hold these items, redrawing both the pallet and the targets on a repaint. Modify the program in this fashion.

6. Currently balls do not test to see if they intersect with other balls. We could support this modification by making PinBall implement the PinBallTarget interface, and adding balls to the list of targets as well as the list of balls. Describe what changes would need to be added to modify the program in this fashion.

7. Another change could allow the programmer to reposition items even after they have been placed in the playing area. If a mouse click occurs on the playing surface over a target, select the target and move it to the location given by the associated mouse up. Be careful that you don't end up placing the element in the target vector twice.

8. Create a program that opens a window, listens for mouse clicks, and when a mouse is released will display the distance (in pixel units) between the location the mouse was pressed and the location it was released.

9. Write a program that places a red circle in the middle of the window. The circle should change color to blue when the mouse enters the window, then return to red when the mouse leaves the window. When the mouse is clicked inside the window, the circle should change color to green and remain green for 1000 milliseconds, before returning to blue. Finally, if the mouse is clicked within the bounds of the circle and released outside the circle, the circle should be moved so as to be centered on the location of the mouse release.

10. Develop a "paddle" target object. When the user clicks the mouse over the paddle, the paddle should move back and forth (perhaps only once). If a paddle encounters a ball, the ball is reflected off the paddle.

III

Understanding Inheritance

8 Understanding Inheritance

The first step in learning object-oriented programming is understanding the basic philosophy of organizing a computer program as the interaction of loosely coupled software components. This idea was the central lesson in the case studies presented in the first part of the book. The next step in learning object-oriented programming is organizing classes into a hierarchical structure based on the concept of inheritance. By *inheritance*, we mean the property that instances of a child class (or subclass) can access both data and behavior (methods) associated with a parent class (or superclass).

Although in Java the term *inheritance* is correctly applied only to the creation of new classes using subclassing (the extends keyword), there are numerous correspondences between subclassification and the designation that classes satisfy an interface (the implements keyword). The latter is sometimes termed "inheritance of specification," contrasted with the "inheritance of code" provided by subclassification. In this chapter we will use the word in a general fashion, meaning both mechanisms.

Although the intuitive meaning of inheritance is clear, and we have used inheritance in many of our earlier case studies, and the mechanics of using inheritance are relatively simple, there are nevertheless subtle features involved in the use of inheritance in Java. In this and subsequent chapters we will explore some of these issues.

8.1 AN INTUITIVE DESCRIPTION OF INHERITANCE

Let us return to Flora the florist from the first chapter. There is a certain behavior we expect florists to perform, not because they are florists but simply because they are shopkeepers. For example, we expect Flora to request money for the transaction and in turn give us a receipt. These activities are not unique to

121

florists, but are common to bakers, grocers, stationers, car dealers, and other merchants. It is as though we have associated certain behavior with the general category Shopkeeper, and as Florists are a specialized form of shopkeepers, the behavior is automatically identified with the subclass.

In programming languages, inheritance means that the behavior and data associated with child classes are always an *extension* (that is, a larger set) of the properties associated with parent classes. A child class will be given all the properties of the parent class, and may in addition define new properties. On the other hand, since a child class is a more specialized (or restricted) form of the parent class, it is also, in a certain sense, a *contraction* of the parent type. For example, the Java library Frame represents any type of window, but a PinBallGame frame is restricted to a single type of game. This tension between inheritance as expansion and inheritance as contraction is a source for much of the power inherent in the technique, but at the same time it causes much confusion as to its proper employment. We will see this when we examine a few of the uses of inheritance in a subsequent section.

Inheritance is always transitive, so that a class can inherit features from superclasses many levels away. That is, if class Dog is a subclass of class Mammal, and class Mammal is a subclass of class Animal, then Dog will inherit attributes both from Mammal and from Animal.

A complicating factor in our intuitive description of inheritance is the fact that subclasses can *override* behavior inherited from parent classes. For example, the class Platypus overrides the reproduction behavior inherited from class Mammal, since platypuses lay eggs. The mechanics of overriding is treated briefly in this chapter in more detail in Chapter 11.

8.2   THE BASE CLASS OBJECT

In Java all classes use inheritance. Unless specified otherwise, all classes are derived from a single root class, named Object. If no parent class is explicitly provided, the class Object is implicitly assumed. Thus, the class declaration for FirstProgram (Chapter 4, Figure 4.1) is the same as the following:

```
class FirstProgram extends Object {
   // ...
   };
```

The class Object provides minimal functionality guaranteed to be common to all objects. These include the following methods:

equals (Object obj)   Determine whether the argument object is the same as the receiver. This method is often overridden to change the equality test for different classes.

getClass ()   Returns the name of the class of the receiver as a string.

hashCode ( )   Returns a hash value for this object (see Section 19.7). This method should also be overridden when the equals method is changed.

toString ( )   Converts object into a string value. This method is also often overridden.

8.3   SUBCLASS, SUBTYPE, AND SUBSTITUTABILITY

The concept of *substitutability* is fundamental to many of the most powerful software development techniques in object-oriented programming. The idea of substitutability is that the type given in a declaration of a variable may not match the type associated with a value the variable is holding. Note that this is never true in conventional programming languages but is a common occurrence in object-oriented programs.

We have seen several examples of substitutability in our earlier case studies. In the Pin Ball Game program described in Chapter 7, the variable target was declared as a PinBallTarget, but in fact held a variety of different types of values that were created using subclasses of PinBallTarget. (These target values were held in the vector named targets.)

```
PinBallTarget target = (PinBallTarget) targets.elementAt(j);
```

Substitutability can also occur through the use of interfaces. An example is the instance of the class FireButtonListener created in the Cannon Game (Chapter 6). The class from which this value was defined was declared as implementing the interface ActionListener. Because it implements the ActionListener interface, we can use this value as a parameter to a function (in this case, addActionListener) that expects an ActionListener value.

```
class CannonWorld extends Frame {
    .
    .
    .
    private class FireButtonListener implements ActionListener {
        public void actionPerformed (ActionEvent e) {
            .
            .
            .
        }
    }

    public CannonWorld () {
        .
        .
        fire.addActionListener(new FireButtonListener());
    }
}
```

Because Object is a parent class to all objects, a variable declared using this type can hold any nonprimitive value. The collection class Vector makes use of this property, holding its values in an array of Object values. Because the array is declared as Object, any object value can be stored in a Vector.

When new classes are constructed using inheritance from existing classes, the argument used to justify the validity of substitutability is as follows:

- Instances of the subclass must possess all data areas associated with the parent class.

- Instances of the subclass must implement, through inheritance at least (if not explicitly overridden) all functionality defined for the parent class. (They can also define new functionality, but that is unimportant for the argument.)

- Thus, an instance of a child class can mimic the behavior of the parent class and should be *indistinguishable* from an instance of the parent class if substituted in a similar situation.

We will see later in this chapter, when we examine the various ways in which inheritance can be used, that this is not always a valid argument. Thus, not all subclasses formed using inheritance are candidates for substitution.

The term *subtype* is used to describe the relationship between types that explicitly recognizes the principle of substitution. That is, a type B is considered to be a subtype of A if two conditions hold. The first is that an instance of B can legally be assigned to a variable declared as type A. And the second is that this value can then be used by the variable with no observable change in behavior.

The term *subclass* refers merely to the mechanics of constructing a new class using inheritance, and is easy to recognize from the source description of a program by the presence of the keyword extends. The *subtype* relationship is more abstract, and is only loosely documented directly by the program source. In the majority of situations a subclass is also a subtype. However, later in this chapter we will discover ways in which subclasses can be formed that are not subtypes. In addition, subtypes can be formed using interfaces, linking types that have no inheritance relationship whatsoever. So it is important to understand both the similarities and the differences between these two concepts.

8.4   FORMS OF INHERITANCE

Inheritance is employed in a surprising variety of ways. Presented in this section are a few of its more common uses. Note that the following list represents general abstract categories and is not intended to be exhaustive. Furthermore, it sometimes happens that two or more descriptions are applicable to a single situation, because some methods in a single class use inheritance in one way while others use it in another. In the following list, pay attention to which uses of inheritance support the subtyping relationship and which do not.

8.4.1   *Inheritance for Specialization*

Probably the most common use of inheritance and subclassification is for specialization. In this form, the new class is a specialized variety of the parent class but it satisfies the specifications of the parent in all relevant respects. Thus, this form always creates a subtype, and the principle of substitutability is explicitly upheld. Along with the following category (subclassification for specification) this is the most ideal form of inheritance, and something that a good design should strive for.

The creation of application window classes using inheritance from the Java library class Frame is an example of subclassification for specialization. The following is from the PinBallGame program in Chapter 7.

```
public class PinBallGame extends Frame {
    .
    .
    .
}
```

To run such an application, an instance of PinBallGame is first created. Various methods inherited from class Frame, such as setSize, setTitle, and show, are then invoked. These methods do not realize they are manipulating an instance of PinBallGame, but instead act as if they were operating on an instance of Frame. The actions they perform would be the same for any instance of class Frame.

Where application-specific behavior is necessary, for example, in repainting the window, a method is invoked that is overridden by the application class. For example, the method in the parent class will invoke the method paint. Although the parent class Frame possesses a method of this name, the parent method is not the one executed. Instead, the function defined in the child class is executed.

We say that subclassification for specialization occurs in this example because the child class (in this example, PinBallGame) satisfies all the properties that we expect of the parent class (Frame). In addition, the new class overrides one or more methods, specializing them with application-specific behavior.

8.4.2   *Inheritance for Specification*

Another frequent use for inheritance is to guarantee that classes maintain a certain common interface—that is, they implement the same methods. The parent class can be a combination of implemented operations and operations that are deferred to the child classes. Often, there is no interface change of any sort between the parent class and the child class—the child merely implements behavior described, but not implemented, in the parent.

This is actually a special case of subclassification for specialization, except that the subclasses are not refinements of an existing type but rather realizations of an incomplete abstract specification. That is, the parent class defines the operation but has no implementation. It is only the child class that provides an implementation. In such cases the parent class is sometimes known as an *abstract specification class*.

There are two different mechanisms provided by the Java language to support the idea of inheritance of specification. The most obvious technique is the use of interfaces. We have seen examples of this in the way that events are handled by the Java library. For instance, the characteristics needed for an ActionListener (the object type that responds to button presses) can be described by a single method, and the implementation of that method cannot be predicted, since it differs from one application to another. Thus, an interface is used to describe only the necessary requirements, and no actual behavior is inherited by a subclass that implements the behavior.

```
interface ActionListener {
    public void actionPerformed (ActionEvent e);
    }
```

When a button is created, an associated listener class is defined. The listener class provides the specific behavior for the method in the context of the current application.

```
class CannonWorld extends Frame {
    .
    .
    .
        // a fire button listener implements the action listener interface
    private class FireButtonListener implements ActionListener {
        public void actionPerformed (ActionEvent e) {
        ... // action to perform in response to button press
        }
    }
}
```

Subclassification for specification can also take place with inheritance of classes formed using extension. One way to guarantee that a subclass must be constructed is to use the keyword abstract. A class declared as abstract must be subclassed; it is not possible to create an instance of such a class using the operator new. In addition, individual methods can also be declared as abstract, and they, too, must be overridden before instances can be constructed.

An example abstract class in the Java library is Number, a parent class for the numeric wrapper classes Integer, Long, Double, and so on. The class description is as follows:

```
public abstract class Number {

    public abstract int intValue( );

    public abstract long longValue( );

    public abstract float floatValue( );

    public abstract double doubleValue( );

    public byte byteValue( )
        { return (byte) intValue( ); }

    public short shortValue( )
        { return (short) intValue( ); }
}
```

Subclasses of Number must override the methods intValue, longValue, floatValue, and doubleValue. Notice that not all methods in an abstract class must themselves be declared abstract. Subclasses of Number need not override byteValue or shortValue, as these methods are provided with an implementation that can be inherited without change.

In general, subclassification for specification can be recognized when the parent class does not implement actual behavior but merely defines the behavior that must be implemented in child classes.

8.4.3 *Inheritance for Construction*

A class can often inherit almost all of its desired functionality from a parent class, perhaps changing only the names of the methods used to interface to the class, or modifying the arguments. This may be true even if the new class and the parent class fail to share any relationship as abstract concepts.

An example of subclassification for construction occurred in the pinball game application described in Chapter 7. In that program, the class Hole was declared as a subclass of Ball. There is no logical relationship between the concepts of a Ball and a Hole, but from a practical point of view much of the behavior needed for the Hole abstraction matches the behavior of the class Ball. Thus, using inheritance in this situation reduces the amount of work necessary to develop the class Hole.

```
class Hole extends Ball implements PinBallTarget {

    public Hole (int x, int y) {
        super (x, y, 12);
        setColor (Color.black);
    }
```

```
    public boolean intersects (Ball aBall)
        { return location.intersects(aBall.location); }

    public void hitBy (Ball aBall) {
            // move ball totally off frame
        aBall.moveTo (0, PinBallGame.FrameHeight + 30);
            // stop motion of ball
        aBall.setMotion(0, 0);
    }
}
```

Another example of inheritance for construction occurs in the Java library. There, the class Stack is constructed using inheritance from the class Vector:

```
class Stack extends Vector {

    public Object push(Object item)
        { addElement(item); return item; }

    public boolean empty ( )
        { return isEmpty( ); }

    public synchronized Object pop() {
        Object obj = peek( );
        removeElementAt(size( ) - 1);
        return obj;
        }

    public synchronized Object peek( )
        { return elementAt(size( ) - 1); }
}
```

As abstractions, the concept of the stack and the concept of a vector have little in common; however, from a pragmatic point of view using the Vector class as a parent greatly simplifies the implementation of the stack.

Inheritance for construction is sometimes frowned upon, since it often directly breaks the principle of substitutability (forming subclasses that are not subtypes). On the other hand, because it is often a fast and easy route to developing new data abstractions, it is nevertheless widely used. See Chapter 10 for a more detailed discussion of the construction of the Stack abstraction.

8.4.4 Inheritance for Extension

Subclassification for extension occurs when a child class only adds new behavior to the parent class and does not modify or alter any of the inherited attributes. An example of inheritance for extension in the Java library is the class Properties, which inherits from class HashTable. A hash table is a dictionary structure (see Section 19.7). A dictionary stores a collection of key/value pairs and allows the user to retrieve the value associated with a given key. Properties represent information concerning the current execution environment. Examples of properties are the name of the user running the Java program, the version of the Java interpreter being used, the name of the operating system under which the Java program is running, and so on. The class Properties uses the parent class, HashTable, to store and retrieve the actual property name/value pairs. In addition, the class defines a few methods specific to the task of managing properties, such as reading or writing properties to or from a file.

```
class Properties extends Hashtable {
    .
    .
    .

    public synchronized void load(InputStream in) throws
        IOException { ... }

    public synchronized void save(OutputStream out, String header)
        { ... }

    public String getProperty(String key) { ... }

    public Enumeration propertyNames() { ... }

    public void list(PrintStream out) { ... }
}
```

As the functionality of the parent remains available and untouched, subclassification for extension does not contravene the principle of substitutability, and so such subclasses are always subtypes.

8.4.5 Inheritance for Limitation

Subclassification for limitation occurs when the behavior of the subclass is smaller or more restrictive than the behavior of the parent class. Like subclassification for extension, subclassification for limitation occurs most frequently when a programmer is building on a base of existing classes that should not, or cannot, be modified.

Although there are no examples of subclassification for limitation in the Java library, we could imagine the following. Suppose you wanted to create the class Set, in a fashion similar to the way the class Stack is subclassed from Vector. Say you also wanted to *ensure* that only Set operations were used on the set, and not vector operations. One way to accomplish this would be to override the undesired methods, so that if they were executed they would generate an exception.[1]

```
class Set extends Vector {
    // methods addElement, removeElement, contains
    // isEmpty and size
    // are all inherited from vector

    public int indexOf (Object obj)
        { throw new IllegalOperation("indexOf"); }

    public int elementAt (int index)
        { throw new IllegalOperation("indexOf"); }
}
```

Where IllegalOperation is a subclass of Exception:

```
class IllegalOperation extends Exception {
    IllegalOperation (String str) { super(str); }
    }
```

Subclassification for limitation is characterized by the presence of methods that take a previously permitted operation and makes it illegal. Because subclassification for limitation is an explicit contravention of the principle of substitutability, and because it builds subclasses that are not subtypes, it should be avoided whenever possible.

8.4.6   *Inheritance for Combination*

When discussing abstract concepts, it is common to form a new abstraction by combining features of two or more abstractions. A teaching assistant, for example, may have characteristics of both a teacher and a student, and can therefore logically behave as both. The ability of a class to inherit from two or more parent classes is known as *multiple inheritance.*

Although the Java language does not permit a subclass to be formed by inheritance from more than one parent class, several approximations to the

---

[1] In actuality, the methods indexOf and elementAt are declared as final in class Vector, so this example will not compile. But it does illustrate the concept.

concept are possible. For example, it is common for a new class to both extend an existing class and implement an interface. We saw this in the example of the class Hole that both extended class Ball and implemented the interface for PinBallTarget.

```
class Hole extends Ball implements PinBallTarget {
   .
   .
   .
}
```

It is also possible for classes to implement more than one interface, and thus be viewed as a combination of the two categories. Many examples occur in the input/output sections of the Java library. A RandomAccessFile, for example, implements both the DataInput and DataOutput protocols.

8.4.7 *Summary of the Forms of Inheritance*

We can summarize the various forms of inheritance by the following list:

Specialization   The child class is a special case of the parent class; in other words, the child class is a subtype of the parent class.

Specification   The parent class defines behavior that is implemented in the child class but not in the parent class.

Construction   The child class makes use of the behavior provided by the parent class but is not a subtype of the parent class.

Extension   The child class adds new functionality to the parent class, but does not change any inherited behavior.

Limitation   The child class restricts the use of some of the behavior inherited from the parent class.

Combination   The child class inherits features from more than one parent class. Although multiple inheritance is not supported directly by Java, it can be simulated in part by classes that use both inheritance and implementation of an interface, or implement two or more interfaces.

The Java language implicitly assumes that subclasses are also subtypes. This means that an instance of a subclass can be assigned to a variable declared as the parent class type. Methods in the child class that have the same name as those in the parent class override the inherited behavior. We have seen that this assumption that subclasses are subtypes is not always valid, and creating subclasses that are not subtypes is a possible source of program error.

8.5   MODIFIERS AND INHERITANCE

The language Java provides several modifiers that can be used to alter aspects of the inheritance process. For example, in the case studies in earlier chapters, we made extensive use of the visibility (or access control) modifiers public, protected, and private.

- A public feature (data field or method) can be accessed outside the class definition. A public class can be accessed outside the package in which it is declared.

- A protected feature can be accessed only within the class definition in which it appears, or within the definition of subclasses.

- A private feature can be accessed only within the class definition in which it appears.

The earlier case studies illustrated how both methods and data fields can be declared as static. A static field is shared by all instances of a class. A static method can be invoked even when no instance of the class has been created. Static data fields and methods are inherited in the same manner as nonstatic items, except that static methods cannot be overridden.

Both methods and classes can be declared to be abstract. An abstract class cannot be instanciated. That is, it is not legal to create an instance of an abstraction class using the operator new. Such a class can only be used as a parent class, to create a new type of object. Similarly, an abstract method must be overridden by a subclass.

An alternative modifier, final, is the opposite of abstract. When applied to a class, the keyword indicates that the class *cannot* be subclassified. Similarly, when applied to a method, the keyword indicates that the method cannot be overridden. Thus, the user is guaranteed that the behavior of the class will be as defined and not modified by a later subclass.

```
final class newClass extends oldClass {
    :
    :
}
```

We have seen that program constants are generally defined by variables that are both static and final:

```
class CannonGame extends Frame {
    :
    :
    public static final int FrameWidth = 600;
```

```
       public static final int FrameHeight = 400;
            .
            .
            .
  }
```

Optimizing compilers can sometimes make use of the fact that a data field, class, or method is declared as final and can thus generate better code than would otherwise be possible.

8.6   PROGRAMMING AS A MULTIPERSON ACTIVITY

When programs are constructed out of reusable, off-the-shelf components, programming moves from an individual activity (one programmer and the computer) to a community effort. A programmer may operate both as the *developer* of new abstractions and as the *user* of a software system created by an earlier programmer. The reader should not confuse the term *user* when applied to a programmer with the same term denoting the application end-user. Similarly, we will often speak of the organization of several objects by describing a *client* object that is requesting the services of a *provider*. Again, the client in this case is likely a programmer (or the code being developed by a programmer) making use of the services developed by an earlier programmer. This should not be confused with the idea of *client/server* computing, as described in Chapter 2.

8.7   THE BENEFITS OF INHERITANCE

In this section we will describe some of the many important benefits of the proper use of inheritance.

8.7.1   *Software Reusability*

When behavior is inherited from another class, the code that provides that behavior does not have to be rewritten. This may seem obvious, but the implications are important. Many programmers spend much of their time rewriting code they have written many times before—for example, to search for a pattern in a string or to insert a new element into a table. With object-oriented techniques, these functions can be written once and reused.

8.7.2   *Increased Reliability*

Code that is executed frequently tends to have fewer bugs than code that is executed infrequently. When the same components are used in two or more applications, the code will be exercised more than code that is developed for a single application. Thus, bugs in such code tend to be discovered more quickly, and latter applications gain the benefit of using components that are more error free. Similarly, the costs of maintenance of shared components can be split among many projects.

8.7.3 Code Sharing

Code sharing can occur on several levels with object-oriented techniques. On one level, many users or projects can use the same classes. (Brad Cox [1986] calls these software-ICs, in analogy to the integrated circuits used in hardware design). Another form of sharing occurs when two or more classes developed by a single programmer as part of a project inherit from a single parent class. For example, a Set and an Array may both be considered a form of Collection. When this happens, two or more types of objects will share the code that they inherit. This code needs to be written only once and will contribute only once to the size of the resulting program.

8.7.4 Consistency of Interface

When two or more classes inherit from the same superclass, we are assured that the behavior they inherit will be the same in all cases. Thus, it is easier to guarantee that interfaces to similar objects are in fact similar and that the user is not presented with a confusing collection of objects that are almost the same but behave, and are interacted with, very differently.

8.7.5 Software Components

Inheritance enables programmers to construct reusable software components. The goal is to permit the development of new and novel applications that nevertheless require little or no actual coding. The Java library offers a rich collection of software components for use in the development of applications.

8.7.6 Rapid Prototyping

When a software system is constructed largely out of reusable components, developers can concentrate their time on understanding the new and unusual portion of the system. Thus, software systems can be generated more quickly and easily, leading to a style of programming known as *rapid prototyping* or *exploratory programming*. A prototype system is developed, users experiment with it, a second system is produced that is based on experience with the first, further experimentation takes place, and so on for several iterations. Such programming is particularly useful in situations where the goals and requirements of the system are only vaguely understood when the project begins.

8.7.7   *Polymorphism and Frameworks*

Software produced conventionally is generally written from the bottom up, although it may be *designed* from the top down. That is, the lower-level routines are written, and on top of these slightly higher abstractions are produced, and on top of these even more abstract elements are generated. This process is like building a wall, where every brick must be laid on top of an already laid brick.

Normally, code portability decreases as one moves up the levels of abstraction. That is, the lowest-level routines may be used in several different projects, and perhaps even the next level of abstraction may be reused, but the higher-level routines are intimately tied to a particular application. The lower-level pieces can be carried to a new system and generally make sense standing on their own; the higher-level components generally make sense (because of declarations or data dependencies) only when they are built on top of specific lower-level units.

Polymorphism in programming languages permits the programmer to generate high-level reusable components that can be tailored to fit different applications by changes in their low-level parts. The Java AWT is an example of a large software framework that relies on inheritance and substitutability for its operation.

8.7.8   *Information Hiding*

A programmer who reuses a software component needs only to understand the nature of the component and its interface. It is not necessary for the programmer to have detailed information concerning matters such as the techniques used to implement the component. Thus, the interconnectedness between software systems is reduced. As mentioned earlier in this book, the interconnected nature of conventional software is one of the principal causes of software complexity.

8.8   THE COSTS OF INHERITANCE

Although the benefits of inheritance in object-oriented programming are great, almost nothing is without cost of one sort or another. For this reason, we must consider the cost of object-oriented programming techniques, and in particular the cost of inheritance.

8.8.1   *Execution Speed*

It is seldom possible for general purpose software tools to be as fast as carefully handcrafted systems. Thus, inherited methods, which must deal with arbitrary subclasses, are often slower than specialized code.

Yet, concern about efficiency is often misplaced.[2] First, the difference in speed or complexity is often small. Second, the reduction in execution speed may be balanced by an increase in the speed of software development. Finally, most programmers actually have little idea of how execution time is being used in their programs. It is far better to develop a working system, monitor it to discover where execution time is being used, and improve those sections, than to spend an inordinate amount of time worrying about efficiency early in a project.

8.8.2 *Program Size*

The use of any software library frequently imposes a size penalty not imposed by systems constructed for a specific project. Although this expense may be substantial, as memory costs decrease, the size of programs becomes less important. Containing development costs and producing high-quality and error-free code rapidly are now more important than limiting the size of programs.

8.8.3 *Message-Passing Overhead*

Much has been made of the fact that passing messages is by nature a more costly operation than simply invoking procedures. As with overall execution speed, however, overconcern about the cost of message passing is frequently penny wise and pound foolish. For one thing, the increased cost is often marginal—perhaps two or three additional assembly-language instructions and a total time penalty of 10 percent. This increased cost, like others, must be weighed against the many benefits of the object-oriented technique.

8.8.4 *Program Complexity*

Although object-oriented programming is often touted as a solution to software complexity, in fact, overuse of inheritance can often simply replace one form of complexity with another. Understanding the control flow of a program that uses inheritance may require several multiple scans up and down the inheritance graph. This is what is known as the *yo-yo* problem, which we will discuss in more detail in a later chapter.

8.9 CHAPTER SUMMARY

Inheritance is a mechanism for relating a new software abstraction being developed to an older, existing abstraction. By stating that the new component

---

[2] The following quote from an article by Bill Wulf is an apt remark on the importance of efficiency: "More computing sins are committed in the name of efficiency (without necessarily achieving it) than for any other single reason—including blind stupidity" [Wulf 1972/1979].

inherits (or *extends*) the older abstraction, the programmer means that all the public and protected properties of the original class are also now part of the new abstraction. In addition, the new class can add new data fields and behavior, and can override methods that are inherited from the original class. Interfaces are a closely related mechanism, which tie the concrete realization of behavior to an abstract description.

All classes in Java use inheritance. If their inheritance is not explicitly stated, classes are assumed to inherit from the fundamental root class Object.

Inheritance is tied to the principle of substitutability. A variable that is declared as one class can be assigned a value that is created from a child class. A similar mechanism also works with interfaces. A class that can be used in lieu of another class is said to be a *subtype*. Java implicitly assumes that all subclasses are subtypes. However, this need not be true (a subclass can override a method in an incompatible fashion, for example). Subtypes can also be constructed from interfaces, avoiding subclasses altogether.

There are many different types of inheritance, used for different purposes. Variations include specialization, specification, construction, extension, limitation, and combination.

A variety of modifiers alter the meaning of inheritance. A private feature is not inherited by subclasses. A static feature (data field or method) is shared by all instances. An abstract method must be overridden. A final feature (data field or method) cannot be overridden.

STUDY QUESTIONS

1. Give an intuitive description of inheritance.

2. What does it mean for a method to override an inherited method?

3. What is the name of the root class for all objects in Java?

4. What behavior is provided by the root class in Java?

5. What does it mean to say that child classes are substitutable for parent classes in Java?

6. What is the difference between a subclass and a subtype?

7. What are the characteristics of inheritance for specialization?

8. What are the characteristics of inheritance for specification? How does this differ from inheritance for specialization?

9. What are the characteristics of inheritance for construction? Why is construction not generally considered to be a good use of inheritance?

10. What are the characteristics of inheritance for extension?

11. What are the characteristics of inheritance for limitation? Why is limitation not generally considered to be a good use of inheritance?

12. Why would it not make sense for a method in Java to be declared both abstract and final?

13. What are some of the benefits of developing classes using inheritance, rather than developing each new class from scratch?

14. What are some of the costs of using inheritance for software development?

EXERCISES

1. Suppose you were required to program a project in a non–object-oriented language, such as Pascal or C. How would you simulate the notion of classes and methods? How would you simulate inheritance? Could you support multiple inheritance? Explain your answer.

2. We noted that the execution overhead associated with message passing is typically greater than the overhead associated with a conventional procedure call. How might you measure these overheads? For a language that supports both classes and procedures (such as C++ or Object Pascal), devise an experiment to determine the actual performance penalty of message passing.

3. Consider the three geometric concepts of a line (infinite in both directions), a ray (fixed at a point, infinite in one direction), and a segment (a portion of a line with fixed end points). How might you structure classes representing these three concepts in an inheritance hierarchy? Would your answer differ if you concentrated more on the data representation or more on the behavior? Characterize the type of inheritance you would use. Explain the reasoning behind your design.

4. Why is the example used in the following explanation not a valid illustration of inheritance?

> Perhaps the most powerful concept in object-oriented programming systems is inheritance. Objects can be created by inheriting the properties of other objects, thus removing the need to write any code whatsoever! Suppose, for example, a program is to process complex numbers consisting of real and imaginary parts. In a complex number, the real and imaginary parts behave like real numbers, so all of the operations (+, −, /, *, sqrt, sin, cos, etc.) can be inherited from the class of objects called REAL, instead of having to be written in code. This has a major impact on programmer productivity.

9

A Case Study: Solitaire

A program for playing the card game *Solitaire* will illustrate the utility and power of inheritance and overriding. A major part of the game of Solitaire is moving cards from one pile of cards to another. There are a number of different types of card piles, each having some features in common with the others, while other features are unique. A parent class can therefore be used to capture the common elements, while inheritance and overriding can be used to produce specialized types of piles. The development of this program will illustrate how inheritance can be used to simplify the creation of these components and ensure that they can all be manipulated in a similar fashion.

9.1 THE CLASS Card

To create a card game, we first need to define a class to represent a playing card. Each instance of class Card (Figure 9.1) maintains a suit value and a rank. To prevent modification of these values, the instance variables maintaining them are declared private and access is mediated through *accessor functions*. The value of the suit and rank fields are set by the constructor for the class. Integer constant values (in Java defined by the use of final static constants) are defined for the height and width of the card as well as for the suits. Another function permits the user to determine the color of the card. The Java library class Color is used to represent the color abstraction. The Color class defines constants for various colors. The values Color.red, Color.black, Color.yellow, and Color.blue are used in the Solitaire program.

There are important reasons that data values representing suit and rank should be returned through an accessor function, as opposed to defining the data fields s and r as public and allowing direct access to the data values. One of the most important is that access through a function ensures that the rank and

```java
import java.awt.*;

public class Card {
     // public constants for card width and suits
   public final static int width = 50;
   public final static int height = 70;
   public final static int heart = 0;
   public final static int spade = 1;
   public final static int diamond = 2;
   public final static int club = 3;
     // internal data fields for rank and suit
   private boolean faceup;
   private int r;
   private int s;

     // constructor
   Card (int sv, int rv) { s = sv; r = rv; faceup = false; }

     // access attributes of card
   public final int rank () { return r; }

   public final int suit() { return s; }

   public final boolean faceUp() { return faceup; }

   public final void flip() { faceup = ! faceup; }

   public final Color color() {
      if (faceUp())
         if (suit() == heart || suit() == diamond)
            return Color.red;
         else
            return Color.black;
      return Color.yellow;
      }

   public void draw (Graphics g, int x, int y) { ... }
}
```

Figure 9.1 Description of the class Card.

suit characteristics of a card can be read but not altered once the card has been created.

Note that many of the methods in the Card abstraction have been declared as final. This modifier serves two important purposes. First, it is a documentation aid, signaling to the reader of the listing that the methods cannot be overridden by subclasses. Second, in some situations the Java compiler can optimize the invocation of final methods, creating faster code than could be generated for the execution of non-final methods.

The only other actions a card can perform, besides setting and returning the state of the card, are to flip over and to display itself. The function flip( ) is a one-line function that simply reverses the value held by an instance variable. The drawing function is more complex, making use of the drawing facilities provided by the Java standard application library. As seen in the earlier case studies, the application library provides a data type called Graphics that provides a variety of methods for drawing lines and common shapes, as well as for coloring. An argument of this type is passed to the draw function, as are the integer coordinates representing the upper left corner of the card.

The card images are simple line drawings, as shown in Figure 9.3. Diamonds and hearts are drawn in red, spades and clubs in black. The hash marks on the back are drawn in yellow. A portion of the procedure for drawing a playing card is shown in Figure 9.2.

The most important feature of the playing-card abstraction is the manner in which each card is responsible for maintaining within itself all card-related information and behaviors. The card knows both its value and how to draw itself. In this manner the information is encapsulated and isolated from the application using the playing card. If, for example, one were to move the program to a new platform using different graphics facilities, only the draw method within the class itself would need to be altered.

9.2   THE GAME

The version of Solitaire we will describe is known as Klondike. The countless variations on this game make it probably the most common version of Solitaire; so much so that when you say "Solitaire," most people think of Klondike. The version we will use is that described in [Morehead and Mott-Smith 1949]; in the exercises we will explore some of the common variations.

The layout of the game is shown in Figure 9.4. A single standard pack of 52 cards is used. The *tableau*, or playing table, consists of 28 cards in 7 piles. the first pile has 1 card, the second 2, and so on up to 7. The top card of each pile is initially face up; all other cards are face down.

The suit piles (sometimes called *foundations*) are built up from aces to kings in suits. They are constructed above the tableau as the cards become available. The object of the game is to build all 52 cards into the suit piles.

```
public class Card {
    .
    .
    .
    public void    draw (Graphics g, int x, int y) {
        String names[] = {"A", "2", "3", "4", "5", "6",
            "7", "8", "9", "10", "J", "Q", "K"};
            // clear rectangle, draw border
        g.clearRect(x, y, width, height);
        g.setColor(Color.blue);
        g.drawRect(x, y, width, height);
            // draw body of card
        g.setColor(color( ));
        if (faceUp( )) {
            g.drawString(names[rank( )], x+3, y+15);
            if (suit( ) == heart) {
                g.drawLine(x+25, y+30, x+35, y+20);
                g.drawLine(x+35, y+20, x+45, y+30);
                g.drawLine(x+45, y+30, x+25, y+60);
                g.drawLine(x+25, y+60, x+5, y+30);
                g.drawLine(x+5, y+30, x+15, y+20);
                g.drawLine(x+15, y+20, x+25, y+30);
                }
            else if (suit( ) == spade) { ... }
            else if (suit( ) == diamond) { ... }
            else if (suit( ) == club) {
                g.drawOval(x+20, y+25, 10, 10);
                g.drawOval(x+25, y+35, 10, 10);
                g.drawOval(x+15, y+35, 10, 10);
                g.drawLine(x+23, y+45, x+20, y+55);
                g.drawLine(x+20, y+55, x+30, y+55);
                g.drawLine(x+30, y+55, x+27, y+45);
                }
            }
        else { // face down
            g.drawLine(x+15, y+5, x+15, y+65);
            g.drawLine(x+35, y+5, x+35, y+65);
            g.drawLine(x+5, y+20, x+45, y+20);
            g.drawLine(x+5, y+35, x+45, y+35);
            g.drawLine(x+5, y+50, x+45, y+50);
            }
        }
    }
```

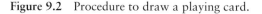

Figure 9.2 Procedure to draw a playing card.

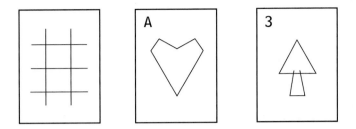

Figure 9.3 Card images for Solitaire.

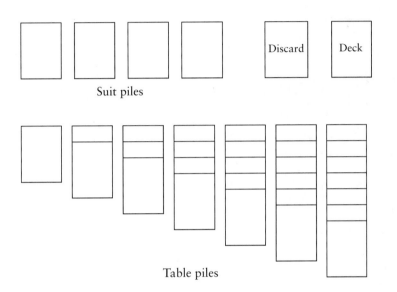

Figure 9.4 Layout for the Solitaire game.

The cards that are not part of the tableau are initially all in the *deck*. Cards in the deck are face down, and are drawn one by one from the deck and placed, face up, on the *discard pile*. From there, they can be moved onto either a tableau pile or a foundation. Cards are drawn from the deck until the pile is empty; at this point, the game is over if no further moves can be made.

Cards can be placed on a tableau pile only on a card of next-higher rank and opposite color. They can be placed on a foundation only if they are the same suit and next higher card or if the foundation is empty and the card is an ace. Spaces in the tableau that arise during play can be filled only by kings.

The topmost card of each tableau pile and the topmost card of the discard pile are always available for play. The only time more than one card is moved is when an entire collection of face-up cards from a tableau (called a *build*) is moved to another tableau pile. This can be done if the bottommost card of the build can be legally played on the topmost card of the destination. Our initial game will not support the transfer of a build, but we will discuss this as a possible extension. The topmost card of a tableau is always face up. If a card is moved from a tableau, leaving a face-down card on the top, the latter card can be turned face up.

From this short description, it is clear that the game of Solitaire mostly involves manipulating piles of cards. Each type of pile has many features in common with the others and a few aspects unique to the particular type. In the next section, we will investigate in detail how inheritance can be used in such circumstances to simplify the implementation of the various card piles by providing a common base for the generic actions and permitting this base to be redefined when necessary.

9.3   CARD PILES—INHERITANCE IN ACTION

Much of the behavior we associate with a card pile is common to each variety of pile in the game. For example, each pile maintains a collection of the cards in the pile (held in a Stack), and the operations of inserting and deleting elements from this collection are common. Other operations are given default behavior in the class CardPile, but they are sometimes overridden in the various subclasses. The class CardPile is shown in Figure 9.5.

Each card pile maintains the coordinate location for the upper left corner of the pile, as well as a Stack. The stack is used to hold the cards in the pile. All three of these values are set by the constructor for the class. The data fields are declared as protected and thus accessible to member functions associated with this class and to member functions associated with subclasses.

The three functions top(), pop(), and isEmpty() manipulate the list of cards, using functions provided by the Stack utility class. Note that these three methods have been declared final, and can not therefore be overridden in subclasses.

The topmost card in a pile is returned by the function top(). This card will be the last card in the underlying container. Note that the function peek() provided by the Stack class returns a value declared as Object. This result must be cast to a Card value before it can be returned as the result.

The method pop() uses the similarly named operation provided by the underlying stack. The stack method generates an exception if an attempt is made to remove an element from an empty stack. The pop() method in the class CardPile catches the exception and returns a null value in this situation.

The five operations that are not declared final are common to the abstract notion of our card piles, but they differ in details in each case. For example, the function canTake(Card) asks whether it is legal to place a card on the given pile. A card can be added to a foundation pile, for instance, only if it is an ace and

```java
import java.util.Stack;
import java.util.EmptyStackException;

public class CardPile {
    protected int x; // coordinates of the card pile
    protected int y;
    protected Stack thePile; // the collection of cards

    CardPile (int xl, int yl) { x = xl; y = yl; thePile = new Stack( ); }

    public final Card top( ) { return (Card) thePile.peek( ); }

    public final boolean isEmpty( ) { return thePile.empty( ); }

    public final Card pop( ) {
        try {
            return (Card) thePile.pop( );
            } catch (EmptyStackException e) { return null; }
        }

        // the following are sometimes overridden
    public boolean includes (int tx, int ty) {
        return x <= tx && tx <= x + Card.width &&
            y <= ty && ty <= y + Card.height;
        }

    public void select (int tx, int ty) { }

    public void addCard (Card aCard)  { thePile.push(aCard); }

    public void display (Graphics g) {
        g.setColor(Color.blue);
        if (isEmpty( )) g.drawRect(x, y, Card.width, Card.height);
        else top( ).draw(g, x, y);
        }

    public boolean canTake (Card aCard) { return false; }
}
```

Figure 9.5 Description of the class CardPile.

the foundation is empty, or if the card is of the same suit as the current topmost card in the pile and has the next-higher value. A card can be added to a tableau pile, on the other hand, only if the pile is empty and the card is a king, or if it is of the opposite color as the current topmost card in the pile and has the next lower value.

The actions of the five non-final functions defined in CardPile can be characterized as follows:

includes   Determines if the coordinates given as arguments are contained within the boundaries of the pile. The default action simply tests the topmost card; this is overridden in the tableau piles to test all card values.

canTake   Tells whether a pile can take a specific card. Only the tableau and suit piles can take cards, so the default action is simply to return no; this is overridden in the two classes mentioned.

addCard   Adds a card to the card list. It is redefined in the discard pile class to ensure that the card is face up.

display   Displays the card deck. The default method merely displays the topmost card of the pile, but it is overridden in the tableau class to display a column of cards. The top half of each hidden card is displayed. So that the playing surface area is conserved, only the topmost and bottommost face-up cards are displayed (this permits us to give definite bounds to the playing surface).

select   Performs an action in response to a mouse click. It is invoked when the user selects a pile by clicking the mouse in the portion of the playing field covered by the pile. The default action does nothing, but it is overridden by the table, deck, and discard piles to play the topmost card, if possible.

Table 9.1 illustrates the important benefits of inheritance. Given five operations and five classes, there are 25 potential methods we might have had to define. By making use of inheritance we need to implement only 13. Further-

Table 9.1   The benefits of inheritance.

	CardPile	SuitPile	DeckPile	DiscardPile	TableauPile
includes	×				×
canTake	×	×			×
addCard	×			×	
display	×				×
select	×		×	×	×

```
class SuitPile extends CardPile {

    SuitPile (int x, int y) { super(x, y); }

    public boolean canTake (Card aCard) {
        if (isEmpty( ))
            return aCard.rank( ) == 0;
        Card topCard = top( );
        return (aCard.suit( ) == topCard.suit( )) &&
            (aCard.rank( ) == 1 + topCard.rank( ));
    }
}
```

Figure 9.6   The class SuitPile.

more, we are guaranteed that each pile will respond in the same way to similar requests.

9.3.1   *The Suit Piles*

We will examine each of the subclasses of CardPile in detail, pointing out various uses of object-oriented features as they are encountered. The simplest subclass is the class SuitPile, shown in Figure 9.6, which represents the pile of cards at the top of the playing surface, the pile being built up in suit from ace to king.

The class SuitPile defines only two methods. The constructor for the class takes two integer arguments and does nothing more than invoke the constructor for the parent class CardPile. Note the use of the keyword super to indicate the parent class. The method canTake determines whether or not a card can be placed on the pile. A card is legal if the pile is empty and the card is an ace (that is, has rank zero) or if the card is the same suit as the topmost card in the pile and of the next higher rank (for example, a three of spades can only be played on a two of spades).

All other behavior of the suit pile is the same as that of our generic card pile. When selected, a suit pile does nothing. When a card is added, it is simply inserted into the collection of cards. To display the pile only the topmost card is drawn.

9.3.2   *The Deck Pile*

The DeckPile (Figure 9.7) maintains the original deck of cards. It differs from the generic card pile in two ways. When constructed, rather than creating an empty pile of cards, it creates the complete deck of 52 cards, inserting them in order into the collection. Once all the cards have been created, the collection is then shuffled. To do this, a *random number generator* is first created. This

```
class DeckPile extends CardPile {

    DeckPile (int x, int y) {
            // first initialize parent
        super(x, y);
            // then create the new deck
            // first put them into a local pile
        for (int i = 0; i < 4; i++)
            for (int j = 0; j <= 12; j++)
                addCard(new Card(i, j));

            // then shuffle the cards
        Random generator = new Random( );
        for (int i = 0; i < 52; i++) {
            int j = Math.abs(generator.nextInt( )) % 52;
            // swap the two card values
            Object temp = thePile.elementAt(i);
            thePile.setElementAt(thePile.elementAt(j), i);
            thePile.setElementAt(temp, j);
            }
        }

    public void select(int tx, int ty) {
        if (isEmpty( ))
            return;
        Solitare.discardPile.addCard(pop( ));
        }
    }
```

Figure 9.7   The class DeckPile.

generator is provided by the Java utility class Random. A loop then examines each card in turn, exchanging the card with another randomly selected card. To produce the index of the latter card, the random number generator first produces a randomly selected integer value (using by the method nextInt). Since this value could potentially be negative, the math library function abs is called to make it positive. The modular division operation is finally used to produce a randomly selected integer value between 0 and 51.

A subtle feature to note is that we are here performing a random access to the elements of a Stack. The conventional view of a stack does not allow access to any but the topmost element. However, in the Java library the Stack container is constructed using inheritance from the Vector class. Thus, any legal operation on a Vector, such as the method elementAt( ), can also be applied to a Stack.

The method select is invoked when the mouse button is used to select the card deck. If the deck is empty, it does nothing. Otherwise, the topmost card is removed from the deck and added to the discard pile.

Java does not have global variables. Where a value is shared between multiple instances of similar classes, such as the various piles used in our Solitaire game, an instance variable can be declared static. As noted in Chapter 4, one copy of a static variable is created and shared among all instances. In the present program, static variables will be used to maintain all the various card piles. These will be held in an instance of class Solitaire, described subsequently. To access these values we use a complete qualified name, which includes the name of the class as well as the name of the variable. This is shown in the select method in Figure 9.7, which refers to the variable Solitare.discardPile to access the discard pile.

9.3.3   *The Discard Pile*

The class DiscardPile (Figure 9.8) is interesting in that it exhibits two very different forms of inheritance. The select method *overrides* or *replaces* the default behavior provided by class CardPile, replacing it with code that when invoked (when the mouse is pressed over the card pile), checks to see if the topmost card can be played on any suit pile or, alternatively, on any tableau pile. If the card cannot be played, it is kept in the discard pile.

The method addCard is a different sort of overriding. Here the behavior is a *refinement* of the default behavior in the parent class. That is, the behavior of the parent class is completely executed, and, in addition, new behavior is added. In this case, the new behavior ensures that when a card is placed on the discard pile it is always face up. After satisfying this condition, the code in the parent class is invoked to add the card to the pile by passing the message to the pseudovariable named super.

Another form of refinement occurs in the constructors for the various subclasses. Each must invoke the constructor for the parent class to guarantee that the parent is properly initialized before the constructor performs its own actions. The parent constructor is invoked by the pseudovariable super being used as a function inside the constructor for the child class. Chapter 12 has much more about the distinction between replacement and refinement in overriding.

9.3.4   *The Tableau Piles*

The most complex of the subclasses of CardPile is that used to hold a tableau, or table pile. It is shown in Figures 9.9 and 9.10 (on pages 151 and 152). Table piles differ from the generic card pile in the following ways:

- When initialized (by the constructor), the table pile removes a certain number of cards from the deck, placing them in its pile. The number of cards

```
class DiscardPile extends CardPile {

    DiscardPile (int x, int y) { super (x, y); }

    public void addCard (Card aCard) {
        if (! aCard.faceUp())
            aCard.flip();
        super.addCard(aCard);
    }

    public void select (int tx, int ty) {
        if (isEmpty())
            return;
        Card topCard = pop();
        for (int i = 0; i < 4; i++)
            if (Solitare.suitPile[i].canTake(topCard)) {
                Solitare.suitPile[i].addCard(topCard);
                return;
            }
        for (int i = 0; i < 7; i++)
            if (Solitare.tableau[i].canTake(topCard)) {
                Solitare.tableau[i].addCard(topCard);
                return;
            }
        // nobody can use it, put it back on our list
        addCard(topCard);
    }
}
```

Figure 9.8   The class DiscardPile.

so removed is determined by an additional argument to the constructor. The topmost card of this pile is then displayed face up.

- A card can be added to the pile (method canTake) only if the pile is empty and the card is a king, or if the card is the opposite color from that of the current topmost card and one smaller in rank.

- When a mouse press is tested to determine if it covers this pile (method includes) only the left, right, and top bounds are checked; the bottom bound is not tested since the pile may be of variable length.

- When the pile is selected, the topmost card is flipped if it is face down. If it is face up, an attempt is made to move the card first to any available suit

```
class TablePile extends CardPile {

    TablePile (int x, int y, int c) {
            // initialize the parent class
        super(x, y);
            // then initialize our pile of cards
        for (int i = 0; i < c; i++) {
            addCard(Solitare.deckPile.pop( ));
            }
            // flip topmost card face up
        top( ).flip( );
        }

    public boolean canTake (Card aCard) {
        if (isEmpty( ))
            return aCard.rank( ) == 12;
        Card topCard = top( );
        return (aCard.color( ) != topCard.color( )) &&
            (aCard.rank( ) == topCard.rank( ) - 1);
        }

    public boolean includes (int tx, int ty) {
            // don't test bottom of card
        return x <= tx && tx <= x + Card.width &&
            y <= ty;
        }

    public void display (Graphics g) {
        int localy = y;
        for (Enumeration e = thePile.elements( ); e.hasMoreElements( ); ) {
            Card aCard = (Card) e.nextElement( );
            aCard.draw (g, x, localy);
            localy += 35;
            }
        }
        .
        .
        .
}
```

Figure 9.9   The class TablePile, part 1.

```
class TablePile extends CardPile {
    .
    .
    .

    public void select (int tx, int ty) {
        if (isEmpty())
            return;

            // if face down, then flip
        Card topCard = top();
        if (! topCard.faceUp()) {
            topCard.flip();
            return;
            }

            // else see if any suit pile can take card
        topCard = pop();
        for (int i = 0; i < 4; i++)
            if (Solitare.suitPile[i].canTake(topCard)) {
                Solitare.suitPile[i].addCard(topCard);
                return;
                }
            // else see if any other table pile can take card
        for (int i = 0; i < 7; i++)
            if (Solitare.tableau[i].canTake(topCard)) {
                Solitare.tableau[i].addCard(topCard);
                return;
                }
            // else put it back on our pile
        addCard(topCard);
        }
}
```

Figure 9.10   The class TablePile, part 2.

pile, and then to any available table pile. Only if no pile can take the card
is it left in place.

■ To display the pile, each card in the pile is drawn in turn, each moving
down slightly. To access the individual elements of the stack, an Enumeration
is created. Enumeration objects are provided by all the containers in the
Java library; they allow the programmer to easily loop over the elements
in the container.

9.4   THE APPLICATION CLASS

Figure 9.11 shows the central class for the Solitaire application. As in our earlier case studies, the control is initially given to the static procedure named main, which creates an instance of the application class. The constructor for the

```
public class Solitare {
   static public DeckPile deckPile;
   static public DiscardPile discardPile;
   static public TablePile tableau [ ];
   static public SuitPile suitPile [ ];
   static public CardPile allPiles [ ];
   private Frame window;

   static public void main (String [ ] args) {
      Solitare world = new Solitare( );
      }

   public Solitare ( ) {
      window = new SolitareFrame( );
      init( );
      window.show( );
      }

   public void init ( ) {
         // first allocate the arrays
      allPiles = new CardPile[13];
      suitPile = new SuitPile[4];
      tableau = new TablePile[7];
         // then fill them in
      allPiles[0] = deckPile = new DeckPile(335, 30);
      allPiles[1] = discardPile = new DiscardPile(268, 30);
      for (int i = 0; i < 4; i++)
         allPiles[2+i] = suitPile[i] =
            new SuitPile(15 + (Card.width+10) * i, 30);
      for (int i = 0; i < 7; i++)
         allPiles[6+i] = tableau[i] =
            new TablePile(15+(Card.width+5)*i, Card.height+35, i+1);
      }

   private class SolitareFrame extends Frame { ... }
}
```

Figure 9.11   The class Solitaire.

application creates a window for the application, by constructing an instance of a nested class SolitareFrame that inherits from the library class Frame. After invoking the init method, which performs the application initialization, the window is given the message show, which will cause it to display itself.

As noted earlier, the variables maintaining the different piles, which are shared in common between all classes, are declared as static data fields in this class. These data fields are initialized in the method name init.

Arrays in Java are somewhat different from arrays in most computer languages. Java distinguishes the three activities of array declaration, array allocation, and assignment to an array location. Note that the declaration statements indicate only that the named objects are an array and not that they have any specific bound. One of the first steps in the initialization routine is to allocate space for the three arrays (the suit piles, the tableau, and the array allPiles we will discuss shortly). The new command allocates space for the arrays, but does not assign any values to the array elements.

The next step is to create the deck pile. Recall that the constructor for this class creates and shuffles the entire deck of 52 cards. The discard pile is similarly constructed. A loop then creates and initializes the four suit piles, and a second loop creates and initializes the tableau piles. Recall that as part of the initialization of the tableau, cards are removed from the deck and inserted in the tableau pile.

The inner class SolitareFrame, used to manage the application window, is shown in Figure 9.12. In addition to the cards, a button will be placed at the bottom of the window. Listeners are created both for mouse events (see Chapter 7) and for the button. When pressed, the button will invoke the button listener method. This method will reinitialize the game, then repaint the window. Similarly, when the mouse listener is invoked (in response to a mouse press) the collection of card piles will be examined, and the appropriate pile will be displayed.

9.5   PLAYING THE POLYMORPHIC GAME

Both the mouse listener and the repaint method for the application window make use of the array allPiles. This array is used to represent all 13 card piles. Note that as each pile is created it is also assigned a location in this array, as well as in the appropriate static variable. We will use this array to illustrate yet another aspect of inheritance. The principle of substitutability is used here: The array allPiles is declared as an array of CardPile, but in fact is maintaining a variety of card piles.

This array of all piles is used in situations where it is not important to distinguish between various types of card piles; for example, in the repaint procedure. To repaint the display, each different card pile is simply asked to display itself. Similarly, when the mouse is pressed, each pile is queried to see if it contains the given position. If the pile does contain the given position, the

```
private class SolitareFrame extends Frame {

    private class RestartButtonListener implements ActionListener {
        public void actionPerformed (ActionEvent e) {
            init();
            repaint();
        }
    }

    private class MouseKeeper extends MouseAdapter {
        public void mousePressed (MouseEvent e) {
            int x = e.getX();
            int y = e.getY();
            for (int i = 0; i < 13; i++)
                if (allPiles[i].includes(x, y)) {
                    allPiles[i].select(x, y);
                    repaint();
                }
        }
    }

    public SolitareFrame() { // constructor for window
        setSize(600, 500);
        setTitle("Solitaire Game");
        addMouseListener (new MouseKeeper());
        Button restartButton = new Button("New Game");
        restartButton.addActionListener(new RestartButtonListener());
        add("South", restartButton);
    }

    public void paint(Graphics g) {
        for (int i = 0; i < 13; i++)
            allPiles[i].display(g);
    }
}
```

Figure 9.12 The inner class SolitareFrame.

pile is selected. Remember, of the piles being queried here seven are tableau piles, four are foundations, and the remaining are the discard pile and the deck. Furthermore, the actual code executed in response to the invocation of the includes and select routines may be different in each call, depending upon the type of pile being manipulated. In other object-oriented languages, such methods are often described as *virtual*.

The use of a variable declared as an instance of the parent class holding a value from a subclass is one aspect of *polymorphism*, a topic we will return to in more detail in a subsequent chapter.

9.6   BUILDING A MORE COMPLETE GAME

The Solitaire game described here is minimal and exceedingly hard to win. A more realistic game would include at least a few of the following variations:

- The method select in class TablePile would be extended to recognize builds. That is, if the topmost card could not be played, the bottommost face-up card in the pile should be tested against each tableau pile; if it could be played, the entire collection of face-up cards should be moved.

- Our game halts after one series of moves through the deck. An alternative would be that when the user selected the empty deck pile (by clicking the mouse in the area covered by the deck pile) the discard pile would be reshuffled and copied back into the deck, allowing execution to continue.

Various other alternatives are described in the exercises.

9.7   CHAPTER SUMMARY

The Solitaire program in this chapter is used as a case study to present many of the features and benefits of inheritance. The various different types of card piles found in the game can all be specialized from one common parent class. This parent class provides default behavior, which can be overridden when a pile requires more specialized code. In the program presented here, the default behavior is overridden less than half the time.

The following are some of the aspects of inheritance discussed in this chapter:

- By creating a common parent class, default behavior can be shared among several different software components.

- Methods can be declared as final, in which case they cannot be overridden in subclasses. (As noted in the previous chapter, methods can also be declared as abstract, in which case they *must* be overridden in subclasses.)

- Overriding methods can be divided into those that *replace* the code inherited from the parent, and those that *refine* the parent code. In the former case only the child code is executed, while in the latter both the child and the parent code is executed. In Java refinement is specified by explicitly executing the parent function, using the pseudovariable super.

- Inheritance is tied to polymorphism through the concept of substitutability. An instance of a child class can be assigned to a variable that is declared as a parent class type. Using this idea, we can create a variable (or, in this case, an array of values) that maintains any type of card pile.

- When an overridden method is applied to a polymorphic variable, the code executed is determined by the value the variable currently holds, not the declared type of the variable. Such methods are sometimes described as *virtual*.

STUDY QUESTIONS

1. What data values are maintained by class Card? What behaviors can a card perform? (That is, what methods are implemented by the class Card?)

2. Explain why the suit and rank data fields are declared private.

3. What is a default constructor? What is a copy constructor?

4. What is an accessor function? What is the advantage of using an accessor function as opposed to direct access to a data member?

5. What are the 13 different card piles that are used in the Solitaire game?

6. What does it mean when a function is declared final?

7. Describe the five non-final functions implemented in class CardPile and overridden in at least one child class.

8. How does the use of inheritance reduce the amount of code that would otherwise be necessary to implement the various types of card piles?

9. Explain the difference between overriding used for replacement and overriding used for refinement. Find another example of each in the methods associated with class CardPile and its various subclasses.

10. Explain how polymorphism is exhibited in the Solitaire game application.

EXERCISES

1. The Solitaire game has been designed to be as simple as possible. A few features are somewhat annoying, but they can be easily remedied with more coding. These include the following:

   (a) The topmost card of a tableau pile should not be moved to another tableau pile if there is another face-up card below it.

   (b) An entire build should not be moved if the bottommost card is a king and there are no remaining face-down cards.

   For each, describe what procedures need to be changed, and give the code for the updated routine.

2. The following are common variations of Klondike. For each, describe which portions of the Solitaire program need to be altered to incorporate the change.

   (a) If the user clicks on an empty deck pile, the discard pile is moved (perhaps with shuffling) back to the deck pile. Thus, the user can traverse the deck pile repeatedly.

   (b) Cards can be moved from the suit pile back into the tableau pile.

   (c) Cards are drawn from the deck three at a time and placed on the discard pile in reverse order. As before, only the topmost card of the discard pile is available for playing. If fewer than three cards remain in the deck pile, all the remaining cards (as many as that may be) are moved to the discard pile. (In practice, this variation is often accompanied by variation 1, permitting multiple passes through the deck.)

   (d) The same as variation 3, but any of the three selected cards can be played. (This requires a slight change to the layout as well as an extensive change to the discard pile class.)

   (e) Any royalty card, not simply a king, can be moved onto an empty tableau pile.

3. The game Thumb and Pouch is similar to Klondike except that a card may be built on any card of next-higher rank, of any suit but its own. Thus, a nine of spades can be played on a ten of clubs, but not on a ten of spades. This variation greatly improves the chances of winning. (According to Morehead and Mott-Smith [1949], the chances of winning Klondike are 1 in 30, whereas the chances of winning Thumb and Pouch are 1 in 4.) What portions of the program need to be changed to accommodate this variation?

4. The game Whitehead is superficially similar to Klondike, in the sense that it uses the same layout. However, it uses different rules for when a card can be played in the tableau:

   (a) A card can be moved onto another face-up card in the tableau only if it has the *same* color and is one smaller in rank. For example, a five of spades can be played on either a six of clubs or a six of spades, but not on a six of diamonds or a six of hearts.

   (b) A build can only be moved if all cards in the build are of the same suit.

   What portions of the program need to be changed to accommodate this variation?

10

Mechanisms for Software Reuse

Object-oriented programming has been billed as the technology that will finally permit software to be constructed from general purpose reusable components. Writers such as Brad Cox have even gone so far as to describe object orientation as heralding the "industrial revolution" in software development [Cox 1986]. While reality may not quite match the expectations of OOP pioneers, it *is* true that object-oriented programming makes possible a level of software reuse that is orders of magnitude more powerful than that permitted by previous software construction techniques. In this chapter, we will investigate the two most common mechanisms for software reuse, which are known as *inheritance* and *composition*.

Inheritance in Java is made more flexible by the presence of two different mechanisms, interfaces and subclassification. In addition to contrasting inheritance and composition, we will contrast inheritance performed using subclassification and inheritance performed using interfaces, and relate all to the concept of substitutability.

10.1 SUBSTITUTABILITY

The concept of substitutability is fundamental to many of the most powerful software development techniques in object-oriented programming. You will recall that substitutability referred to the situation that occurs when a *variable* declared as one type is used to hold a *value* derived from another type.

In Java, substitutability can occur either through the use of classes and inheritance, or through the use of interfaces. Examples of both occurred in the case studies in earlier chapters. In the PinBall Game program described in Chapter 7, the variable targets was declared a PinBallTarget, but in fact it held a variety of

159

different types of values that were created using subclasses of PinBallTarget. In the Solitaire program from Chapter 9, the variable allPiles was declared as holding a CardPile, but in fact it held values that were subclasses of CardPile, such as DeckPile and DiscardPile as follows:

```
public class Solitare {
   static public CardPile allPiles [ ];

   public void init () {
         .
         .
      allPiles = new CardPile[13];
      // then fill them in
      allPiles[0] = new DeckPile(335, 30);
      allPiles[1] = new DiscardPile(268, 30);
   }
      .
      .
}
```

We have also seen examples of substitutability arising through interfaces. An example is the instance of the class FireButtonListener created in the Cannon Game (Chapter 6). The class from which this value was defined was declared as implementing the interface ActionListener. Because it implements the ActionListener interface, we can use this value as a parameter to a function (in this case, addActionListener) that expects an ActionListener value.

```
class CannonWorld extends Frame {
      .
      .
   private class FireButtonListener implements ActionListener {
      public void actionPerformed (ActionEvent e) {
            .
            .
      }
   }

   public CannonWorld () {
         .
         .
      fire.addActionListener(new FireButtonListener());
   }
}
```

We will return to the distinction between inheritance of classes and inheritance of interfaces in Section 10.1.2.

10.1.1 *The* Is-a *Rule and the* Has-a *Rule*

A commonly employed rule of thumb that can be used to understand when inheritance is an appropriate software technique is known colloquially as *is-a* and *has-a* (or *part-of*) relationship.

The *is-a* relationship holds between two concepts when the first is a specialized instance of the second. That is, for all practical purposes the behavior and data associated with the more specific idea form a subset of the behavior and data associated with the more abstract idea. For example, all the examples of inheritance described in the early chapters satisfy the *is-a* relationship (a Florist *is-a* Shopkeeper, a Dog *is-a* Mammal, a PinBall *is-a* Ball, and so on). The relationship derives its name from a simple rule of thumb that tests the relationship. To determine if concept X is a specialized instance of concept Y, simply form the English sentence "*An* X *is a* Y". If the assertion "sounds correct," that is, if it seems to match your everyday experience, you may judge that X and Y have the *is-a* relationship.

The *has-a* relationship, on the other hand, holds when the second concept is a component of the first but the two are not in any sense the same thing, no matter how abstract the generality. For example, a Car *has-a* Engine, although clearly it is not the case that a Car *is-a* Engine or that an Engine *is-a* Car. A Car, however, *is-a* Vehicle, which in turn *is-a* MeansOfTransportation. Once again, the test for the *has-a* relationship is to simply form the English sentence "*An* X *has a* Y", and let common sense tell you whether the result sounds reasonable.

Most of the time, the distinction is clear-cut. But, sometimes it may be subtle or may depend on circumstances. In Section 10.2 we will use one such indefinite case to illustrate the two software development techniques that are naturally tied to these two relationships.

10.1.2 *Inheritance of Code and Inheritance of Behavior*

There are at least two different ways in which a concept can satisfy the *is-a* relationship with another concept, and these are reflected in two different mechanisms in the Java language. Inheritance is the mechanism of choice when two concepts share *structure* or *code* relationship with each other, while an interface is the more appropriate technique when two concepts share the *specification of behavior*, but no actual code.

This can be illustrated with examples from the Java run-time library. The class Frame, from which most Java windows inherit, provides a great deal of code, in the form of methods that are inherited and used without being overridden. Thus, inheritance using the extends modifier in the class heading is the appropriate mechanism to use in this situation.

```
    // a cannon game is a type of Frame
public class CannonGame extends Frame {
    .
    .
    .
}
```

On the other hand, the characteristics needed for an ActionListener (the object type that responds to button presses) can be described by a single method, and the implementation of that method cannot be predicted, since it differs from one application to another. Thus, an interface is used to describe only the necessary requirements, and no actual behavior is inherited by a subclass that implements the behavior.

```
class CannonWorld extends Frame {
    .
    .
    .

        // a fire button listener implements the action listener interface
    private class FireButtonListener implements ActionListener {
        public void actionPerformed (ActionEvent e) {
            .
            .
            .
        }
    }
}
```

In general, the class-subclass relationship should be used whenever a subclass can usefully inherit code, data values, or behavior from the parent class. The interface mechanism should be used when the child class inherits only the specification of the expected behavior, but no actual code.

10.2   COMPOSITION AND INHERITANCE DESCRIBED

Two different techniques for software reuse are *composition* and *inheritance*. Although uses of inheritance were explicitly noted in earlier chapters, and composition was used in several places as well, this was not pointed out. One way to view these two different mechanisms is as manifestations of the *has-a* rule and the *is-a* rule, respectively.

Although in most situations the distinction between *is-a* and *has-a* is clear-cut, it does happen occasionally that it can be difficult to determine which mechanism is most appropriate to use in a particular situation. By examining one such indefinite case, we can more easily point out the differences between the use of inheritance and the use of composition. The example we will use is taken from the Java library and concerns the development of a Stack abstraction from an existing Vector data type.

The Vector data type is described in detail in Chapter 19. While abstractly a vector is most commonly thought of as an indexed collection, the Java implementation also permits values to be added or removed from the end of the collection, growing and shrinking the container as necessary. The methods of interest for this discussion can be described as follows:

```java
class Vector {
    // see if collection is empty
    public boolean isEmpty () { ... }

    // return size of collection
    public int size () { ... }

    // add element to end of collection
    public void addElement (Object value) { ... }

    // return last element in collection
    public Object lastElement () { ... }

    // remove element at given index
    public Object removeElementAt (int index) { ... }

        .
        .
        .
}
```

A *stack* is an abstract data type that allows elements to be added or removed from one end only. If you think about a stack of dishes sitting on a counter, you can get a good intuitive image. It is easy to access the topmost dish, or to place a new dish on the top. It is much more difficult to access any dish other than the topmost dish. In fact, it might be that the only way to do this is to remove dishes one by one until you reach the dish you want.

The Stack abstractions defined here will be slightly simpler than the version provided by the Java library. In particular, the library abstraction will generate an exception if an attempt is made to access or remove an element from an empty stack, a condition we will ignore. The Java library stack routine names the empty test method *empty*, instead of the method isEmpty from class Vector, and finally the Stack abstraction provides a method to search the stack to determine if it includes a given element. We will not describe this method here.

10.2.1   *Using Composition*

We will first investigate how the stack abstraction can be formed with composition. Recall from our earlier discussion that an object is simply an encapsulation of data values and behavior. When composition is employed to reuse an existing data abstraction in the development of a new data type, a portion of the state of the new data structure is simply an instance of the existing structure. This is illustrated in Figure 10.1, where the data type Stack contains a private instance field named theData, which is declared to be of type Vector.

Because the Vector abstraction is stored as part of the data area for our stack, it must be initialized in the constructor. The constructor for class Stack allocates space for the vector, giving a value to the variable theData.

Operations that manipulate the new structure are implemented by making use of the existing operations provided for the earlier data type. For example, the implementation of the isEmpty operation for our stack data structure simply invokes the similarly named function already defined for vectors. The peek operation is known by a different name, but the task is already provided by the lastElement operation in the Vector class. Similarly, the push operation is simply performed by executing an addElement on the vector.

```
class Stack {
    private Vector theData;

    public Stack ()
       { theData = new Vector( ); }

    public boolean isEmpty ()
       { return theData.isEmpty( ); }

    public Object push (Object newValue)
       { theData.addElement (newValue); }

    public Object peek ()
       { return theData.lastElement( ); }

    public Object pop () {
       Object result = theData.lastElement( );
       theData.removeElementAt(theData.size( )-1);
       return result;
       }
}
```

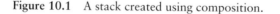

Figure 10.1   A stack created using composition.

The only operation that is slightly more complex is popping an element from the stack. This involves using two methods provided by the Vector class, namely obtaining the topmost element and removing it from the collection. Notice that to remove the element we must first determine its index position, then remove the element by naming its position.

The important point to emphasize is the fact that composition provides a way to leverage off an existing software component in the creation of a new application. By use of the existing Vector class, we have already addressed the majority of the difficult work in managing the data values for our new component.

But composition makes no explicit or implicit claims about substitutability. When formed in this fashion, the data types Stack and Vector are entirely distinct and neither can be substituted in situations where the other is required.

10.2.2 *Using Inheritance*

An entirely different mechanism for software reuse in object-oriented programming is the concept of inheritance, with which a new class can be declared a *subclass*, or *child class*, of an existing class. In this way, all data areas and functions associated with the original class are automatically associated with the new data abstraction. The new class can, in addition, define new data values or new functions; it can also *override* functions in the original class, simply by defining new functions with the same names as those of functions that appear in the parent class.

These possibilities are illustrated in the class description shown in Figure 10.2, which implements a different version of the Stack abstraction. By naming the class Vector in the class heading, we indicate that our Stack abstraction is an extension, or a refinement, of the existing class Vector. Thus, all data fields and operations associated with vectors are immediately applicable to stacks as well.

The most obvious features of this class in comparison to the earlier are the items that are missing. There are no local data fields. There is no constructor, since no local data values need be initialized. The method isEmpty need not be provided, since the method is inherited already from the parent class Vector.

Compare this function with the earlier version, shown in Figure 10.1. Both techniques are powerful mechanisms for code reuse, but unlike composition, inheritance carries an implicit assumption that subclasses are, in fact, subtypes. This means that instances of the new abstraction should react similarly to instances of the parent class.

In fact, the version using inheritance provides more useful functionality than the version using composition. For example, the method size in the Vector class yields the number of elements stored in a vector. With the version of the Stack formed using inheritance we get this function automatically for free, while the composition version needs to explicitly add a new operation if we want to include this new ability. Similarly, the ability to access intermediate values

```
class Stack extends Vector {

   public void push (Object value)
      { addElement (value); }

   public Object peek ()
      { return lastElement(); }

   public Object pop () {
      Object result = lastElement();
      removeElementAt(theData.size()-1);
      return result;
      }
}
```

Figure 10.2   A stack created using inheritance.

directly using an index is in this version possible with a stack, but not permitted in the abstraction created using composition.

10.3   COMPOSITION AND INHERITANCE CONTRASTED

Having illustrated two mechanisms for software reuse, and having seen that they are both applicable to the implementation of stacks, we can comment on some of the advantages and disadvantages of the two approaches.

- Inheritance carries with it an implicit, if not explicit, assumption of substitutability. That is, classes formed by inheritance are assumed to be subtypes of the parent class, and therefore candidates for values to be used when an instance of the parent class is expected. No such assumption of substitutability is associated with the use of composition.

- Composition is the simpler of the two techniques. Its advantage is that it more clearly indicates exactly what operations can be performed on a particular data structure. Looking at the declaration for the Stack data abstraction, it is clear that the only operations provided for the data type are the test for emptiness, push, peek, and pop. This is true regardless of what operations are defined for vectors.

- In inheritance the operations of the new data abstraction are a superset of the operations of the original data structure on which the new object is built. Thus, to know exactly what operations are legal for the new structure, the programmer must examine the declaration for the original. An examination of the Stack declaration, for example, does not immediately indicate that the size method can be legally applied to stacks. It is only by examination of the declaration for the earlier Vector data abstraction that the entire set of legal operations can be ascertained.

The difficulty that occurs when, to understand a class constructed using inheritance, the programmer must frequently flip back and forth between two (or more) class declarations has been labeled the "yo-yo" problem by Taenzer, Ganti, and Podar [Taenzer 1989].

- The brevity of data abstractions constructed with inheritance is, in another light, an advantage. Using inheritance it is not necessary to write any code to access the functionality provided by the class on which the new structure is built. For this reason, implementations using inheritance are almost always, as in the present case, considerably shorter in code than are implementations constructed with composition, and they often provide greater functionality. For example, the inheritance implementation makes available not only the size test for stacks but also the index-related operations (inserting, modifying, or removing elements by giving their index locations).

- Inheritance does not prevent users from manipulating the new structure using methods from the parent class, even if these are not appropriate. For example, when we use inheritance to derive the class Stack from the class Vector, nothing prevents users from adding new elements to the stack using the inherited method insertElementAt, and thereby placing elements in locations other than the top of the stack.

- In composition the fact that the class Vector is used as the storage mechanism for our stack is merely an implementation detail. With this technique it would be easy to reimplement the class to make use of a different technique (such as a linked list), with minimal impact on the users of the Stack abstraction. If users counted on the fact that a Stack is merely a specialized form of Vector, such changes would be more difficult to implement.

- A component constructed using inheritance has access to fields and methods in the parent class that have been declared as protected. A component constructed using composition can only access the public portions of the included component.

- Inheritance may allow us to use the new abstraction as an argument in an existing *polymorphic* function. We will investigate this possibility in more detail in Chapter 12. Because composition does not imply substitutability, it usually precludes polymorphism.

- Understandability and maintainability are difficult to judge. Inheritance has the advantage of brevity of code but not of protocol. Composition code, although longer, is the only code that another programmer must understand to use the abstraction. A programmer faced with understanding the inheritance version needs to ask whether any behavior inherited from the parent class was necessary for proper utilization of the new class, and would thus have to understand both classes.

- Data structures implemented through inheritance tend to have a very small advantage in execution time over those constructed with composition, since one additional function call is avoided (although optimization techniques, such as inline functions, can in theory be used to eliminate much of this overhead).

Of the two possible implementation techniques, can we say which is better in this case? One answer involves the substitution principle. Ask yourself whether, in an application that expected to use a Vector data abstraction, it is correct to substitute instead an instance of class Stack.

The bottom line is that the two techniques are very useful, and an object-oriented programmer should be familiar with both of them.

10.4   COMBINING INHERITANCE AND COMPOSITION

The Java input/output system, which we will investigate in more detail in Chapter 14, provides an interesting illustration of the way in which inheritance and composition can interact with each other, and the particular problems each mechanism is designed to solve.

To begin with, there is an abstract concept, and several concrete realizations of the concept. For the file input system the abstract concept is the idea of reading a stream of bytes in sequence, one after the other. This idea is embodied in the class InputStream, which defines a number of methods for reading byte values. The concrete realizations differ in the source of the data values. Values can come from an array of bytes being held in memory, from an external file, or from another process that is generating values as needed. There is a different subclass of InputStream for each of these, as shown in Figure 10.3.

Because each of these is declared as a subclass of InputStream, they can be substituted for a value of type InputStream. In this fashion procedures can be written to process a stream of byte values, without regard to where the values originate (whether in memory, or from an external file, or from another process).

However, there is an additional source of variation among input streams. Or rather, there is additional functionality that is sometimes required when using an input stream. Furthermore, this functionality is independent of the source for the byte values. One example is the ability to keep track of line numbers, so that the programmer can determine on which line of the input the current byte originates. Another useful function is the ability to buffer input so as to have the possibility of rereading recently referenced bytes once again.

These features are provided by defining a subclass of InputStream, named FilterInputStream. A FilterInputStream is formed as a subclass of InputStream. Thus,

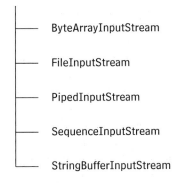

InputStream

├──── ByteArrayInputStream

├──── FileInputStream

├──── PipedInputStream

├──── SequenceInputStream

└──── StringBufferInputStream

Figure 10.3   Subclasses of InputStream.

using the principle of substitutability, a FilterInputStream can be used in places where an InputStream is expected. On the other hand, a FilterInputStream holds as a component another instance of InputStream, which is used as the source for data values. Thus, the class InputStream is both parent and component to FilterInputStream. As requests for values are received, the FilterInputStream will access the InputStream it holds to get the values it needs, performing whatever additional actions are required (for example, counting newline characters in order to keep track of the current line number).

```
class FilterInputStream extends InputStream {

    protected InputStream in;
    .
    .
    .
}
```

Because the component held by the FilterInputStream can be any type of InputStream, this additional functionality can be used to augment and type of InputStream, regardless of where the byte values originate. This idea of *filters* (sometimes called *wrappers* in other object-oriented literature) can be quite powerful when there are orthogonal sources of variation. Here the two reasons of variation are (1) the source of the input values and (2) the additional functionality that may or may not be needed in any particular application.

10.5   NOVEL FORMS OF SOFTWARE REUSE

There are several novel ways in which composition, or inheritance, or both, are used to achieve different effects.

```
class Frog {
   private FrogBehavior behavior;

   public Frog () {
      behavior = new TadpoleBehavior();
      }

   public grow () { // see if behavior should change
      if (behavior.growUp())
         behavior = new AdultFrogBehavior();
      behavior.grow(); // behavior does actual work
      behavior.swim();
      }
}
```

Figure 10.4   Class Frog holds dynamically changing behavior component.

10.5.1   *Dynamic Composition*

One advantage of composition over inheritance concerns the delay in binding time. With inheritance, the link between child class and parent class is established at compile time and cannot later be modified. With composition, the link between the new abstraction and the older abstraction is created at run time, and is therefore much weaker, since it can also be changed at run time. This is sometimes called *dynamic composition*.

To illustrate, imagine a class that is simulating the behavior of a Frog. Although the frog interface can be fixed throughout its life, the actual actions it performs might be very different when the frog is a tadpole or when it is an adult. One way to model this is to create a class Frog (Figure 10.4) that uses composition to hold a value of type FrogBehavior. The Frog class is largely a facade, invoking the FrogBehavior object to do the majority of the real work.

The novel idea is that the variable holding the instance of FrogBehavior can actually be polymorphic. There might be more than one class that implements the FrogBehavior specification, such as TadpoleBehavior and AdultFrogBehavior. Figure 10.5 illustrates these classes. The parent class FrogBehavior is here declared *abstract*, which means that it *must* be overridden before any instances can be created. As the frog "grows," it can dynamically change behavior by reassigning the value behavior to a different value (for example, moving from a TadpoleBehavior to an AdultFrogBehavior). The user of the Frog abstraction need not know about this change, or even be aware when it occurs.

Dynamic composition is a useful technique if the behavior of an object varies dramatically according to some internal concept of "state," and the change in state occurs infrequently.

```
abstract class FrogBehavior {
   public boolean growUp () { return false; }

   public void grow ();

   public void swim ();
}

class TadpoleBehavior extends FrogBehavior {
   private int age = 0;

   public boolean growUp () { if (++age > 24) return true; }

   public void grow () { ... }

   public void swim () { ... }
}

class AdultFrogBehavior extends Behavior {

   public void grow () { ... }

   public void swim () { ... }
}
```

Figure 10.5   Class FrogBehavior can dynamically change

10.5.2   *Inheritance of Inner Classes*

We have seen another combination of inheritance and composition in some
of the case studies presented in earlier chapters. For example, the "listener"
classes that responded to events were constructed using inheritance, but were
themselves components in the application class. The following is a skeleton of
the class PinBallGame from Chapter 7.

```
public class PinBallGame extends Frame {
   .
   .
   .
   private class MouseKeeper extends MouseAdapter { ... }

   private class PinBallThread extends Thread { ... }
}
```

The classes MouseKeeper and PinBallThread are each constructed using inheritance. Each is then used to create a new component, which will be held as part of the state of the pinball game. When used in this fashion, inner classes combine aspects of both inheritance and composition.

10.5.3   *Unnamed Classes*

In several of the earlier case studies we have seen situations where inheritance is used to override an existing class, yet only one instance of the new class is created. An alternative to naming the new class and then creating an instance of the named class is to use a class definition expression. Such an expression places the entire class definition inside the instance creation expression.

An example where this could be used is in the definition of an event listener. For example, the Cannon Game described in Chapter 6 contained the following code:

```
class CannonWorld extends Frame {
    .
    .
    .

    private class FireButtonListener implements ActionListener {
        public void actionPerformed (ActionEvent e) {
            .
            .
            .
        }
    }

    public CannonWorld ( ) {
        fire.addActionListener(new FireButtonListener( ));
        .
        .
        .
    }
}
```

Note how the constructor for the class CannonWorld creates an instance of the inner class FireButtonListener. This is the only instance of this class created. An alternative way to achieve the same effect would be as follows:

```
class CannonWorld extends Frame {
    .
    .
    .

    public CannonWorld ( ) {
        fire.addActionListener(new ActionListener( ){
```

```
public void actionPerformed (ActionEvent e) {
    .
    .
    .
            }
      });
    .
    .
    .
    }
}
```

Notice that in this example the object being created is declared only as being an instance of ActionListener. However, a class definition follows immediately the ending parenthesis, indicating that a new and *unnamed* class is being defined. This class definition would have exactly the same form as before, ending with a closing curly brace. The parenthesis that follows this curly brace ends the argument list for the addActionListener call. (The reader should carefully match curly braces and parenthesis to see how this takes place.)

An advantage to the use of the class definition expression in this situation is that it avoids the need to introduce a new class name (in this case, the inner class name FireButtonListener). A disadvantage is that such expressions tend to be difficult to read, since the entire class definition must be wrapped up as an expression, and the close of the expressions occurs after the end of the class definition.

10.6 CHAPTER SUMMARY

The two most common techniques for reusing software abstractions are inheritance and composition. Both are valuable techniques, and a good object-oriented system will usually have many examples of each.

A good rule of thumb for deciding when to use inheritance is the *is-a* rule. Form the sentence "An X is a Y", and if it sounds right to your ear, then the two concepts X and Y can probably be related using inheritance. The corresponding rule for composition is the *has-a* rule.

The decision whether to use inheritance or not is not always clear. By examining one borderline case, one can more easily see some of the advantages and disadvantages of the two software structuring techniques.

The idea of *filters*, found in the portion of the Java library used for input and output, is an interesting technique that combines features of both inheritance and composition.

STUDY QUESTIONS

1. Explain in your own words the principle of substitutability.

2. What is the *is-a* rule? What is the *has-a* rule? How are these two rules related to inheritance and composition?

3. How are interfaces and inheritance related?

4. What are some of the advantages of composition over inheritance?

5. What are some of the advantages of using inheritance that are not available when composition is used?

6. How does a FilterStream combine inheritance and composition?

EXERCISES

1. A set is simply an unorganized collection of values. Describe how one could use a Vector to implement a set. Would inheritance or composition be the more appropriate mechanism in this case?

2. Modify the Stack data abstractions given in this chapter so that they will throw a EmptyStackException if an attempt is made to read or remove a value from an empty stack.

11 Implications of Inheritance

The decision to support inheritance and the principle of substitutability in a language sets off a series of chain reactions that end up impacting almost every aspect of a programming language. In this chapter, we will illustrate this point by considering some of the implications of the decision to support in a natural fashion the idea of the polymorphic variable.

The links between inheritance and other language features can be summarized as follows:

- In order to make the most effective use of object-oriented techniques, the language must support the polymorphic variable. A polymorphic variable is a variable that is declared as one type but actually maintains a value derived from a subtype of the declared type.

- Because at compile time we cannot determine the amount of memory that will be required to hold the value assigned to a polymorphic variable, all objects must reside on the heap, rather than on the stack.

- Because values reside in heaps, the most natural interpretation of assignment and parameter passing uses reference semantics, rather than copy semantics.

- Similarly, the most natural interpretation of equality testing is to test object identity. However, since often the programmer requires a different meaning for equality, two different operators are necessary.

- Because values reside on the heap, there must be some memory management mechanism. Because assignment is by reference semantics, it is difficult for the programmer to determine when a value is no longer being

175

used. Therefore a garbage collection system is necessary to recover unused memory.

Each of these points will be more fully developed in the following sections.

11.1   THE POLYMORPHIC VARIABLE

As we will see in Chapter 12, a great deal of the power of the object-oriented features of Java comes through the use of a *polymorphic variable*. A polymorphic variable is declared as maintaining a value of one type but in fact holds

```
class Shape {
   protected int x;
   protected int y;

   public Shape (int ix, int iy)
      { x = ix; y = iy; }

   public String describe ()
      { return "unknown shape"; }
}

class Square extends Shape {
   protected int side;

   public Square (int ix, int iy, int is)
      { super(ix, iy); side = is; }

   public String describe ()
      { return "square with side " + side; }
}

class Circle extends Shape {
   protected int radius;

   public Circle (int ix, int iy, int ir)
      { super(ix, iy); radius = ir; }

   public String describe ()
      { return "circle with radius " + radius; }
}
```

Figure 11.1 Shape classes and polymorphic variable.

a value from another type. We have seen many such examples in the sample programs presented in Part 1. For instance, much of the standard user interface code thinks only that an application is an instance of class Frame, when in fact each program we created used inheritance to create a new type of application. Similarly, in the Pin Ball Game Construction Kit program (Chapter 7) a variable was declared as holding a value of type PinBallTarget, when in fact it would hold a Hole or a ScorePad.

Figure 11.1 provides a class hierarchy consisting of three classes, Shape and two subclasses Circle and Square. In the small test program shown below variable named form is declared as type Shape, then assigned a value of type Circle. As expected, when the function describe( ) is invoked, the method that is executed is the procedure in class Circle, not the function inherited from class Shape. We will use this example class in the subsequent discussion in this chapter.

```
class ShapeTest {
    static public void main (String [ ] args) {
        Shape form = new Circle (10, 10, 5);
        System.out.println("form is " + form.describe( ));
    }
}
```

11.2 MEMORY LAYOUT

Before we can observe the impact of the polymorphic variable on memory management, it is first necessary to review how variables are normally represented in memory in most programming languages. From the point of view of the memory manager, there are two major categories of memory values. These are *stack-based* memory locations, and *heap-based* memory values.

Stack-based memory locations are tied to procedure entry and exit. When a procedure is started, space is allocated on a run-time stack for local variables. These values exist as long as the procedure is executing, and are erased, and the memory recovered, when the procedure exits. Figure 11.2 shows, for example, a snapshot of the run-time stack for the following simple recursive algorithm:

```
class FacTest {
    static public void main (String [ ] args) {
        int f = factorial(3);
        System.out.println("Factorial of 3 is " + f);
    }

    static public int factorial (int n) {
        int c = n - 1;
        int r;
        if (c > 0)
```

```
0                n: 1
                            third
4                r: 1        activation
                            record
8                c: 0
---            ----------    ---------------
0                n: 2
                            second
4                r: ?        activation
                            record
8                c: 1
---            ----------    ---------------
0                n: 3
                            first
4                r: ?        activation
                            record
8                c: 2
```

Figure 11.2   A snapshot of the activation frame stack.

```
        r = n * factorial(c);
    else
        r = 1;
    return r;
    }
}
```

The snapshot is taken after the procedure has recursed three times, just as the innermost procedure is starting to return. The data values for three procedures are shown. In the innermost procedure the variable r has been assigned the value 1, while for the two pending procedures the value of r has yet to be determined.

There are a number of advantages of stack-based memory allocation. All local variables can be allocated or deallocated as a block, for example, instead of one by one. This block is commonly called an *activation record*. Internally, variables can be described by their numeric offset within the activation record, rather than by their symbolic address. These numeric offsets have been noted in Figure 11.2. Most machines are much more efficient at dealing with numeric offsets than with symbolic names. Notice that each new activation record creates a new set of offsets, so that the offset is always relative to the activation frame in which a variable appears.

Stack-based allocation has one serious disadvantage: These numeric offsets associated with variables must be determined at compile time, not at run time. In order to do this, the compiler must know the amount of memory to assign to each variable. In Figure 11.2, the compiler only knows that variable c can be found at address 8 because it knows that variable r, which starts at location 4, requires only four bytes.

But, this is exactly the information we do not know for a polymorphic variable. The storage requirements for a polymorphic variable value are determined when the value is created at run time, and can even change during the course of execution. Recall the classes shown in Figure 11.1, and the memory requirements for the procedure main in the sample program described earlier. Here the variable form, which is declared as holding a Shape, can at one moment be holding a circle, at another a square, and so on. Both the subclasses add more data fields that are not found as part of the parent class. Thus the translator cannot know at compile time exactly how much memory will be required to hold the variable form.

In Java the solution to this problem is that objects are not stored on the activation record stack but are instead stored on the heap. A heap is an alternative memory-management system, one that is not tied to procedure entry and exit. Instead, memory is allocated on the heap when explicitly requested (to create a new object, using the new operator) and is freed, and recycled, when no longer needed. At run time, when the memory is requested, the Java system knows precisely how much memory is required to hold a value. In this fashion the Java language avoids the need to predict, at compile time, the amount of memory that will be needed at run time.

The code generated by the compiler, however, must still be able to access variables through numeric offsets, even through the actual heap addresses will not be known until run time. The solution to this dilemma is to use one level of indirection. Local variables are represented on the stack as pointer values. The size of a pointer is known at compile time and is independent of the size of the object it points to. This pointer field is filled when an object is created.

It is said that the programming language Java has no pointers. This is true as far as the language the programmer sees is concerned. But ironically, this is only possible because *all* object values are, in fact, represented internally by pointers.

11.2.1 *An Alternative Technique*

It should be noted that the solution to this problem selected by the designers of Java is not the only possibility. This can be illustrated by considering the language C++, which uses an entirely different approach. C++ treats assignment of *variables* and assignment of *pointers* very differently.

The designers of C++ elected to store variable values on the stack. Thus, the memory allocated to a variable of type Shape is only large enough to hold a value of type Shape, not the additional fields added by the subclass Circle. During the process of assignment these extra fields are simply sliced off and discarded. Of course, the resulting value is then no longer a Circle. For this reason, when we try to execute a member function, such as the describe function, the code executed will be that associated with class Shape, not the value associated with class Circle, as in Java. The programmer who uses both C++ and Java should be aware of this subtle, but nevertheless important difference.

11.3 ASSIGNMENT

In Section 11.2 we saw why values in Java are most naturally maintained on the heap, rather than being held in the activation record stack. Because to the compiler the underlying "value" of a variable is simply a pointer into the heap, the most natural semantics for assignment simply copy this pointer value. In this manner, the right and left sides of an assignment statement end up referring to the same object. This is often termed *reference* semantics (sometimes also called *pointer* semantics). The consequences of this interpretation of assignment are subtle but are, again, a key point for Java programmers to remember. Suppose we create a simple class Box as follows:

```
public class Box {
   private int value;

   public Box () { value = 0; }
   public void setValue (int v) { value = v; }
   public int getValue () { return value; }
}
```

Now imagine that we create a new box, assign it to a variable x, and set the internal value to 7. We then assign the box held by x to another variable, named y. Since both x and y now hold non-null values of type Box, the programmer might assume that they are distinct. But, in fact, they are exactly the same box, as can be verified by changing the value held in the y box and printing the value held by the x box:

```
public class BoxTest {
   static public void main (String [ ] args) {

      Box x = new Box( );
      x.setValue (7);      // set value of x

      Box y = x;      // assign y the same value as x
      y.setValue (11);      // change value of y

      System.out.println("contents of x " + x.getValue( ));
      System.out.println("contents of y " + y.getValue( ));
   }
}
```

The key observation is that the two variables, although assigned separate locations on the activation record stack, nevertheless point to the same location on the heap, as shown in Figure 11.3.

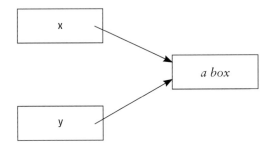

Figure 11.3   Two variables pointing to the same location.

11.3.1   *Clones*

If the desired effect of an assignment is indeed a copy, then the programmer must indicate this. One way would be to explicitly create a new value, copying the internal contents from the existing value:

```
// create new box with same value as x
Box y = new Box (x.getValue());
```

If making copies is a common operation, it might be better to provide a method in the original class:

```
public class Box {
    .
    .
    .
    public Box copy() { // make copy of box
        Box b = new Box();
        b.setValue (getValue());
        return b;
    }
    .
    .
    .
}
```

A copy of a box is then created by invoking the copy() method:

```
// create new box with same value as x
Box y = x.copy();
```

There is no general mechanism in Java to copy an arbitrary object; however, the base class Object does provide a protected method named clone() that creates a bitwise copy of the receiver, as well as an interface Cloneable that represents objects that can be cloned. Several methods in the Java library require that arguments be values that are cloneable.

To create a class that is cloneable, the programmer must not only override the clone method to make it public but also explicitly indicate that the result satisfies the Cloneable interface. The following, for example, shows how to create a cloneable box.

```
public class Box implements Cloneable {
    private int value;

    public Box () { value = 0; }
    public void setValue (int v) { value = v; }
    public int getValue () { return value; }

    public Object clone () {
        Box b = new Box();
        b.setValue (getValue());
        return b;
    }
}
```

The clone method is declared as yielding a result of type Object. This property cannot be modified when the method is overridden. As a consequence, the result of cloning a value must be cast to the actual type before it can be assigned to a variable.

```
public class BoxTest {
    static public void main (String [ ] args) {

        Box x = new Box();
        x.setValue (7);

        Box y = (Box) x.clone(); // assign copy of x to y

        y.setValue (11); // change value of x

        System.out.println("contents of x " + x.getValue());
        System.out.println("contents of y " + y.getValue());
    }
}
```

As always, subtleties can trap the unwary programmer. Consider the object that is being held by our box. Imagine, instead of simply an integer, that it is something more complex, such as a Shape. Should a clone also clone this value, or just copy it? A copy results in two distinct boxes, but ones that share a common value. This is called a *shallow copy* (Figure 11.4).

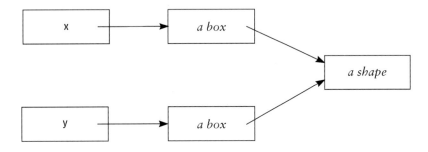

Figure 11.4 A shallow copy.

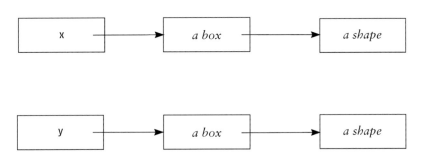

Figure 11.5 A deep copy.

Cloning the contents of the box (which must therefore be itself a type that is cloneable) results in two box values which are not only themselves distinct, but which point to values that are also distinct. This is termed a *deep copy* (Figure 11.5).

Whether a copy should be shallow or deep is something that must be determined by the programmer when overriding the clone interface.

11.3.2 *Parameters as a Form of Assignment*

Note that passing a variable as an argument to a member function can be considered to be a form of assignment, in that parameter passing, like assignment, results in the same value being accessible through two different names. Thus, the issues raised in Section 11.3 regarding assignment apply equally to parameter values. Consider the function sneaky in the following example, which modifies the value held in a box that is passed through a parameter value.

```
public class BoxTest {
    static public void main (String [ ] args) {
```

```
        Box x = new Box( );
        x.setValue (7);

        sneaky (x);

        System.out.println("contents of x " + x.getValue( ));
    }

    static void sneaky (Box y) {
        y.setValue (11); // change value of parameter
        }
    }
```

A programmer who passes a box to this function, as shown in the `main` procedure, could subsequently see the resulting change in a local variable.

A Java programmer should always keep in mind that when a value is passed to a procedure, a certain degree of control over the variable is lost. In particular, the procedure is free to invoke any method applicable to the parameter type, which could result in the state of the variable being changed, as in this example.

11.4   EQUALITY TEST

For basic data types the concept of equality is relatively simple. The value 7 should clearly be equivalent to $3 + 4$, for example, because we think of integers as being unique entities—there is one and only one 7 value. This is true even when there are two syntactic representations for the same quantity, for example the ASCII value of the letter *a* is 141, and thus `'\141'` is the same as `'a'`.

The situation becomes slightly more complicated when the two values being defined are not the same type. For example, should the value 2 (an integer constant) be considered equal to 2.0 (a floating-point constant)? The Java language says that the two values are equivalent in this case, since the integer value can be *converted* into a floating-point value, and the two floating values compared. Thus, all the following expressions will yield a true result.

```
    7 == (3 + 4)
    'a' == '\141'
    2 == 2.0
```

When the concept of equality testing is expanded to include objects, the most natural interpretation becomes less obvious. In Section 11.3 it was argued that because objects are internally represented by pointers, the natural interpretation of assignment uses reference semantics. One interpretation of equality testing follows the same reasoning. That is, two objects can be considered equal if they are identically the same. This form of equality testing is often termed "testing object *identity*," and is the interpretation provided by the operator == and its inverse, the operator ! =. This can cause certain anomalies. For example, although 7 is equal to $3 + 4$, the following code fragment will nevertheless show that an Integer value 7 is a distinct object from a different Integer object, even if it has the same value:

```
Integer x = new Integer(7);
Integer y = new Integer(3 + 4);
if (x == y)
   System.out.println("equivalent");
else
   System.out.println("not equivalent");
```

The Java compiler does apply type checking rules to the two arguments, which will help detect many programming errors. For example, although a numeric value can be compared to another numeric, a numeric cannot be compared to a different type of object (for example, a String). Two object values can be compared if they are the same type, or if the class of one can be converted into the class of the second. For example, a variable that was declared to be an instance of class Shape could be compared with a variable of type Circle, since a Circle would be converted into a Shape. A particular instance of the conversion rule is one of the more frequent uses of the == operator; namely, any object can be compared to the constant null, since the value null can be assigned to any object type.

Often object identity is not the relation one would like to test, and instead one is interested in object *equality*. This is provided by the method equals, which is defined by the base class Object and redefined by a number of classes. The following, for example, would return true using the equals function but would not be true using the == operator:

```
String a = "abc";
String b = "abc";
Integer c = new Integer(7);
Integer d = new Integer(3 + 4);
if (a.equals(b))
   System.out.println("strings are equal");
if (c.equals(d))
   System.out.println("integers are equal");
```

Because the equals function is defined in class Object, it can be used with any object type. However, for the same reason, the argument is declared only as type Object. This means that any two objects can be compared for equality, even if there is no possible way that for either to be assigned to the other:

```
if (a.equals(c)) // can never be true
    System.out.println("string equal to integer");
```

The developer of a class is free to override the equals operator and thereby allow comparison between objects. Since the argument is an Object it must first be tested to ensure it is the correct type. By convention, the value false is returned in cases where the type is not correct. The following, for example, would be how one could define a function to compare two instances of class Circle (Figure 11.1).

```
class Circle extends Shape {
    .
    .
    .
    public boolean equals (Object arg) {
        if (arg instanceof Circle) {
                // convert argument to circle
            Circle argc = (Circle) arg;
            if (radius == argc.radius)
                return true;   // just test radius
        }
        return false; // return false otherwise
    }
}
```

Because the type of the argument is not necessarily the same as the type of the receiver, unusual situations can occur if the programmer is not careful. For example, suppose we defined equals in class Shape from Figure 11.1 to test equality of the x and y values, but forgot to also override the function in class Square. It could happen in this situation that if we tried to compare a square and a circle, the comparison would be true one way and false the other.

```
Square s = new Square(10, 10, 5);
Circle c = new Circle(10, 10, 5);
if (s.equals(c)) // true, since method in shape is used
    System.out.println("square equal to circle");
if (c.equals(s)) // false, since method in circle is used
    System.out.println("circle equal to square");
```

When overriding the equals method the programmer should be careful to avoid this problem and should ensure that the resulting functions are both symmetric (if x is equal to y, then y is equal to x) and associative (if x is equal to y and y is equal to z, then x is equal to z).

A good rule of thumb is to use $==$ when testing numeric quantities, and when testing an object against the constant null. In all other situations the function equals should be used.

11.5 GARBAGE COLLECTION

In Section 11.2 it was argued that support for polymorphic variables naturally implies that values are allocated to the heap, rather than to the stack. Memory of any type is always a finite resource, which must be managed if a program is to avoid running out of storage. In order to prevent this problem, both stack-based and heap-based memory is recycled, with new memory requests being assigned the same locations as previous memory values that are no longer being used.

Unlike stack-based memory allocation, heap-based memory management is not tied to procedure activation, and is thus not automatically recovered when a procedure returns. This means an alternative mechanism must be introduced.

Two different approaches to the recovery of heap-based memory values are found in programming languages. In languages such as Object Pascal or C++, it is up to the programmer to explicitly indicate when a memory value is no longer being used and can therefore be reused to satisfy new memory requests. In Object Pascal, for example, this is accomplished by means of the statement dispose:

```
var
    aShape : Shape;
begin
    new (aShape); (* allocate a new shape *)
    .
    .
    .
    dispose (aShape); (* free memory used by variable *)
end.
```

In such languages, if an object is to be freed, it must be "owned" by some variable (the variable that will be the target for the free request). But Java values are simply references, and are shared equally by all variables that refer to the same value. If a programmer assigns a value to another variable, or passes the value as an argument, the programmer may no longer be aware of how many references a value might have.

Leaving to the programmer the responsibility for freeing memory in this situation exposes a program to a number of common errors, such as freeing the same memory location twice. Even more commonly, programmers avoid committing this error by simply never freeing memory, causing long-running programs to slowly degrade as they consume more and more memory resources.

For these reasons, the designers of Java elected a different approach. Rather than having the programmer indicate when a value is no longer needed, a run-time system is provided that periodically searches the memory being used by a program to discover which heap values are being accessed and, more importantly, which heap values are no longer being referenced by any variable and can therefore be recovered and recycled. This mechanism is known as the *garbage collection* system.

The use of a garbage collection system in Java is a compromise. The task of garbage collection does exact a toll in execution time. However, in return a garbage collection system greatly simplifies the programming process and eliminates several categories of common programming errors. For most programs, the improvements in reliability are well worth the execution time overhead.

11.6 CHAPTER SUMMARY

The idea of a polymorphic variable is an extremely powerful concept, one we will explore in detail in later chapters. However, the decision to support the concept of a polymorphic variable raises a number of subtle and difficult issues in other aspects of the language. In this chapter we have investigated some of these, showing how inheritance alters the way the language must handle storage management, the concept of assignment, and the testing of two values for equality.

STUDY QUESTIONS

1. What is a polymorphic variable?

2. From the language implementation point of view, what are the two major categories of memory values?

3. How does the idea of a polymorphic variable conflict with the ability to determine memory requirements at compile time?

4. What does it mean to say that Java uses reference semantics for assignment?

5. What must a programmer do to create a class that supports the Cloneable interface?

6. What is the difference between a deep and shallow copy?

7. In what way is passing a parameter similar to assignment?

8. What is the difference between the == operator and the equals( ) method?

9. What task is being performed by the garbage collection system in the Java run-time library?

10. What are some advantages of a language that uses garbage collection? What are some disadvantages?

EXERCISES

1. Rewrite the Shape classes shown in Figure 11.1 so that they support the Cloneable interface.

2. Rewrite the class Box so that it holds values that are Cloneable, and when cloned it creates a deep copy.

IV

Understanding Polymorphism

12 Polymorphism

The term *polymorphic* has Greek roots and means roughly "many forms." (*poly* = many, *morphos* = form. Morphos is related to the Greek god Morphus, who could appear to sleeping individuals in any form he wished and hence was truly polymorphic.) In biology, a polymorphic species is one, such as *Homo sapiens*, that is characterized by the occurrence of different forms or color types in individual organisms or among organisms. In chemistry, a polymorphic compound is one that can crystallize in at least two distinct forms, such as carbon, which can crystallize both as graphite and as diamond.

12.1 VARIETIES OF POLYMORPHISM

In object-oriented languages, polymorphism is a natural result of the *is-a* relationship and of the mechanisms of message passing, inheritance, and the concept of substitutability. One of the great strengths of the OOP approach is that these devices can be combined in a variety of ways, yielding a number of techniques for code sharing and reuse.

Pure polymorphism occurs when a single function can be applied to arguments of a variety of types. In pure polymorphism, there is one function (the code body) and a number of interpretations. The other extreme occurs when we have a number of different functions (code bodies) all denoted by the same name—a situation known as *overloading* or sometimes *ad hoc polymorphism*. Between these two extremes are *overriding* and *deferred methods*.[1]

---

[1] Note that there is little agreement regarding terminology in the programming language community. In [Horowitz 1984], [Marcotty and Ledgard 1987], [MacLennan 1987], and [Pinson and Wiener 1988] for example, *polymorphism* is defined in a manner roughly equivalent to what we are here calling *overloading*. In [Sethi 1989] and [Meyer 1988] and in the functional programming languages community (such as [Wikström 1987] and [Milner, Tofte, and Harper 1990]), the term is reserved for what we are calling *pure polymorphism*. Other authors use the term for one, two, or all of the mechanisms described in this chapter. Two complete, but technically daunting, analyses are [Cardelli and Wegner 1985] and [Danforth and Tomlinson 1988].

12.2 POLYMORPHIC VARIABLES

With the exception of overloading, polymorphism in object-oriented languages is made possible only by the existence of *polymorphic variables* and the idea of substitutability. A polymorphic variable is one with many faces; that is, it can hold values of different types. Polymorphic variables embody the principle of substitutability. In other words, although there is an expected type for any variable, the actual type can be from any value that is a subtype of the expected type.

In dynamically bound languages (such as Smalltalk), all variables are potentially polymorphic—any variable can hold values of any type. In these languages the desired type is defined by a set of expected behaviors. For example, an algorithm may make use of an array value, expecting the subscripting operations to be defined for a certain variable; any type that defines the appropriate behavior is suitable. Thus, the user could define his or her own type of array (for example, a sparse array) and, if the array operations were implemented using the same names, use this new type with an existing algorithm.

In statically typed languages, such as Java, the situation is slightly more complex. Polymorphism occurs in Java through the difference between the declared (static) class of a variable and the actual (dynamic) class of the value the variable contains.

A good example of a polymorphic variable is the array allPiles in the Solitaire game presented in Chapter 9. The array was declared as maintaining a value of type CardPile, but in fact it maintains values from each of the different subclasses of the parent class. A message presented to a value from this array, such as display in the example code shown below, executes the method associated with the dynamic type of the variable and not that of the static class.

```
public class Solitaire extends Applet {
    .
    .
    static CardPile allPiles [ ];
    .
    .
    public void paint(Graphics g) {
        for (int i = 0; i < 13; i++)
            allPiles[i].display(g);
    }
    .
    .
}
```

12.3 OVERLOADING

We say a function name is *overloaded* if two or more function bodies are associated with it. Note that overloading is a necessary part of overriding, described in the next section, but the two terms are not identical and overloading can occur without overriding.

In overloading, it is the function *name* that is polymorphic—it has many forms. Another way to think of overloading and polymorphism is that there is a single abstract function that takes various types of arguments; the actual code executed depends on the arguments given. The fact that the compiler can often determine the correct function at compile time (in a strongly typed language) and the fact that it can therefore generate only a single code sequence are simply optimizations.

12.3.1 *Overloading Messages in Real Life*

In Chapter 1 we saw an example in which overloading occurred without overriding, when I wanted to surprise my friend with flowers for her birthday. One possible solution was to send the message sendFlowersTo to my local florist; another was to give the *same* message to my wife. Both my florist and my wife (an instance of class Spouse) would have understood the message, and both would have acted on it to produce a similar result. In a certain sense, I could have thought of sendFlowersTo as being one function understood by both my wife and my florist, but each would have used a different algorithm to respond to my request.

Note, in particular, that there was no inheritance involved in this example. The first common superclass for my wife and my florist was the category Human. But certainly the behavior sendFlowersTo was not associated with all humans. My dentist, for example, who is also a human, would have been very puzzled by the message.

12.3.2 *Overloading and Coercion*

As an example more closely tied to programming languages, suppose a programmer is developing a library of classes representing common data structures. A number of data structures can be used to maintain a collection of elements (sets, bags, dictionaries, arrays, and priority queues, for example), and these might all define a method, add, to insert a new element into the collection.

This situation—in which two totally separate functions are used to provide semantically similar actions for different data types—occurs frequently in all programming languages, not simply in object-oriented languages. Perhaps the most common example is the overloading of the addition operator, +. The code generated by a compiler for an integer addition is often radically different from the code generated for a floating-point addition, yet programmers tend to think of the operations as a single entity, the "addition" function.

In this example it is important to point out that overloading may not be the only activity taking place. A semantically separate operation, *coercion*, is also usually associated with arithmetic operations. It occurs when a value of one type is converted into one of a different type. If mixed-type arithmetic is permitted, the addition of two values may be interpreted in a number of different ways:

- There may be four different functions, corresponding to integer + integer, integer + real, real + integer, and real + real. In this case, there is overloading but no coercion.

- There may be two different functions for integer + integer and real + real. In integer + real and real + integer, the integer value is coerced by being changed into a real value. In this situation there is a combination of overloading and coercion.

- There may be only one function, for real + real addition. All arguments are coerced into being real. In this case there is coercion only, with no overloading.

12.3.3   *Overloading from Separate Classes*

Two different forms of overloading can be distinguished. One form occurs when the same function name is found in two or more classes that are not linked by inheritance. The second form occurs when two or more functions with the same name are found within one class definition. The latter form will be described in the next section.

A good example of overloading of the first type is the method isEmpty. This method is used to determine if an object is empty; however, the exact meaning of empty will differ depending upon circumstances. The message is understood by the classes Vector, Hashtable, and Rectangle. The first two are collection classes, and the message returns true when there are no elements in the collection. In the class Rectangle the message returns true if either the height or width of a rectangle is zero, and thus the rectangle has no area.

```
Rectangle r1 = new Rectangle ();
if (r1.isEmpty()) ...
```

Overloading Does Not Imply Similarity

There is nothing intrinsic to overloading that requires the functions associated with an overloaded name to have any semantic similarity. Consider a program that plays a card game, such as the Solitaire game we examined in Chapter 9. The method draw was used to draw the image of a card on the screen. In another application we might also have included a draw method for the pack of cards, that is, to draw a single card from the top of the deck. This draw method is not even remotely similar in semantics to the draw method for the single card, and yet they share the same name.

Note that this overloading of a single name with independent and unrelated meanings should *not* necessarily be considered bad style, and generally it will not contribute to confusion. In fact, the selection of short, clear, and meaningful names such as add, draw, and so on, contributes to ease of understanding and correct use of object-oriented components. It is far simpler to remember that you can add an element to a set than to recall that to do so requires invoking the addNewElement method, or, worse, that it requires calling the routine Set_Module_ Addition_Method.

All object-oriented languages permit the occurrence of methods with similar names in unrelated classes. In this case the resolution of overloaded names is determined by observation of the class of the receiver for the message. Nevertheless, this does not mean that functions or methods can be written that take arbitrary arguments. The statically typed nature of Java still requires specific declarations of all names.

12.3.4 *Parametric Overloading*

Another style of overloading, in which procedures (or functions or methods) in the same context are allowed to share a name and are disambiguated by the number and type of arguments supplied, is called *parametric overloading*; it occurs in Java as well as in some imperative languages (such as Ada) and many functional languages. Parametric overloading is most often found in constructor functions. A new Rectangle, for example, can be created either with no arguments (generating a rectangle with size zero and northwest corner 0,0), with two integer arguments (a width and height), with four integer arguments (width, height, northwest corner), with a Point (the northwest corner, size is zero), with a Dimension (height and width, corner 0,0), or with both a Point and a Dimension.

```
Rectangle r1 = new Rectangle ();
Rectangle r2 = new Rectangle (6, 7);
Rectangle r3 = new Rectangle (10, 10, 6, 7);
Point p1 = new Point (10, 10);
Dimension d1 = new Dimension (6, 7);
Rectangle r4 = new Rectangle (p1);
Rectangle r5 = new Rectangle (d1);
Rectangle r6 = new Rectangle (p1, d1);
```

There are six different constructor functions in this class, all with the same name. The compiler decides which function to execute based on the number and type of arguments used with the function call.

Overloading is a necessary prerequisite to the other forms of polymorphism we will consider: overriding, deferred methods, and pure polymorphism. It is also often useful in reducing the "conceptual space," that is, in reducing the amount of information that the programmer must remember. Often, this reduction in programmer-memory space is just as significant as the reduction in computer-memory space permitted by code sharing.

12.4   OVERRIDING

In Chapter 8 we described the mechanics of overriding, so it is not necessary to repeat that discussion here. Recall, however, the following essential elements of the technique. In one class (typically an abstract superclass), a general method is defined for a particular message that is inherited and used by subclasses. In at least one subclass, however, a method with the same name is defined that hides access to the general method for instances of this class (or, in the case of refinement, subsumes access to the general method). We say the second method *overrides* the first.

Overriding is often transparent to the user of a class, and, as with overloading, frequently the two functions are thought of semantically as a single entity.

12.4.1   *Replacement and Refinement*

In Chapter 9 it was briefly noted that overriding can occur in two different forms. A method can *replace* the method in the parent class, in which case the code in the parent is not executed at all. Alternatively, the code from the child can be used to form a *refinement*, which combines the code from the parent and the child classes.

Normally, overridden methods use replacement semantics. If a refinement is desired, it can be constructed by explicitly invoking the parent method as a function. This is accomplished by using the pseudovariable super as the receiver in a message-passing expression. An example from the Solitaire program described in Chapter 9 showed this:

```
class DiscardPile extends CardPile {

    public void addCard (Card aCard) {
        if (! aCard.faceUp( ))
            aCard.flip( );
        super.addCard(aCard);
    }

}
```

Constructors, on the other hand, *always* use refinement semantics. A constructor for a child class will always invoke the constructor for the parent class. This invocation will take place *before* the code for the constructor is executed. If the constructor for the parent class requires arguments, the pseudovariable super is used as if it were a function:

```
class DeckPile extends CardPile {

    DeckPile (int x, int y) {
            // first initialize parent
        super(x, y);
            // then create the new deck
            // first put them into a local pile
        for (int i = 0; i < 4; i++)
            for (int j = 0; j <= 12; j++)
                addCard(new Card(i, j));

            // then shuffle the cards
        Random generator = new Random( );
        for (int i = 0; i < 52; i++) {
            int j = Math.abs(generator.nextInt( )) % 52;
                // swap the two card values
            Object temp = thePile.elementAt(i);
            thePile.setElementAt(thePile.elementAt(j), i);
            thePile.setElementAt(temp, j);
            }
        }

    }
```

When used in this fashion, the call on the parent constructor must be the first statement executed. If no call on super is made explicitly and there exist two or more overloaded forms of the constructor, the constructor with no arguments (sometimes called the *default* constructor) will be the form used.

12.5   ABSTRACT METHODS

A method that is declared as *abstract* can be thought of as defining a method that is *deferred*; it is specified in the parent class but must be implemented in the child class. Interfaces can also be viewed as a method for defining deferred classes. Both can be considered to be a generalization of overriding. In both cases, the behavior described in a parent class is modified by the child class. In an abstract method, however, the behavior in the parent class is essentially null, a place holder, and *all* useful activity is defined as part of the code provided by the child class.

One advantage of abstract methods is conceptual, in that their use allows the programmer to think of an activity as associated with an abstraction at a higher level than may actually be the case. For example, in a collection of classes representing geometric shapes, we can define a method to draw the shape in each of the subclasses Circle, Square, and Triangle. We could have defined a similar method in the parent class Shape, but such a method cannot, in actuality, produce any useful behavior since the class Shape does not have sufficient information to draw the shape in question. Nevertheless, the mere presence of this method permits the user to associate the concept *draw* with the single class Shape, and not with the three separate concepts Square, Triangle, and Circle.

There is a second, more practical reason for using abstract methods. In statically typed object-oriented languages, such as Java, a programmer is permitted to send a message to an object only if the compiler can determine that there is in fact a corresponding method that matches the message selector. Suppose the programmer wishes to define a polymorphic variable of class Shape that will, at various times, contain instances of each of the different shapes. Such an assignment is possible, according to our rule of substitutability; nevertheless, the compiler will permit the message draw to be used with this variable only if it can ensure that the message will be understood by any value that may be associated with the variable. Assigning a method to the class Shape effectively provides this assurance, even when the method in class Shape is never actually executed.

12.6   PURE POLYMORPHISM

Many authors reserve the term *polymorphism* (or *pure polymorphism*) for situations where one function can be used with a variety of arguments, and the term *overloading* for situations where multiple functions are all denoted by a single name.[2] Such facilities are not restricted to object-oriented languages. In Lisp or ML, for example, it is easy to write functions that manipulate lists of arbitrary elements; such functions are polymorphic, because the type of the argument is not known at the time the function is defined. The ability to form polymorphic functions is one of the most powerful techniques in object-oriented programming. It permits code to be written once, at a high level of abstraction, and to be tailored as necessary to fit a variety of situations. Usually, the programmer accomplishes this tailoring by sending further messages to the receiver for the method. These subsequent messages often are not associated with the class at the level of the polymorphic method, but rather are deferred methods defined in the lower classes.

---

[2] The extreme cases may be easy to recognize, but discovering the line that separates overloading from polymorphism can be difficult. In both Java and ML a programmer can define a number of functions, each having the same name, but which take different arguments. Is it overloading in Java because the various functions sharing the same name are not defined in one location, whereas in ML-style polymorphism they must all be bundled together under a single heading?

An example will help us to illustrate this concept. As we noted in Chapter 8, the class Number is an abstract class, parent to the wrapper classes such as Integer, Double, Float. The definition of the class is similar to the following:

```
public abstract class Number {

    public abstract int intValue( );

    public abstract long longValue( );

    public abstract float floatValue( );

    public abstract double doubleValue( );

    public byte byteValue( )
        { return (byte) intValue( ); }

    public short shortValue( )
        { return (short) intValue( ); }
}
```

The method intValue, on the one hand, is abstract and deferred—each type of number must provide its own implementation of this method. The method byteValue, on the other hand, is not overridden. It is a purely polymorphic algorithm. Regardless of whether the receiver is an integer, a double-precision floating-point value, or some other type of number, this is the only definition that will be found. For all of these different types, when byteValue is invoked this will be the algorithm that is executed.

The important defining characteristic of pure polymorphism, as opposed to overloading and overriding, is that there is one function with the given name, used with a variety of different arguments. Almost always, as in this case, the body of such an algorithm will make use of other forms of polymorphism, such as the invocation of abstract functions shown here.

12.7   EFFICIENCY AND POLYMORPHISM

An essential point to note is that programming always involves compromises. In particular, programming with polymorphism involves compromises among ease of development and use, readability, and efficiency. In large part, efficiency has been already considered and dismissed; however, it would be remiss not to admit that it is an issue, however slight.

A function, such as the byteValue method described in the last section, that does not know the type of its arguments can seldom be as efficient as a function that has more complete information. Nevertheless, the advantages of rapid development and consistent application behavior and the possibilities of code reuse usually more than make up for any small losses in efficiency.

12.8 CHAPTER SUMMARY

Polymorphism is an umbrella term used to describe a variety of different mechanisms found in programming languages. In object-oriented languages the most important forms of polymorphism are tied to the polymorphic variable—a variable that can hold many different types of values. For example, overloading occurs when two or more functions share the same name. If these functions happen to be found in classes that have a parent class/child class relationship, then it is called overriding. If an overridden function is used with a polymorphic variable, then the particular function executed will be determined by the run-time value of the variable, not the compile-time declaration for the variable.

Other forms of polymorphism include overloading from independent classes, parametric overloading (overloading that is disambiguated by the types of arguments used in a function call), and abstract methods.

Note that the use of polymorphism tends to optimize program development time and reliability, at the cost of run-time efficiency. For most programs, the benefits far exceed the costs.

FURTHER READING

In the interests of completeness, it should be mentioned that there is at least one important style of polymorphism, found in other computer languages, that is not found in Java. A *generic* (sometimes called a template) is a technique that allows a class description to be parameterized with a type. In C++, for example, one could declare a class as follows:

```
template <class T> class box {
public:
    box (T init) { value = initial; }
    T getValue( ) { return value; }
private
    T value;
};
```

The result is a "box of T", and not simply a box. To create such a value, one must also specify a type for the parameter value T:

```
box<int> aBox(5); // create a box with an integer
box<Shape> aBox(Circle); // create a box with a circle
```

One important place where this mechanism is useful is in the creation of collection classes (see Chapter 19). A language with generics, for example, would allow one to declare a vector *of Cards*, rather than (as in Java) simply a vector of objects. The compiler can then verify that the collection contains only the indicated type of values. More importantly, the compiler can avoid the cast necessary in Java when an object is removed from a container.

A discussion of generics in relation to other forms of polymorphism can be found in [Budd 1997].

STUDY QUESTIONS

1. What does the term *polymorphic* mean in common usage?

2. What is a polymorphic variable?

3. How is the characterization of polymorphic variables different in dynamically typed languages than in statically typed languages?

4. What does it mean to say that a function name is overloaded?

5. What does it mean to say that a value has been coerced to a different type?

6. What is parametric overloading?

7. What is overriding, and how is it different from overloading?

8. What is the difference between overriding using replacement and overriding using refinement?

9. What is the default semantics for overriding for methods? For constructors?

10. What is an abstract method?

11. How is an abstract method denoted?

12. What characterizes pure polymorphism?

13. Why should a programmer not be overly concerned with the loss of efficiency due to the use of polymorphic programming techniques?

EXERCISES

1. Describe the various types of polymorphism found in the PinBall Game application presented in Chapter 7.

2. Describe the various types of polymorphism found in the Solitaire application presented in Chapter 9.

13 The AWT

Java's Abstract Windowing Toolkit, or AWT, is the portion of the Java run-time library that is involved with creating, displaying, and facilitating user interaction with window objects. The AWT is an example of a software *framework*. A framework is a way of structuring generic solutions to a common problem, using polymorphism as a means of creating specialized solutions for each new application. Thus, examining the AWT will illustrate how polymorphism is used in a powerful and dynamic fashion in the language Java.

13.1 THE AWT CLASS HIERARCHY

From the very first, we have said that class Frame represents the Java notion of an application window, a two-dimensional graphical surface that is shown on the display device and through which the user interacts with a computer program. All our applications have been formed by inheriting from Frame, overriding various methods, such as the paint method for repainting the window. In actuality, much of the behavior provided by class Frame is inherited from parent classes (see Figure 13.1). Examining each of these abstractions in turn will help illustrate the functioning of the Java windowing system, as well as illustrate the power of inheritance as a mechanism for code reuse and sharing.

The class Object is the parent class of all classes in Java. It provides the ability to compare two objects for equality, compute a hash value for an object, and determine the class of an object. Methods defined in class Object include the following:

equals (anObject)	Return true if object is equal to argument
getClass ( )	Return the name of the class of an object
hashCode ( )	Return a hash value for an object
toString ( )	Return a string representation of an object

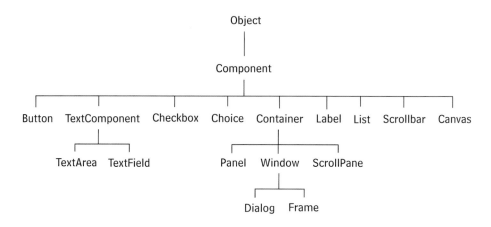

Figure 13.1   The AWT class hierarchy.

A Component is something that can be displayed on a two-dimensional screen and with which the user can interact. Attributes of a component include a size, a location, foreground and background colors, whether or not it is visible, and a set of listeners for events. Methods defined in class Component include the following:

enable( ), disable( )	Enable/disable a component
setLocation(int,int), getLocation( )	Set and get component location
setSize(int,int), getSize( )	Set and get size of component
setVisible(boolean)	Show or hide the component
setForeground(Color), getForegound( )	Set and get foreground colors
setBackground(Color), getBackground( )	Set and get background colors
setFont(Font), getFont( )	Set and get font
repaint(Graphics)	Schedule component for repainting
paint(Graphics)	Repaint component appearance
addMouseListener(MouseListener)	Add a mouse listener for component
addKeyListener(KeyListener)	Add a keypress listener for component

Besides frames, other types of components include buttons, checkboxes, scroll bars, and text areas.

A Container is a type of component that can nest other components within it. A container is the way that complex graphical interfaces are constructed. A

Frame is a type of Container, so it can hold objects such as buttons and scroll bars. When more complicated interfaces are necessary, a Panel (another type of container) can be constructed, which might hold, for example, a collection of buttons. Since this Panel is both a Container and a Component, it can be inserted into the Frame. A container maintains a list of the components it manipulates, as well as a layout manager to determine how the components should be displayed. Methods defined in class Container include the following:

setLayout (LayoutManager)	Set layout manager for display
add (Component), remove (Component)	Add or remove component from display

A Window is a type of Container. A window is a two-dimensional drawing surface that can be displayed on an output device. A window can be stacked on top of other windows and can be moved either to the front or back of the visible windows. Methods defined in class Window include the following:

show( )	Make the window visible
toFront( )	Move window to front
toBack( )	Move window to back

Finally, a Frame is a type of window with a title bar, a menu bar, a border, a cursor, and other properties. Methods defined in class Frame include:

setTitle(String), getTitle( )	Set or get title
setCursor(int)	Set cursor
setResizable( )	Make the window resizable
setMenuBar(MenuBar)	Set menu bar for window

If we consider a typical application, such as the CannonWorld application of Chapter 6, we see that it uses methods from a number of different levels of the class hierarchy:

setTitle(String)	Inherited from class Frame
setSize(int, int)	Inherited from class Component
show( )	Inherited from class Window
repaint( )	Inherited from class Component
paint( )	Inherited from Component, overridden in application class

The power of the AWT, indeed the power of any framework, comes through the use of a polymorphic variable. When the method show in class Window is invoked, it calls the method setVisible in class Component. This method calls

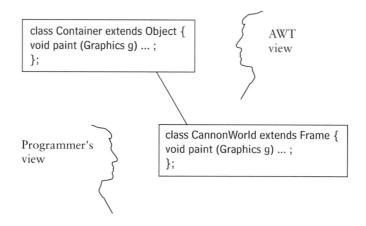

Figure 13.2   Two views of a component.

repaint, which in turn calls paint. The code for the algorithm used by setVisible and repaint resides in class Component. When it is being executed, the framework "thinks" that it is dealing only with an instance of Component. However, in actuality the method paint that is being executed is the version that has been overridden in the application class. Thus, there are two views of the function being executed, as described in Figure 13.2.

The code in the parent classes (Component, Container, Window, and Frame) can all be written without reference to any particular application. Thus, this code can be easily carried from one application to the next. To specialize the design framework to a new application it is only necessary to override the appropriate methods (such as paint or event listeners) to define application-specific behavior. Thus, the combination of inheritance, overriding, and polymorphism permits design and software reuse on a grand scale.

13.2 THE LAYOUT MANAGER

The idea of a layout manager, which is the technique used by the AWT to assign the locations of components within a container, is an excellent illustration of the combination of polymorphic techniques of composition and inheritance. The layout manager is charged with assigning the list of components held in a container positions on the surface covered by the container. There are a variety of standard layout managers, each of which will place components in slightly different ways. The programmer developing a graphical user interface creates an instance of a layout manager and hands it to a container. Generally, the task of creation is the only direct interaction the programmer will have with the layout manager, as thereafter all commands will be handled by the container itself.

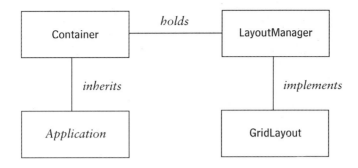

Figure 13.3   Relationships between Layout Manager Components

The connections between the application class, the container, and the layout manager illustrate yet again the many ways that inheritance, composition, and interfaces can be combined (Figure 13.3). The application class may inherit from the container (as is usually the case when an application is formed using inheritance from class Frame) or it may hold the container as a component. The container itself, however, holds the layout manager as a data field, as part of the internal state of the container. But in actual fact, the variable that holds the layout manager is polymorphic. While the Container thinks that it is maintaining a value of type LayoutManager, in fact it will be holding a value from some other type, such as GridLayout, that is implementing the LayoutManager interface.

There are three different mechanisms at work here: inheritance, composition, and implementation of an interface. Each is serving a slightly different purpose. Inheritance is the *is-a* relation that links the application class to the parent window class. This allows the code written in the AWT class Window to perform application-specific actions, by invoking methods in the application class that override methods in the parent class (paint( ), for example). The fact that composition is used to link the container with the layout manager makes the link between these two items very dynamic—the programmer can easily change the type of layout manager being employed by a container. This dynamic behavior is very difficult to achieve using inheritance alone, since the inheritance relationship between a parent and child is established at compile time. Finally, the fact that LayoutManager is simply an interface; and as well as the fact that various different classes of objects implement this interface, means that the programmer is free to develop alternative layout managers using a wide variety of techniques. (This freedom would be much more constrained if, for example, LayoutManager was a class that alternative layout managers needed to extend.)

13.2.1   *Layout Manager Types*

There are five standard types of layout managers: BorderLayout, GridLayout, Card-Layout, FlowLayout, and GridBagLayout. The BorderLayout manager can manage no

Figure 13.4   Locations recognized by Border Layout Manager.

more than five different components. This is the default layout manager for applications constructed by subclassing from Frame. The five locations are shown in Figure 13.4. They correspond to the left and right, top and bottom, and center of the display. Not all five locations need be filled. If a location is not used, the space is allocated to the remaining components.

When a border layout manager is employed, the first argument in the add method is used to specify which position a component is filling in a collection:

```
add("North", new Button("quit"));
add("Center", colorField);
```

The next most common type of layout is the GridLayout. The manager for this layout creates a rectangular array of components, each occupying the same size portion of the screen. Using arguments with the constructor, the programmer specifies the number of rows and the number of columns in the grid. Two additional integer arguments can be used to specify a horizontal and vertical space between the components. An example of a panel formatted using a GridLayout is shown in Figure 13.12 on page 223. The section of code for that application that creates the layout manager is as follows:

```
Panel p = new Panel( );
    // make a 4 by 4 grid,
    // with 3 pixels between each element
p.setLayout (new GridLayout(4, 4, 3, 3));

p.add (new ColorButton(Color.black, "black"));
p.add (new ColorButton(Color.blue, "blue"));
```

A FlowLayout manager places components in rows left to right, top to bottom. Unlike the layout created by a GridLayout manager, the components managed by a flow layout manager need not all have the same size. When a component cannot be completely placed on a row without truncation, a new row is created. The flow manager is the default layout manager for the class Panel (as opposed to Frame, where the default manager is a BorderLayout).

A CardLayout manager stacks components vertically. Only one component is visible at any one time. The components managed by a card layout manager can be named (using the string argument to the add method). Subsequently, a named component can be made the visible component. This is one of the few instances where the programmer would have direct interaction with the layout manager.

```
CardLayout lm = new CardLayout();
Panel p = new Panel (lm);
p.add ("One", new Label ("Number One"));
p.add ("Two", new Label ("Number Two"));
p.add ("Three", new Label ("Number Three"));
    .
    .
lm.show ("Two"); // show component "Two"
```

The most general type of layout manager is the GridBagLayout manager. This manager allows the programmer to create a nonuniform grid of squares, and place components in various positions within each square. However, the details of the use of this manager are complex and will not be described here.

13.3 USER INTERFACE COMPONENTS

The variety of user interface components in the Java AWT library are again a good illustration of the power of polymorphism provided both through inheritance and interfaces. With the exception of menu bars, all the user interface components are subclasses of the parent class Component (Figure 13.1). Containers assume only that the elements they will hold are instances of class Component. In fact, the values they maintain are polymorphic and represent more specialized values, such as buttons or scroll bars. Thus, the design of the user interface construction system depends upon the mechanisms of inheritance, polymorphism, and substitutability.

13.3.1 *Labels*

The simplest type of user interface component is a Label. A label has only the text it will display. It will display as much of the text as it can in the area it is given.

```
Label lab = new Label("score: 0 to 0");
add ("South", lab); // put label on top of window
```

Unlike other components, a label does not respond to any type of event, such as a mouse click or a key press. However, the text of the label can be changed using the function setText(String), and the current text of a label can be retrieved using getText( ).

13.3.2 *Button*

A Button is a labeled component, usually represented by a rounded box, that can respond to user interaction. As we have seen in earlier programs, interaction with a button is achieved by attaching an ActionListener object to the button. The ActionListener object is then notified when the button is pressed.

```
Button b = new Button ("do it!");
b.addActionListener (new doIt( ));
    .
    .
    .
private class doIt implements ActionListener {
   public void actionPerformed (ActionEvent e) {
      // whatever doIt does
      .
      .
      .
   }
}
```

A useful technique is to combine the button object and the button listener in one new class. This new class both subclasses from the original Button class and implements the ActionListener interface. For example, in the case study presented in Section 13.5, we create a set of buttons for different colors. Each button holds a color value, and when pressed it invokes a method using the color as argument. This class is written as follows:

```
private class ColorButton
      extends Button implements ActionListener {
   private Color ourColor;

   public ColorButton (Color c, String name) {
      super (name); // create the button
      ourColor = c; // save the color value
      addActionListener (this); // add ourselves as listener
      }

   public void actionPerformed (ActionEvent e) {
         // set color for middle panel
      setFromColor (ourColor);
      }
}
```

Notice how the object registers itself as a listener for button actions. The pseudovariable this is used when an object needs to denote itself. When pressed, the button will invoke the method actionPerformed, which will then invoke the procedure setFromColor that is found in the surrounding class.

We can even take this technique one step further, and define a generic ButtonAdapter class that is both a button and a listener. The actions of the listener will be encapsulated by an abstract method, which must be implemented by a subclass:

```
abstract class ButtonAdapter
       extends Button implements ActionListener {
    public ButtonAdapter (String name) {
       super (name);
       addActionListener (this);
       }

    public void actionPerformed (ActionEvent e) { pressed(); }

    public abstract void pressed ();
}
```

To create a button using this abstraction, the programmer must create a subclass and override the method pressed. This, however, can be done easily using a class definition expression. The following, for example, creates a button that when pressed will halt the application.

```
Panel p = new Panel();

p.add (new ButtonAdapter("Quit"){
    public void pressed () { System.exit(0); }});
```

13.3.3 *Canvas*

A Canvas is a simple type of component, having only a size and the ability to be a target for drawing operations. Among other uses, the class Canvas is often subclassified to form new types of components. An illustration of one use of a Canvas occurs in the discussion of the class ScrollPane (Section 13.4.1).

13.3.4 *Scroll Bars*

A ScrollBar is a slider, used to specify integer values over a wide range. Scroll bars can be displayed in either a horizontal or a vertical direction. The maximum and minimum values can be specified, as well as the line increment (the amount the scroll bar will move when it is touched in the ends), and the page increment (the amount it will move when it is touched in the background area between the slider and the end). Like a button, interaction is provided for a scroll bar by defining a listener that will be notified when the scroll bar is modified.

The case study at the end of this chapter uses a technique similar to the one described earlier in the section on buttons. Figure 13.12 offers a a snapshot of this application, which includes three vertical scroll bars. The class ColorBar represents a scroll bar for maintaining colors. The constructor for the class creates a vertical scroll bar with an initial value of 40 and a range between 0 and 255. The background color for the scroll bar is set using a given argument. Finally, the object itself is made a listener for scroll bar events. When the scroll bar is changed, the method adjustmentValueChanged will be executed. Typically, within this method the current value of the scroll bar would be accessed using getValue(). In this particular application, a bank of three scroll bars will be created, and the value of all three will be recovered in a shared procedure named setFromBar.

```
private class ColorBar
        extends Scrollbar implements AdjustmentListener {
    public ColorBar (Color c) {
        super (Scrollbar.VERTICAL, 40, 0, 0, 255);
        setBackground (c);
        addAdjustmentListener (this);
    }

    public void adjustmentValueChanged (AdjustmentEvent e) {
        // method setFromBar will get scroll bar
        // value using getValue( );
        setFromBar ( );
    }
}
```

13.3.5   Text Components

A text component is used to display editable text. There are two varieties of text components, TextField and TextArea. The first is a fixed-size block, while the second uses scroll bars to display a larger block of text, not all of which might be viewable at any one time. Figure 13.5 illustrates these two types of items.

The text in a text component can be set or accessed by the program using the functions setText(String) and getText( ). Additional text can be added to the text area using the method append(String). Various other methods can be used to indicate whether or not the text is editable and to select a subportion of the text. A TextListener can be attached to a text component. The listener must implement the TextListener interface:

```
interface TextListener extends EventListener {
    public void textValueChanged (TextEvent e);
    }
```

Figure 13.5   A window with two text components.

Figure 13.6   A window with a checkbox.

13.3.6   *Checkbox*

A Checkbox is a component that maintains and displays a labeled binary state. The state described by a checkbox can be either on or off. The current state of the checkbox can be set or tested by the programmer. A checkbox is typically used in an application to indicate a binary (on/off, yes/no) choice (see Figure 13.6).

Both the label and the state of the checkbox can be set by the programmer, using the functions getLabel, setLabel, getState, and setState. Changing the state of a checkbox creates an ItemEvent, that is registered with any ItemListener objects. The following simple application illustrates the use of these methods:

```
class CheckTest extends Frame {
    private Checkbox cb = new Checkbox ("the checkbox is off");

    public static void main (String [ ] args)
       { Frame world = new CheckTest( ); world.show( ); }

    public CheckTest ( ) {
       setTitle("Check box example"); setSize(300, 70);
       cb.addItemListener (new CheckListener( ));
       add ("Center", cb);
       }
```

```
private class CheckListener implements ItemListener {

    public void itemStateChanged (ItemEvent e) {
        if (cb.getState())
            cb.setLabel ("The checkbox is on");
        else cb.setLabel ("The checkbox is off");
        }
    }
}
```

13.3.7   *Checkbox Groups, Choices, and Lists*

Three types of interface components are typically employed to allow the user to select one item from a large number of possibilities. The first is a group of connected checkboxes with the property that only one can be set at any one time. Such a collection is sometimes called a *radio button* group, since their behavior is similar to the way buttons in car radios work. The second form is termed a Choice. A Choice object displays only one selection, but when the user clicks the mouse in the selection area, a pop-up menu appears that allows the choice to be changed to a different selection. A third possibility is termed a List. A List is similar to a Choice, however several possibilities out of the range can be displayed at one time.

Figure 13.7 illustrates all three possibilities. The code to produce this example is shown in Figure 13.8.

Figure 13.7   Three selection possibilities: radio button Checkbox group, Choice object, and a List.

```java
class ChoiceTest extends Frame {
   public static void main (String [ ] args)
      { Window world = new ChoiceTest( ); world.show( ); }

   private String [ ] choices = {"One", "Two", "Three", "Four",
      "Five", "Six", "Seven", "Eight", "Nine", "Ten"};
   private Label display = new Label( );
   private Choice theChoice = new Choice( );
   private List theList = new List( );
   private CheckboxGroup theGroup = new CheckboxGroup( );
   private ItemListener theListener = new ChoiceListener( );

   public ChoiceTest ( ) {
      setTitle ("selection example ");
      setSize (300, 300);
      for (int i = 0; i < 10; i++) {
         theChoice.addItem (choices[i]);
         theList.addItem (choices[i]); }
      theChoice.addItemListener (theListener);
      theList.addItemListener (theListener);
      add ("West", makeCheckBoxes( )); add ("North", theChoice);
      add ("East", theList); add ("South", display);
      }

   private class ChoiceListener implements ItemListener {
      public void itemStateChanged (ItemEvent e) {
         display.setText (theGroup.getSelectedCheckboxGroup( ).getLabel( )
            + theList.getSelectedItem( ) + theChoice.getSelectedItem( ));
         }
      }

   private Panel makeCheckBoxes( ) {
      Panel p = new Panel (new GridLayout(5,2));
      for (int i = 0; i < 10; i++) {
         Checkbox cb = new Checkbox(choices[i], theGroup, false);
         cb.addItemListener (theListener); p.add (cb); }
      return p;
      }
}
```

Figure 13.8   Alternative ways to display choices.

A Checkbox group should be used when the number of alternatives is small. A choice or a list should be used if the number of alternatives is five or more. A choice takes up less space in the display, but makes it more difficult to view all the alternatives.

To create a Choice or a List object, the programmer specifies each alternative using the method addItem. An ItemListener can be attached to the object. When a selection is made, the listener will be informed using the method item-StateChanged. The text of the selected item can be recovered using the method getSelectedItem.

To structure a group of checkboxes as a group, the programmer first creates a CheckboxGroup. This value is then passed as argument to each created checkbox, along with a third argument that indicates whether or not the checkbox should be initially active. If more than one button is made active (as here) only the last button will remain active. The current checkbox can be accessed using the method getSelectedCheckbox.

As a checkbox group is constructed out of several components, it is almost always laid out on a Panel. The Panel is then placed as a single element in the original layout. This is shown in Figure 13.8. Here a 5 by 2 grid is used as layout for the 10 checkboxes.

13.4   PANELS

A Panel is a Container that acts like a Component. A panel represents a rectangular region of the display. Each panel holds its own layout manager, which can differ from the layout manager for the application display. Items can be inserted into the panel. The panel, as a single unit, is then inserted into the application display.

The use of a panel is illustrated by the application described in Figure 13.8. Here the method makeCheckBoxes creates a panel to hold the 10 checkboxes that make up the checkbox group. This panel is structured, using a GridLayout as a 5 by 2 element matrix. This group of 10 components can then be treated as a single element, and is placed on the left side of the application layout.

More examples of the use of panels will be provided by the application that will be described in the next section. A snapshot of the window for this application is shown in Figure 13.12. The three scroll bars on the left are placed on a panel. This panel is laid out using a BorderLayout manager. The procedure to create and return this panel is described as follows:

```
private Panel makeScrollBars () {
    Panel p = new Panel();
    p.setLayout (new BorderLayout());
    p.add("West", redBar);
    p.add("Center", greenBar);
```

```
        p.add("East", blueBar);
        return p;
    }
```

The panel returned as the result of this method is then placed on the left side of the application window.

13.4.1 ScrollPane

A ScrollPane is in many ways similar to a Panel. Like a panel, it can hold another component. (See Figure 13.9.) However, a ScrollPane can only hold one component, and it does not have a layout manager. If the size of the component being held is larger than the size of the ScrollPane itself, scroll bars will be automatically generated to allow the user to move the underlying component.

We illustrate the use of a ScrollPane with a simple test program, shown in Figure 13.10. The application window in this program will be set to 300 by 300 pixels, but a scroll pane is created that holds a canvas that has been sized to 1000 by 1000 pixels. Scroll bars will therefore be added automatically that allow the user to see portions of the underlying canvas. As mouse events are detected by the canvas, points will be added to a Polygon. To paint the application window, the canvas simply draws the polygon values.

Figure 13.9 A ScrollPane test.

```
class BigCanvas extends Frame {
    public static void main ( String [ ] args) {
        Frame world = new BigCanvas();
        world.show();
    }

    private Polygon poly = new Polygon();
    private Canvas cv = new Canvas();

    public BigCanvas() {
        setSize (300, 300);
        setTitle ("Scroll Pane Test");
            // make canvas larger than window
        cv.setSize (1000, 1000);
        cv.addMouseListener (new MouseKeeper());
            // make scroll pane to manage canvas
        ScrollPane sp = new ScrollPane();
        sp.add(cv);
        add("Center", sp);
    }

    public void paint (Graphics g) {
            // redraw canvas
        Graphics gr = cv.getGraphics();
        gr.drawPolygon (poly);
    }

    private class MouseKeeper extends MouseAdapter {
        public void mousePressed (MouseEvent e) {
            poly.addPoint (e.getX(), e.getY());
            repaint();
        }
    }
}
```

Figure 13.10   Test program for scrollpanes.

13.5   CASE STUDY: A COLOR DISPLAY

A simple test program will illustrate how panels and layout managers are used in developing user interfaces. The application will also illustrate the use of scroll bars and the use of methods provided by the class Color. Finally, we can also use this program to illustrate how nested classes can be employed to combine the actions of creating a new graphical component (such as a button or a slider) and listening for actions relating to the component.

The class ColorTest (Fig. 13.11) creates a window to display color values. The window (Fig. 13.12) is divided into four regions. The regions are managed by the default layout manager for class Frame, which is a value of type BorderLayout.

At the top (the "north" side) is a text region, a component of type TextField,

```
class ColorTest extends Frame {
   static public void main (String [ ] args)
      { Frame window = new ColorTest( ); window.show( ); }

   private TextField colorDescription = new TextField( );
   private Panel colorField = new Panel( );
   private Color current = Color.black;
   private Scrollbar redBar = new ColorBar(Color.red);
   private Scrollbar greenBar = new ColorBar(Color.green);
   private Scrollbar blueBar = new ColorBar(Color.blue);

   public ColorTest( ) {
      setTitle ("color test"); setSize (400, 600);
      add("North", colorDescription);
      add("East", makeColorButtons( ));
      add("Center", colorField);
      add("West", makeScrollBars( ));
      setFromColor (current);
      }

   private void setFromColor (Color c) {
      current = c; colorField.setBackground (current);
      redBar.setValue(c.getRed( )); greenBar.setValue(c.getGreen( ));
      blueBar.setValue(c.getBlue( ));
      colorDescription.setText(c.toString( ));
      }

   private void setFromBar ( ) {
      int r = redBar.getValue( ); int g = greenBar.getValue( );
      int b = blueBar.getValue( ); setFromColor (new Color(r, g, b));
      }

   private Panel makeColorButtons ( ) { ... }
   private Panel makeScrollBars ( ) { ... }
private class BrightenButton extends Button implements ActionListener ...
private class ColorButton extends Button implements ActionListener ...
private class ColorBar extends Scrollbar implements AdjustmentListener ...
}
```

Figure 13.11 The class ColorTest.

Figure 13.12   Snapshot of ColorTest application.

that describes the current color. To the left (the "west" region) is a trio of sliders that can be used to set the red, green, and blue values. To the right (the "east" region) is a 4 by 4 bank of 16 buttons. These are constructed on a Panel that is organized by a GridLayout manager. Thirteen of the buttons represent the predefined color values. Two more represent the actions of making a color brighter and darker. The final button will halt the application. Finally, in the middle will be a square panel that represents the specified color.

The class ColorTest holds six data fields. The first represents the current color in the middle panel, while the remaining five represent different graphical objects. Three represent the slider, one represents the text field at the top of the page, and one represents the color panel in the middle.

The three sliders make use of the class ColorBar described earlier in Section 13.3.4. The argument used with the constructor for each class is the color to be used in painting the buttons and background for the scroll bar. You will recall that when adjusted, the scroll bar will invoke its listener, which will execute the method adjustmentValueChanged. This method will then execute the procedure setFromBar.

A method makeScrollBars, used to create the panel that holds the three scroll bars, was described earlier in Section 13.4.

The idea of combining inheritance and implementation of an interface is used in creating the buttons that represent the 13 predefined colors. Each instance of ColorButton, shown earlier in Section 13.3.2, both extends the class Button and implements the ActionListener interface. When the button is pressed, the method setFromColor will be used to set the color of the middle panel using the color stored in the button.

The class BrightenButton is slightly more complex. An index value is stored with the button. This value indicates whether the button represents the "brighten" button or the "darken" button. When pressed, the current color is modified by the appropriate method, and the new value used to set the current color.

```
private class BrightenButton
        extends Button implements ActionListener {
    private int index;
    public BrightenButton (int i) {
        super ( i == 0 ? "brighter" : "darker");
        index = i;
        addActionListener(this);
        }

    public void actionPerformed (ActionEvent e) {
        if (index == 0)
            setFromColor (current.brighter( ));
        else
            setFromColor (current.darker( ));
        }
}
```

A panel is used to hold the 16 button values. In this case the layout is described by a 4 by 4 grid pattern. Thirteen represent the predefined buttons. Two represent the brighter and darker buttons. And the final creates a button that when pressed exits the application.

```
private Panel makeColorButtons ( ) {
    Panel p = new Panel( );
    p.setLayout (new GridLayout(4,4,3,3));
    p.add (new ColorButton(Color.black, "black"));
    p.add (new ColorButton(Color.blue, "blue"));
    p.add (new ColorButton(Color.cyan, "cyan"));
    p.add (new ColorButton(Color.darkGray, "darkGray"));
    p.add (new ColorButton(Color.gray, "gray"));
    p.add (new ColorButton(Color.green, "green"));
    p.add (new ColorButton(Color.lightGray, "lightGray"));
    p.add (new ColorButton(Color.magenta, "magenta"));
    p.add (new ColorButton(Color.orange, "orange"));
    p.add (new ColorButton(Color.pink, "pink"));
    p.add (new ColorButton(Color.red, "red"));
    p.add (new ColorButton(Color.white, "white"));
    p.add (new ColorButton(Color.yellow, "yellow"));
    p.add (new BrightenButton(0));
    p.add (new BrightenButton(1));
```

```
        p.add (new ButtonAdapter("Quit"){
          public void pressed( ) { System.exit(0); }});
        return p;
    }
```

13.6   DIALOGS

A Dialog is a special purpose window that is displayed for a short period of time during the course of execution, disappearing thereafter. Dialogs are often used to notify the user of certain events, or to ask simple questions. A dialog must always be attached to an instance of Frame, and disappears automatically when the frame is hidden (such as when the application halts).

Dialog windows can be modal or nonmodal. A modal dialog demands a response from the user, and it prevents the user from performing any further action until the dialog is dismissed. A nonmodal dialog, sometimes called a modeless dialog, can be ignored by the user. The processing of actions for a nonmodal dialog is often placed in a separate Thread (see Chapter 20), so that the actions produced by the dialog will not disrupt the continuing processing of the rest of the application. Whether or not a dialog is modal is determined when the dialog is created. The two arguments used in the constructor for the dialog are the application Frame and a Boolean value that is true if the dialog is modal.

```
        // create a new nonmodal dialog in current application
        Dialog dig = new Dialog (this, false);
```

Because a Dialog is a type of Window, graphical components can be placed in the dialog area, just as in a Frame or Panel. The default layout manager for a dialog is BorderLayout, the same as with Frame.

The most common functions used with a dialog are not actually defined in the class Dialog but are inherited from parent classes. These include the following:

setSize(int, int)	Set window size
show( )	Display window
setVisible(false)	Remove window from display
setTitle(String), getTitle( )	Set or get title of window

For modal dialogs, the show method does not return until the dialog is dismissed. Such dialogs must therefore invoke the setVisible(false) method sometime during their processing.

13.6.1   *Example Program for Dialogs*

An example program will illustrate the creation and manipulation of dialogs. The application shown in Figure 13.14, on page 226, creates a window with

Figure 13.13   Dialog example window.

a checkbox, a button, and a text area. The application window, as well as an example dialog box window, is shown in Figure 13.13. The checkbox allows the user to specify either a modal or modeless dialog box should be created. The button creates the dialog, while the text area records button presses performed by the dialog.

The procedure makeDialog creates the dialog box. The size of the box is set at 100 by 100 pixels, and four buttons are placed on the box. Three buttons simply type text into the display when pressed, while the last button will hide the dialog. For a modal dialog hiding the dialog is the same as dismissing the dialog box, and it returns control to the procedure that created the dialog.

13.7   THE MENU BAR

Although a menu bar is a graphical component, it is not declared as a subclass of Component. This is because platforms differ in how they handle menu bars, so the implementation must be more constrained. Both menu bars and menus act like containers. A menu bar contains a series of menus, and each menu contains a series of menu items.

An instance of *MenuBar* can be attached to a Frame using the method set-MenuBar:

```
        .
        .
        .
MenuBar bar = new MenuBar( );
setMenuBar (bar);
        .
        .
        .
```

```
class DialogTest extends Frame {
    static public void main (String [ ] args)
        { Frame world = new DialogTest( ); world.show( ); }

    private TextArea display = new TextArea( );
    private Checkbox cb = new Checkbox("Modal Dialog?");

    public DialogTest( ) {
        setTitle ("Dialog Test Program");
        setSize (300, 220);

        add ("West", cb);
        add ("East", new Makebutton( ));
        add ("South", display);
        }

    private class Makebutton extends ButtonAdapter {
        public Makebutton ( ) { super ("Make Dialog"); }
        public void pressed ( ) { makeDialog (cb.getState( )); }
        }

    private void makeDialog (boolean modalFlag) {
        final Dialog dlg = new Dialog (this, modalFlag);
        dlg.setSize (100, 100);
        dlg.add ("North", new CountButton(1));
        dlg.add ("West", new CountButton(2));
        dlg.add ("East", new CountButton(3));
        dlg.add ("South", new ButtonAdapter("Hide") {
            public void pressed ( ) { dlg.setVisible(false); }});
        dlg.show( );
        }

    private class CountButton extends ButtonAdapter {
        public CountButton (int val) { super ("" + val); }
        public void pressed ( ) {
            display.append("Button " + getLabel( ) + " pressed\n");}
        }
    }
```

Figure 13.14 Example program for creating dialogs.

Individual menus are named, and are placed on the menu bar using the method add:

```
     .
     .
     .

Menu helpMenu = new Menu ("Help");
bar.add (helpMenu);
     .
     .
     .
```

Menu items are created using the class MenuItem. Each menu item maintains a list of ActionListener objects, the same class used to handle Button events. The listeners will be notified when the menu item is selected.

```
     .
     .
     .

MenuItem quitItem = new MenuItem ("Quit");
quitItem.addActionListener (new QuitListener( ));
helpMenu.add (quitItem);
     .
     .
     .
```

A number of techniques can be used to create special purpose menus, such as tear-off menus, cascading menus, and so on. However, these will not be described here.

13.7.1   *A Quit Menu Facility*

On many platforms it is sometimes difficult to stop a running Java application. For this reason, it is useful to define a general purpose "Quit" menu bar facility. The class QuitItem (Figure 13.15, on page 228) creates a listener that will halt the running application when the associated menu item is selected. By overloading the constructor, we make it trivial to add this functionality to any application.

The constructor for QuitItem can be given a MenuItem as argument. In this case it merely attaches itself as a listener to the menu item. Alternatively, it can be given a Menu, in which case it creates a menu item labeled "Quit." Or it can be given a MenuBar, in which case it creates a new menu labeled "Quit" that contains only the quit menu item. Finally, the constructor can be given an application as argument, in which case it creates a new menu bar containing only the one menu that contains only the single quit item. Using the application

```
class QuitItem implements ActionListener {

    public QuitItem (Frame application) {
        MenuBar mbar = new MenuBar( );
        application.setMenuBar (mbar);
        Menu menu = new Menu("Quit");
        mbar.add (menu);
        MenuItem mitem = new MenuItem("Quit");
        mitem.addActionListener (this);
        menu.add (mitem);
        }

    public QuitItem (MenuBar mbar) {
        Menu menu = new Menu("Quit");
        mbar.add (menu);
        MenuItem mitem = new MenuItem("Quit");
        mitem.addActionListener (this);
        menu.add (mitem);
        }

    public QuitItem (Menu menu) {
        MenuItem mitem = new MenuItem("Quit");
        mitem.addActionListener (this);
        menu.add (mitem);
        }

    public QuitItem (MenuItem mitem)
        { mitem.addActionListener (this); }

    public void actionPerformed (ActionEvent e)
        { System.exit(0); }
}
```

Figure 13.15   A general purpose QuitItem class.

constructor, a quit menu selection can be added to an application by placing only a single line in the constructor for the application:

```
class ColorTest extends Frame {
    .
    .
    public ColorTest ( ) {
        .
        .
```

```
        // add quit menu item to application
    new QuitItem (this);
        .
        .
        .
    }
}
```

13.8 CHAPTER SUMMARY

The Abstract Windowing Toolkit, or AWT, is the portion of the Java library used for the creation of graphical user interfaces. The design of the AWT is an excellent illustration of the power of object-oriented techniques. In this chapter we have described the various AWT components, and the way in which they are used to develop user interfaces.

STUDY QUESTIONS

1. What do the letters *AWT* stand for?

2. What are the parent classes of class Frame?

3. In what AWT class is the method setBackground defined?

4. How is a container different from other types of components?

5. Explain why in a framework there are two views of an overridden method, such as paint.

6. What is the task performed by the layout manager?

7. Explain how the three mechanisms of inheritance, composition, and implementation of an interface are all involved in the task of attaching a layout manager to a container.

8. What are the five different layout manager types? Which mangers use the one argument add method, and which use the method in which the first argument is a String value and the second a component?

9. What is the difference between a TextArea and a TextField?

10. What are the three different types of components that allow the user to select one item out of many possibilities?

11. What is a Panel?

12. What are the 13 predefined values provided by class Color?

13. What do the three numerical values that define a color represent?

14. In what ways is a MenuBar similar to a Component? In what ways is it different?

EXERCISES

1. Add a menu bar to the Solitaire program described in Chapter 9. Then, add two menu items, one to quit the application, and one to reset the application for a new game.

2. Using a text box and a grid of buttons, create a simple calculator application. Buttons correspond to digits and the four arithmetic functions +, −, * and /, as well as the equals sign.

14 Input and Output Streams

At first glance, the input/output facilities in Java seem to present a confusing profusion of alternatives. Over two dozen classes are used to implement stream I/O. However, standing behind this multitude is an elegant logical structure that makes efficient and effective use of inheritance and polymorphism. Understanding how to manipulate the file facilities will be much easier once you appreciate the structure and purpose of these classes.

14.1 INPUT STREAMS

The class InputStream is a virtual class, parent to 10 subclasses in the Java library (Figure 14.1). Each class implements roughly the same behavior. This input stream protocol can be described as follows:

```
abstract class InputStream {

    // read a single byte from the input
    int read( ) throws IOException;

    // read a buffer of values from the input
    int read (byte [ ] buffer) throws IOException

    // skip the indicated number of values from input
    long skip (long n) throws IOException

    // determine number of bytes readable without blocking
    int available( ) throws IOException
```

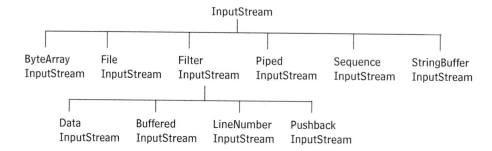

Figure 14.1   Subclasses of input stream.

```
    // close this input stream
  void close( ) throws IOException
}
```

An IOException will be thrown (generated) if a file cannot be opened, or if an interrupt is encountered while reading from a pipe, or in similar situations.

The differences among the variety of input stream classes can best be understood by dividing them into two major categories. The first are classes tied to a *physical* input source. These read values from a string buffer, a byte array, a file, or a pipe. The second are those input streams that are *virtual*, depending upon another input stream for the actual reading operations but extending the functionality of the input stream in some fashion. For example, a LineNumberInputStream reads values from another input stream but watches for newline characters as values are read. As each newline character is seen, a counter is incremented. This counter therefore indicates the number of lines that have been processed.

14.1.1   *Physical Input Streams*

There are four input stream classes that read from actual data areas. These are distinguished by their names and the arguments used in their constructors. A ByteArrayInputStream, for example, must be given an array of byte values as an argument. A FileInputStream requires either a file or a file name, and so on.

```
    // constructors for various input stream
  ByteArrayInputStream (byte [ ] buffer);
  ByteArrayInputStream (byte [ ] buffer, int offset, int count);
  FileInputStream (File f);
  FileInputStream (String fileName);
  StringBufferInputStream (String s);
  PipedInputStream (PipedOutputStream p);
```

Each of the input stream classes supports the common InputStream protocol. Some of the classes augment this with additional methods. For example, a StringBufferInputStream can be reset() back to the beginning of the underlying string.

Note that for simple reading and writing, a FileInputStream or FileOutput-Stream can be manipulated without first creating a File object. Generally, a File is necessary only if one is doing operations to the file itself, such as renaming or removing the file. Another reason for creating a File object would be to test whether a file is readable or writable before beginning a sequence of input/output operations.

14.1.2   *Virtual Input Streams*

The class SequenceInputStream and the four subclasses of FilterInputStream can be thought of as *virtual* input classes. None of these actually read characters from any input area, but instead they rely on one or more underlying input streams for their data source. Each adds useful functionality as values are passed through the class.

For example, a SequenceInputStream takes a sequence of two or more input streams, and logically places them end to end. When one input stream is exhausted, the next stream in sequence is started without interruption or any action on the users' part. The underlying streams can be specified either as two arguments to the constructor (if there are only two input streams to be catenated) or as an enumeration to an underlying collection of input streams (if there are more than two input streams).

```
InputStream f1 = new FileInputStream ("file1.text");
InputStream f2 = new FileInputStream ("file2.text");
InputStream f3 = new SequenceInputStream (f1, f2);
    // f3 now represents the catenation of file1 and file2
Vector fv = new Vector ( );
fv.addElement (f1); fv.addElement (f2);
InputStream f4 = new SequenceInputStream (fv.elements());
    // f4 also now represents the same catenation
```

The structure of the class SequenceInputStream is an example of the *composition* design pattern (see Section 15.2).

As noted in Chapter 10, the subclasses of FilterInput represent an interesting combination of the object-oriented mechanisms of inheritance and composition, characteristic of the *wrapper* design pattern (see Section 15.9). Because each class inherits from InputStream, they can be used in all situations where an input stream is expected. But each also holds as a component an underlying input stream, used to read the actual character values. One way to envision these classes is as an adapter, or filter, that sits between the client (the code making the request for values) and the physical input stream producing the values.

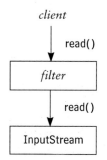

Because they support the interface common to all input streams, such filters can be easily added or removed as needed.

Perhaps the easiest filter to understand is the class LineNumberInputStream. The underlying input stream must be given as an argument to the constructor when an instance of this class is created. The filter simply scans the input for newline characters as values are read. Each time a newline character is found, a counter is incremented. The value of this counter can be retrieved by the method getLineNumber( ).

The PushbackInputStream allows a single character to be unread. A value pushed back into the input stream will subsequently be returned as the result of the next read operation. This facility is useful when scanning textual input. Imagine, for example, reading the textual representation of a numeric value, such as 456. It is only *after* the first nondigit character is read that one knows that all of the digits of the number have been seen. But the last character, the nondigit, should not be considered part of the number. Thus, this value is "pushed back" into the input, to be read again later.

The PushbackInputStream only allows a single character to be reprocessed. The BufferedInputStream is a more general facility, allowing the input operations to be backed up over a larger range. The method mark( ) tells the stream to begin saving the values of characters as they are read. A subsequent reset( ) then resets the input back to the marked location. All characters between the mark and the reset will then be read again. The standard input stream System.in is an example of a buffered input stream. On most platforms, characters cannot be read from this input stream until an entire line of text has been entered.

The input filter that adds the most new functionality is the class DataInput-Stream. In this class, methods are provided to read the binary representation of all of the primitive data types:

```
class DataInputStream extends FilterInputStream
    implements DataInput {
    .
    .
    .
    public boolean readBoolean () throws IOException
```

```
    public byte readByte () throws IOException

    public char readChar () throws IOException

    public double readDouble () throws IOException

    public int readInt () throws IOException

    public int readLong () throws IOException

    public String readLine () throws IOException
}
```

Note that these methods read a binary representation, not a textual representation of the values. Most generally, the input stream being processed was produced using a DataOutputStream. However, DataInputStreams are also useful with purely textual files. In particular, the method readLine () can be used when textual input must be processed in a line by line fashion. An example was shown in Section 19.7.1. The DataInput interface is also used by the class RandomAccess-File.

14.1.3 *Stream Tokenizer*

Although not specifically an InputStream, the class StreamTokenizer provides a useful mechanism for breaking a textual file into a sequence of tokens. The stream tokenizer recognizes words (sequences of letters separated by nonletter characters), numbers (sequences of digit characters), and can even be set up to recognize comments or convert all tokens to lower case. Each token returned is characterized by a token type, which is either one of several symbol constants defined in the class or the integer value of the last character read. The following program illustrates several of the methods provided by this class:

```
class TokenTest {
  public static void main (String [ ] args) {
    StreamTokenizer tok = new StreamTokenizer (System.in);
    try {
    while (tok.nextToken( ) != tok.TT_EOF) {
      switch (tok.ttype) { // ttype is token type
        case tok.TT_NUMBER: // nval is numeric value
          System.out.println("number " + tok.nval);
          break;
        case tok.TT_EOL:
          System.out.println("end of line");
          break;
        case tok.TT_WORD: // sval is text value
```

```
                    System.out.println("word " + tok.sval);
                    break;
                default:
                    System.out.println("token " + (char) tok.ttype);
                    break;
                }
            }
        } catch (IOException e) { }
    }
}
```

Giving this program the input "23-skido, kid!" yields the output:

```
number 23.0
token -
word skido
token ,
word kid
token !
```

14.2   OUTPUT STREAMS

Although not as extensive as the input stream classes, the subclasses of
OutputStream (Figure 14.2) also exhibit the same interesting use of polymorphism
and inheritance. Like InputStream, the abstract parent class OutputStream defines
minimal functionality:

```
abstract class OutputStream {
        // write a single byte value:w%added 2 lines to cause break
```

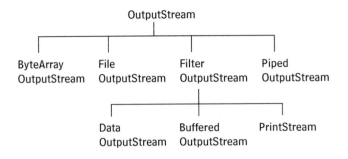

Figure 14.2   Subclasses of OutputStream.

```
        public abstract void write (int b) throws IOException

            // write an array of byte values
        public void write (byte [ ] buffer) throws IOException

            // flush all output from buffers
        public void flush () throws IOException

            // close stream
        public void close () throws IOException
    }
```

As we did with input streams, we can divide the description of output streams into two major categories, those classes that characterize the physical location of the output, and those classes that add more behavior to an output stream.

In the first group are the three classes ByteArrayOutputStream, FileOutputStream, and PipedOutputStream. The first writes values into an in-memory byte array, the second on to an external file, and the third to a pipe (see Section 14.3).

The second category is represented by the class FilterOutputStream and its subclasses. Just as FilterInputStream provided an orthogonal way of adding additional functionality to an input stream regardless of the physical source of the data, a filtered output stream adds new functionality to an output operation. Whereas a filtered input stream generally performs new operations after reading from the underlying stream, a filtered output stream generally performs some task *before* sending the (perhaps transformed) values to the underlying output stream. There are three subclasses of FilterOutputStream. These are BufferedOutputStream, DataOutputStream, and PrintStream.

A BufferedOutputStream maintains an internal buffer of values that have been output. Rather than writing bytes one by one, values are written to the underlying output stream only when the buffer becomes full or when the output is flushed. This is useful if writing an individual byte to the output stream involves a high overhead that can be amortized if many characters are written at once.

A DataOutputStream is the output equivalent of DataInputStream. This class adds methods to write the binary values for each of the primitive data types. The output will be read subsequently by a DataInputStream. A program in Section 14.3 will illustrate the use of a DataOutputStream.

A PrintStream is similar but generates a textual representation rather than a binary representation. The methods print( ) and println( ) are overloaded with functions specific to each of the primitive data types. Typically, a print stream is used to generate output that will be read by human users, as opposed to processing by another program. Both the streams System.out and System.err are instances of PrintStream.

```
class PrintStream extends FilterOutputStream  {
    .
    .
    // print textual representation of primitive value
    public void print (boolean bool)
    public void print (int inum)
    public void print (float fnum)
    public void print (double dnum)
    public void print (String str)
    public void print (Object obj) { print (obj.toString( )); }
    .
    .
}
```

The implementation of the method print( ) when used with an object as argument is an example of parametric polymorphism combined with an abstract, or deferred method. Because all objects are subclasses of Object, any value can be used as argument with this method. When executed, the procedure uses the function toString( ) to convert the object into a string representation. The implementation of this method in class Object simply returns the name of the class of the receiver. However, this method is overridden in many classes to provide more meaningful output. The function executed will be determined by the dynamic, run-time type of the argument, not by the static type Object. In this fashion, whatever text the programmer has provided using the toString( ) method will be the output produced.

14.3 PIPED INPUT AND OUTPUT

In some types of applications a common situation is for one portion of a program to be producing values that are being consumed by a different portion of the same program. Such an arrangement is called a *producer/consumer* relationship. Java provides an elegant way of organizing this type of program, through the use of multiple threads of execution and pipes. The producer and consumer each run in their own thread of execution, communicating through a pipe.

A *pipe* is a buffered data area that is used for both reading and writing. A pipe can hold only a limited number of values. Either reading from or writing to a pipe can cause a thread to be temporarily suspended. A write will be suspended if the current pipe buffer is full, whereas a read operation will be suspended if the buffer is empty. In both cases, execution will continue when the condition is resolved, for example when a subsequent read frees up space in the buffer, or a subsequent write adds a new element.

Each pipe is manifest by a matched pair of stream pointers, a PipedOutputStream and a PipedInputStream. The second value created (either input or output pipe) is passed the first value as argument, and the connection is thereby made between the two:

```
PipedInputStream in = new PipedInputStream( );
PipedOutputStream out = new PipedOutputStream (in);
```

Values can subsequently be written to the piped output stream as if it were any other type of output stream, and these values can then be read, in the same order they were inserted, from the corresponding input stream.

We can illustrate the use of pipes by means of a program designed to find all the integers smaller than 100,000 that are both prime numbers and Fibonacci numbers. A prime number, you will recall, is a value with no divisors other than 1 and itself. A Fibonacci number [1] is defined by the recurrence relation $f_0 = 0$, $f_1 = 1$, $f_n = f_{n-2} + f_{n-1}$.

A separate thread of control (see Chapter 20) is created to generate both sequences of numbers. The thread, in fact, need not even know that it is dealing with a pipe. The Fibonacci thread simply creates a sequence of values and writes them to an output stream. Using a DataOutputStream makes it easier to write integer values. Although it looks as if the thread produces all the values at once, a print( ) statement placed inside the loop will demonstrate that this is not so, and that production of values will be delayed until they are required.

```
class FibMaker extends Thread {
    private DataOutputStream out;

    public FibMaker (DataOutputStream o) { out = o; }

    public void run ( ) {
        int n = 0;
        int m = 1;
        try {
            out.writeInt (m);
            while (m < 100000) {
                int newValue = n + m;
                n = m;
                m = newValue;
                System.out.println("writing new Fibonacci " + newValue);
                out.writeInt (newValue);
            }
```

---

[1] Tradition has it that Fibonacci numbers describe the population growth of rabbits. Rabbits take two years to mature. Once mature, they give birth each year to a single offspring. Thus, each new year the number of rabbits is the number of rabbits in the previous year plus the number of mature rabbits in the previous year, each of which has given birth. Hardly realistic, but the sequence of numbers produced by this relation has some fascinating properties.

```
            out.close( );
          } catch (IOException e) { return; }
      }
}
```

A similar thread creates prime numbers:

```
class PrimeMaker extends Thread {
   private DataOutputStream out;

   public PrimeMaker (DataOutputStream o) { out = o; }

   public void run () {
      int newValue = 1;
      try {
         while (newValue < 100000) {
            newValue = newValue + 1;
            boolean isPrime = true;
            for (int i = 2; i * i <= newValue; i++)
               if (newValue % i == 0) {
                  isPrime = false; break; // no use checking further
                  }
            if (isPrime) {
               System.out.println("writing new prime " + newValue);
               out.writeInt (newValue);
               }
            }
         out.close( );
         } catch (IOException e) { return; }
      }
}
```

The main program shows how these are connected. The thread for each generator and for the pipes as well is created in the methods makeFibs( ) and makePrimes( ). Note how all the pipe mechanism is encapsulated in these two routines, and the remainder of the program simply views input as coming from a DataInputStream. The main program simply reads values as long as they are available, comparing them and outputting those that match.

```
class PipeTest {
   static public void main (String [ ] args)
      { PipeTest world = new PipeTest(System.out); }

   private PipeTest (PrintStream out) {
      DataInputStream fibs = makeFibs( );
```

```
      DataInputStream primes = makePrimes( );
      try {
         int x = fibs.readInt( );
         int y = primes.readInt( );
         while (x < 100000) {
            if (x == y) {
               out.println ("integer " + x + " is both fib
                  and prime");
               x = fibs.readInt( );
               }
            else if (x < y)
               x = fibs.readInt( );
            else
               y = primes.readInt( );
            }
         } catch (IOException e) { System.exit(0); }
      }

   private DataInputStream makeFibs ( ) {
      try {    // create the Fibonacci number generator
         PipedInputStream in = new PipedInputStream( );
         PipedOutputStream out = new PipedOutputStream (in);
         Thread fibThread = new FibMaker
            (new DataOutputStream(out));
         fibThread.start( );
         return new DataInputStream (in);
         } catch (IOException e) { return null; }
      }

   private DataInputStream makePrimes ( ) {
      try {    // create the prime number generator
         PipedInputStream in = new PipedInputStream( );
         PipedOutputStream out = new PipedOutputStream (in);
         Thread primeThread = new PrimeMaker
            (new DataOutputStream(out));
         primeThread.start( );
         return new DataInputStream (in);
         } catch (IOException e) { return null; }
      }
}
```

An examination of the output will show that values are being generated on demand, rather than being all computed at once.

```
writing new Fibonacci 1
writing new Fibonacci 2
writing new prime 2
writing new prime 3
writing new prime 5
writing new prime 7
writing new Fibonacci 3
writing new Fibonacci 5
writing new prime 11
writing new prime 13
writing new prime 17
writing new Fibonacci 8
writing new Fibonacci 13
writing new Fibonacci 21
integer 2 is both fib and prime
integer 3 is both fib and prime
integer 5 is both fib and prime
integer 13 is both fib and prime
writing new Fibonacci 34
  .
  .
  .
writing new prime 19
writing new prime 23
  .
  .
writing new prime 31
writing new Fibonacci 233
  .
  .
integer 89 is both fib and prime
  .
  .
integer 233 is both fib and prime
```

14.4   CHAPTER SUMMARY

Although the number of different classes can initially make the input/output facilities of Java seem confusing, the structure of these classes is very simple and a good illustration of the use of inheritance and polymorphism.

Input streams can be divided into those based on a physical input source (reading input from a file, for example), and those based on adding new functionality to a logical input stream. An example of the latter is the class LineNumberInputStream, which adds the ability to count line numbers to an existing input stream. The design of the subclasses of FilterInputStream combines both the techniques of inheritance and composition.

Although not specifically an input stream, the class StreamTokenizer provides a way to break a stream into individual tokens. A similar facility for strings will be described in Chapter 17.

Like input streams, the various subclasses of output stream differ in the physical location to which the output is directed.

Pipes provide a mechanism for structuring programs that include both the production and consumption of a given resource. The producer writes values to the pipe, while the consumer reads values. The pipe facility will automatically suspend either the producer or the consumer tasks if values are not available or the pipe buffer becomes full.

STUDY QUESTIONS

1. Describe the functions that are common to all subclasses of InputStream.

2. What are the different types of physical locations from which an input stream can read?

3. Describe how a FilterInputStream combines both inheritance and composition.

4. What new functionality is provided by the class LineNumberInputStream?

5. What task is performed by a StreamTokenizer?

6. Describe the different targets to which an output stream can write.

7. In what ways is a pipe different from a file? In what ways are they the same?

EXERCISES

1. Create a new subclass of FilterInputStream that reads values from an input stream and converts all uppercase characters to lowercase. How would you test your program?

2. Using DataInputStream.readLine() and a StringTokenizer, write an application that will count and display the number of lines, words, and characters in a file. The name of the file should be taken from the argument list for the application.

3. Write the class description for SequenceOutputStream, which is the output analog to SequenceInputStream. The constructor for this class will take two output streams as argument. Each write to the SequenceOutputStream will thereafter be translated into a write on each of the argument streams.

4. Extend the class you developed in the preceding exercise so that the constructor can take an enumeration of output streams as argument.

5. Write a subclass of FilterInputStream that looks for positive integer digit characters, such as "4231", and replaces them with the textual equivalent, in this example the words "four thousand two hundred and thirty one". Do this in several steps:

(a) Convert the input stream into a PushbackInputStream.

(b) As long as the source input stream is not a digit character, return it.

(c) When a digit character is encountered, read the number until the end of digit is found.

(d) Push the terminating nondigit character back into the input.

(e) Translate the number into its textual equivalent, stored in a String. Create a StringBufferInputStream to read characters from this string.

(f) For subsequent requests, read from the string buffer input stream until no further characters remain, then revert to reading from the original push back input stream.

15 Design Patterns

Like most complex structures, good computer programs are often formed by imitating the structure of older, similar programs that have already proven successful. A *design pattern* is an attempt to capture and formalize this process of imitation. The basic idea is to characterize the features of a proven solution to a small problem, summarizing the essential elements and omitting the unnecessary detail. A catalog of design patterns is a fascinating illustration of the myriad ways that software can be structured so as to address different problems. Later, patterns can give insight into how to approach new problems that are similar to those situations described by the pattern.

This chapter will introduce the idea of design patterns by describing several found in the Java library. The terminology used in describing the patterns is adapted from the book *Design Patterns: Elements of Reusable Object-Oriented Software*, by Erich Gamma, Richard Helm, Ralph Johnson and John Vlissides [1995]. This was one of the first books to describe the concept of design patterns and provide a systematic cataloging of patterns. Many more patterns than are described in the present chapter can be found in this book, as well as in the recent literature on design patterns.

The format used in describing each pattern is to first characterize the problem the pattern is addressing, then to summarize the essential features of the solution. In some cases this is followed by a discussion of some of the context for the problem or of alternative design possibilities. This is followed by a more detailed description of the pattern as it is manifest in the Java Library. Finally, a sentence or two summarizes the situations where the pattern is applicable.

15.1 ADAPTER

Problem: How do you use an object that provides appropriate behavior but uses a different interface than is required in some situation?

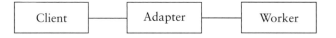

Figure 15.1   The adapter pattern.

Solution: Define an *adapter* class that acts as an intermediary. The adapter does little work itself but merely translates commands from one form into the other.

Discussion: International travelers frequently overcome the problem of differing electrical plug and voltage standards by using adapters for their appliances. These adapters are connectors that allow an electrical appliance with a plug for one type of outlet to be plugged into a different type of electrical outlet. The software equivalent is similar. An adapter is concerned mostly with changes in the interface to an object, and less with the actual functionality being provided. (See Figure 5.1)

Example: An example of adapters in the Java library are the wrapper classes, Boolean, Integer, and so on. These adapt a primitive type (such as boolean or int) so that they can be used in situations where an Object is required. For example, wrappers are necessary to store primitive values as elements in a Vector.

   Another form of adapter is the class MouseAdapter used in the pinball game described in Chapter 7, as well as in the Solitaire program presented in Chapter 9. Here the adapter reduces the interface, by implementing default behavior for methods that are unneeded in the current application. The client can therefore concentrate on the one method that is used in the program.

   An adapter can be used whenever there is the need for a change in interface, but no, or very little, additional behavior beyond that provided by the worker.

15.2   COMPOSITION

Problem: How do you permit the creation of complex objects using only simple parts?

Solution: Provide a small collection of simple components, but also allow these components to be nested arbitrarily. The resulting composite objects allow individual objects and compositions of objects to be treated uniformly. Frequently, an interesting feature of the *composition* pattern is the merging of the *is-a* relation with the *has-a* relation.

Example: A good example of composition in the Java library is the creation of design layouts through the interaction of Components and Containers. Only five simple types of layouts are provided by the standard library, and of these five only two, border layouts and grid layouts, are commonly used. Each item in a layout is a Component. Composition occurs because Containers are also

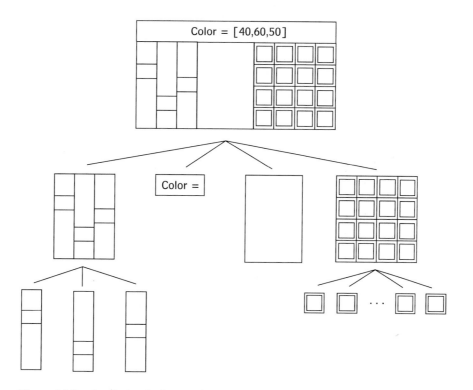

Figure 15.2   An Example Composition.

Components. A container holds its own layout, which is again one of only a few simple varieties. Yet the container is treated as a unit in the original layout.

The structure of a composite object is often described in a treelike format. Consider, for example, Figure 15.2, the layout of the window shown in Figure 13.12 of Chapter 13. At the application level there are four elements to the layout. These are a text area, a simple blank panel, and two panels that hold composite objects. One of these composite panels holds three scroll bars, while the second is holding a grid of 16 buttons.

By nesting panels one within another, arbitrarily complex layouts can be created. Another example of composition is the class SequenceInputStream, which is used to catenate two or more input streams so that they appear to be a single input source (see Section 14.1.2). A SequenceInputStream *is-a* InputStream (meaning it extends the class InputStream). But a SequenceInputStream also *has-a* InputStream as part of its internal state. By combining inheritance and composition, the class permits multiple sequences of input sources to be treated as a single unit.

This pattern is useful whenever it is necessary to build complex structures out of a few simple elements. Note that the merging of the *is-a* and *has-a* relations is

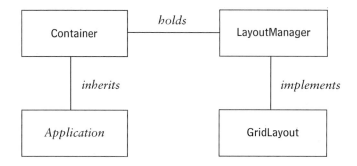

Figure 15.3   An example of the strategy pattern.

characteristic of the *wrapper* pattern (Section 15.9), although wrappers can be constructed that are not composites.

15.3   STRATEGY

Problem: How do you allow the algorithm that is used to solve a particular problem to be easily and dynamically changed by the client?

Solution: Define a family of algorithms with a similar interface. Each algorithm provides a different strategy for solving the problem at hand. Encapsulate each algorithm, and let the client select the strategy to be used in any situation.

Discussion: If a complex algorithm is embedded in a larger application, it may be difficult to extract the algorithm and replace it with another, alternative version. If several alternative algorithms are included in the same object, both the complexity and the code of the resulting object may be increased unnecessarily. Separating problem and solution makes it easier for the client to select the solution (strategy algorithm) appropriate for any particular situation.

Example: An example of the use of the strategy pattern is the creation of layout managers in the AWT. Rather than coding in the component library the details of how items are laid out on the screen, these decisions are left to the layout manager. An interface for LayoutManager is defined, and five standard layout managers are provided. The ambitious programmer is even allowed, should he or she choose, to define a new object that satisfies the LayoutManager interface. (See Figure 15.3.)

The activities of the design component (such as a Panel or a Window) are independent of the particular layout manager that is being used. This both simplifies the container component and permits a much greater degree of flexibility in the structure of the resulting layout than would be possible if layout decisions were an intrinsic part of the container.

The strategy pattern is useful whenever it is necessary to provide a set of alternative solutions to a problem and the algorithms used to address the problem can be encapsulated with a simple interface.

15.4 OBSERVER

Problem: How do you allow two or more independent and loosely coupled objects to change in synchrony with each other?

Solution: Maintain a list of objects that are tied, or dependent, on another object. When the target object changes, the dependents, or observers, are notified that they should update themselves.

Discussion: It is easy to maintain tightly coupled objects in synchrony. For example, if a new class is defined as a subclass of an existing parent class, modifications of the parent that are made via method invocations can be monitored by simply overriding the methods. It is much more difficult to keep objects in step with one another when links are formed and broken dynamically at run time, or when no obvious class relationship exists between the separate elements.

Example: There are two good examples of the use of the observer pattern in the Java library. The first we have seen in many earlier case studies, such as the Cannon World examined in Chapter 6. Each of the user interface components that permits interaction, such as buttons, scroll bars, and checkboxes, maintains a collection of *listener* objects. This list is dynamic; listeners for any component can be easily added or removed at run time. Furthermore, the structure of the listeners is not specified, they are only required to satisfy the necessary interface. When the component changes state (the button is pressed, the slider moved, the checkbox changed), each of the listeners is notified that a change has occurred. It is up to the listener to decide what action should be taken as a result of the change.

The idea behind listeners is also found in a more general facility that can be used by programmers for situations that do not involve user interaction. The library class Observable represents objects that can be "observed," the equivalent of the components in the AWT mechanism. Programmers can either subclass a new class from Observable, or simply create an Observable field within a class. Other objects can implement the Observer interface. These correspond to "listener" objects. An instance of Observer registers itself with the object being observed.

At any time, the Observable object can indicate that it has changed, by invoking the message notifyObservers(). An optional argument can be passed along with this message. Each observer is passed the message update(Observable, Object), where the first argument is the Observable that has changed, and the second is the optional argument provided by the notification. The observer takes whatever action is necessary to bring the state into synchrony with the observed object.

The *observer* pattern is applicable whenever two or more objects must be loosely coupled but must still maintain synchronization in some aspect of their behavior or state.

15.5   FLYWEIGHT

Problem: How can one reduce the storage costs associated with a large number of objects that have similar state?

Solution: Share state in common with similar objects, thereby reducing the storage required by any single object.

Example: With the exception of primitive values, all objects in Java are an instance of some class. With each class it is necessary to associate certain information. Examples of information is the name of the class (a String), and the description of the interface for the class. If this information were duplicated in each object, the memory costs would be prohibitive. Instead, this information is defined once by an object of type Class, and each instance of the class points to this object.

The objects that share the information are known as *flyweights*, since their memory requirements are reduced (often dramatically) by moving part of their state to the shared value. The flyweight pattern can be used whenever there are a large number of objects that share a significant common internal state.

15.6   ABSTRACT FACTORY

Problem: How to provide a mechanism for creating instances of families of related objects without specifying their concrete representations.

Solution: Provide a method that returns a new value that is characterized only by an interface or parent class, not by the actual type produced.

Discussion: There are several instances where the value returned by a function in the standard library is characterized by either an abstract class or an interface. Clearly the actual value being returned is a different type, but normally the client using the function is not concerned with the actual type, but only the behavior described by the characterizing attributes.

Example: Two examples out of the many found in the Java library will be described. Each of the collection classes Vector, Hashtable, and Dictionary define a method named elements( ) that is described as returning a value of type Enumeration. As Enumeration is only an interface, not a class, the value returned is clearly formed as an instance of some other class. Almost always, the client has no interest in the actual type being yielded by elements( ) and is only interested in the behavior common to all values that satisfy the Enumeration interface.

A similar situation occurs with the classes Font and FontMetrics. The class Font-Metrics is used to describe the characteristics of a Font, such as the height and width of characters, the distance characters extend above or below the baseline, and so on. A FontMetrics is an abstract class, one that cannot be instanciated directly by the programmer using the new command. Instead, a value of type FontMetric is returned by a Graphics object in response to the message getFontMetrics. Clearly, the graphics object is returning a value derived from a subclass of FontMetric, but the particular value returned is normally of no concern to the client.

A similar facility is used by class Applet, which can return an AppletContext that describes the current execution environment.

The abstract factory pattern should be used whenever the type of the actual value to be created cannot be predicted in advance and therefore must be determined dynamically.

15.7 FACTORY METHOD

Problem: You have a method that returns a newly created object, but you want subclasses to have the ability to return different types of object.

Solution: Allow the subclass to override the creation method and return a different type of object.

Discussion: This pattern is very similar to the abstract factory but is specialized for the situation where new abstractions are formed using inheritance.

Example: The method clone() is a good example of a factory method. This method returns a copy of an object, provided the object supports the Cloneable interface. The default method in class Object raises an exception, indicating that the cloneable interface is not supported. Subclasses that wish to permit clones must override this method and return a different type of value.

Note that the value returned by a factory method must be the same for all classes. For the Cloneable interface this type is Object. Any class that permits cloning will still return a value of type Object in response to the message clone(). This value must then be cast to the appropriate type.

The factory method pattern is useful when there is a hierarchy of abstractions formed using inheritance, and part of the behavior of these abstractions is the creation of new objects.

15.8 ITERATOR

Problem: How to provide a way to access elements of an aggregate object sequentially without exposing the underlying representation.

Solution: Provide a mediator object for the sole purpose of sequential access. This mediator can be aware of the representation of the aggregate although the client using the object need not be aware of these details.

Example: The Enumeration interface for container access actually addresses two related problems. It provides a uniform means of accessing elements from many different types of container, and it hides the details of the underlying container representation. It is the second aspect that makes the Enumeration a good example of the iterator pattern.

Consider, for example, an enumeration that is generating elements from a Hashtable. Internally, a hash table is implemented as an array, each element of the array being a list. Values that hash into the same locations are found on the same list. (See Figure 15.4.)

The programmer who uses a hash table and wishes to iterate over the values should not be concerned with the representation, such as moving from one list to the next when the elements in one hash location have been exhausted. The hash table enumeration hides these difficulties behind a simple interface. The programmer sees only the two methods hasMoreElements() and nextElement(). With these, a loop can be written that does not even hint at the complex actions needed to access the underlying elements.

```
HashTable htab = new HashTable( );
    .
    .
    .
for (Enumeration e = htab.elements( ); e.hasMoreElements( ); ) {
   Object val = e.nextElement( );
    .
    .
    .
   }
```

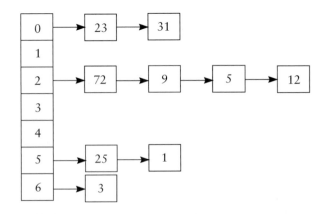

Figure 15.4   Internal Representation of a hash table.

The fact that the method elements returns a value that is not directly an Enumeration, but is rather a value from another class that implements the Enumeration interface, is an example of the *abstract factory* pattern (Section 15.6).

The iterator pattern is useful whenever an aggregate object is created that can hold an arbitrary number of values, and it is necessary to provide access to values without exposing the underlying representation.

15.9 DECORATOR (FILTER OR WRAPPER)

Problem: How can you attach additional responsibilities to an object dynamically?

Solution: By combining the *is-a* and *has-a* relations, create an object that wraps around an existing value, adding new behavior without changing the interface.

Discussion: Inheritance is one technique for providing new functionality to an existing abstraction. But inheritance is rather heavyhanded, and is often not flexible enough to accommodate situations that must dynamically change during the course of execution. A decorator wraps around an existing object and satisfies the same requirements (for example, is subclassed from the same parent class or implements the same interface). The wrapper delegates much of the responsibility to the original but occasionally adds new functionality. (See Figure 15.5.)

Example: The class InputStream provides a way to read bytes from an input device, such as a file. The class BufferedInputStream is a subclass of InputStream, adding the ability to buffer the input so that it can be reset to an earlier point and values can be reread two or more times. Furthermore, a BufferedInputStream can take an InputStream as argument in its constructor.

Because a BufferedInputStream both *is* an InputStream and *has* an input stream as part of its data, it can be easily wrapped around an existing input stream. Due to inheritance and substitutability, the BufferedInputStream can be used where the original InputStream was expected. Because it holds the original input stream, any

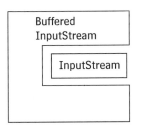

Figure 15.5 Buffered InputStream as an example of the wrapper or filter pattern.

Figure 15.6   The proxy pattern.

actions unrelated to the buffering activities are simply passed on to the original stream.

A decorator, or wrapper class, is often a flexible alternative to the use of subclassing. Functionality can be added or removed simply by adding or deleting wrappers around an object.

15.10   PROXY

Problem: How do you hide details such as transmission protocols to remote objects?

Solution: Provide a proxy that acts as a surrogate or placeholder for another object.

Discussion: A proxy is an object that stands in place of another. The first object receives requests for the second, and generally forwards the requests to the second, after processing them in some fashion. (See Figure 15.6.)

Example: An example proxy in the Java Library is the Remote Method Invocation (RMI) system. RMI is a mechanism that can be used to coordinate Java programs running on two or more machines. RMI creates a proxy object that runs on the same machine as the client. When the client invokes a method on the proxy, the proxy transmits the method across the network to the server on another machine. The server handles the request, then transmits the result back to the proxy. The proxy hands the result back to the client. In this fashion, the details of transmission over the network are handled by the proxy and the server, and are hidden from the client.

15.11   BRIDGE

Problem: How to decouple an abstraction from its implementation so that the latter can vary independently.

Solution: Remove implementation details from the abstraction, placing them instead in an object that is held as a component in the abstraction.

Example: Most of the component classes in the AWT make use of the *bridge* pattern. Fundamentally, this is because the actions necessary to implement a graphical component vary in great detail from one platform to another. For example, the actions needed to display a window are different depending upon whether the underlying display is X-Windows/Motif, Windows-95, or the Macintosh. Rather than placing platform specific details in the class Window, instead each window maintains a component of type WindowPeer. The interface Window-Peer has different implementations, depending upon the platform on which the application is being executed. This separation allows a Java program that depends only on the class Window to be executed in any environment for which there is a corresponding peer.

The bridge pattern is in many ways similar to the strategy pattern described earlier. Differences are that bridges are almost always hidden from the client (for example, the average Java programmer is generally unaware of the existence of the peer classes), and are generally dictated by environmental issues rather than reflecting design decisions.

15.12   Chapter Summary

An emerging new area of study in object-oriented languages is the concept of design patterns. A design pattern captures the salient characteristics of a solution to a commonly observed problem, hiding details that are particular to any one situation. By examining design patterns, programmers learn about techniques that have proven to be useful in previous problems, and are therefore likely to be useful in new situations.

Further Reading

The most important reference for design patterns is the 1995 book of the same name by Gamma, Helm, Johnson, and Vlissides (commonly known as the Gang of Four, or GOF). Another recent book on patterns is by Richard Gabriel [1996].

Study Questions

1. In what ways is an adapter similar to a proxy? In what ways are they different?

2. In what way is the composition design pattern similar to the idea of composition examined in Chapter 10?

3. In what ways is a strategy design pattern similar to a bridge pattern? In what ways are they different?

4. In what ways is an iterator similar to an adapter?

Exercise

1. What design pattern is exhibited by the class PrintStream (see Section 14.2)? Explain your answer.

V

Understanding the Java World

16 Exception Handling

From the start, Java was designed with the understanding that errors occur, that unexpected events happen, and that programmers should always be prepared for the worst. Part of this outlook is the inclusion in the language of a simple yet powerful mechanism for handling *exceptions*.

An exception is an event that occurs during the execution of a program that disrupts the flow of instructions and prevents the program from continuing along its normal course. An example that is easy to understand is the exception that occurs when a file cannot be opened. The programmer developing a file-processing application starts out with a structure that perhaps looks something like the following:

```
ask the user for the name of a file
open the file
read the contents
do something with the contents
close the file
```

The programmer probably develops the application using some simple test cases and might not even think about the possibility that the file cannot be opened. What happens if the user enters incorrect values, a name that is not a valid file name? In most languages, the likely answer is that the program will fail in totally unexpected and inexplicable ways.

In Java, the programmer cannot simply forget to think about this possibility, because the language will not allow the programmer to write a statement that opens a file without providing the code that will be executed should a failure occur. The file-opening method is declared as a function that can potentially "throw an exception", and the compiler will refuse to recognize any use of the method that does not handle the exception.

259

As we saw earlier in the case study described in Chapter 7, a method that can potentially raise an exception must be invoked within the framework of a *try/catch* block. This is written as a nested statement following the keyword try, and an associated set of statements following the keyword catch:

```
try {
    File fd = new File(filename);
} catch (fileOpenFailed e)
    { System.err.println("Cannot open file " + filename); }
```

The exception mechanism is in fact dealing with an actual object, which is an instance of class Throwable. When an error occurs, the value of this object is assigned to the variable e in the statements shown above.

Multiple statements can be nested within the try block. In fact, often almost the entire application will be held within a surrounding block.

```
try {
    File fd = new File(filename);
    processFile (fd);
    fd.close( );
} catch (fileOpenFailed e)
    { System.err.println("Cannot open file " + filename); }
```

Multiple exceptions can also be tested, by writing a series of catch clauses

```
try {
    File fd = new File(filename);
    processFile (fd);
    fd.close( );
} catch (FileNotFoundException e)
    { System.err.println("Cannot find file " + filename); }
catch (FileOpenFailed e)
    { System.err.println("Cannot open file " + filename); }
```

Exceptions are a useful programming construct because the location where an error is detected is usually not the place where the appropriate solution is known. For example, suppose you are the programmer developing the file-processing library routines. That is, you are the person developing the code for the class File. Certainly you are aware of the fact that the string passed to the constructor for your class might not represent a valid file name. But what should you do in this situation? Without knowledge of the surrounding application, there is no good answer.

One common solution is to return a special value, such as the value null, when a command cannot be processed. But constructors are not permitted to return a null value, furthermore there might be multiple reasons for a failure. Does a null value returned by a file open operation mean the file does not exist, or that it exists but cannot be read? Finally, what if a null value is perfectly legal? How would one indicate an error in that case?

The exception mechanism not only gives the programmer who detects the message the ability to return precise information, it also places responsibility for dealing with the error on the shoulders of the programmer, who knows the appropriate action to take.

16.1   INFORMATION TRANSMITTED TO THE CATCH BLOCK

You will note that a catch block looks something like a procedure declaration. Like a procedure, the catch block defines a *variable* that is given a value when the exception is handled. Each of the various exceptional conditions is in fact a class name, a subclass of Throwable. The variable that is thrown often contains useful information pertaining to the exception, such as the name of the file that cannot be opened, or the value of an illegal array index. If the exception is converted to a String value, as in many of the examples shown in this chapter, then this information will be printed.

The class Throwable also defines several methods. One of the most useful is a method that will print a stack trace, which describes the sequence or procedure calls up to the point where the exception occurred. The following shows how this could be used:

```
try {
    File fileOne = new File (fileName);
    processfile (fileOne);
    fileOne.close( );
    } catch (FileNotFoundException e)
        { System.error.println("Cannot find file " + e);
            e.printStackTrace( );
            }
```

16.2   CATCHING MULTIPLE ERRORS

There need not be a one-to-one correspondence between methods that can throw an exception and the try block that handles the error. The Java language only requires that the statement that can throw the exception must be handled somewhere. For example, if two or more files are being opened, they can be surrounded by a single try/catch statement. An error opening either file will be handled in the same way.

```
try {
    File fileOne = new File (filenameOne);
    File fileTwo = new File (filenameTwo);
```

```
    processFile (fileOne, fileTwo);
    fileOne.close( );
    fileTwo.close( );
} catch (FileNotFoundException e)
    { System.err.println("Cannot find file " + e); }
} catch (FileOpenFailed e)
    { System.err.println("Cannot open file " + e); }
```

16.3   TERMINATION OR RESUMPTIVE MODELS

When an exception is thrown, control transfers directly to the catch block that handles the error. Unless the programmer explicitly reinvokes the same procedure, control will not return to the point at which the error occurred. This is sometimes referred to as the *termination model* of exception handling. There exist other programming languages that permit control to be returned to the point of error. Such languages are said to use the *resumptive model* of exception handling.

16.4   EXCEPTIONS THROWN IN THE STANDARD LIBRARY

Exceptions come in several varieties, which are all subclasses of the class Throwable. The two major subclasses of Throwable are Error and Exception. Some of the more common exceptions are described in Figure 16.1.

The subclasses of Error represent "hard" failures, such as the virtual machine detecting an error in the bytecode representation. Processing will immediately halt once such an error is detected. Fortunately, it is unlikely that a typical Java program will ever see or throw such an error.

Most programmers will write code to throw and catch objects that derive from the class Exception. Once again, these can be divided into categories, the two most important being RuntimeException and IOException.

The subclasses of RuntimeException represent conditions that arise within the Java virtual machine itself during the processing of the bytecodes that represent a program. Examples include the use of a variable that has not been initialized (NullPointerException), an improper cast conversion, or an arithmetic operation that overflows. Because the source for such an error could potentially be almost any Java statement, the compiler does not insist that programmer test for or catch these errors. (Think about what a program would look like if every variable reference needed to be surrounded by a try statement to detect null value possibilities.)

The subclasses of IOException represent errors that can occur during the processing of input and output statements. Examples include not being able to open files, attempting to read past the end of a file, or attempting to access information across the network using a badly formed URL.

```
Throwable
   Error
      LinkageError
         IncompatibleClassChangeError
            InstantiationError
      VirtualMachineError
         InternalError
         OutOfMemoryError
         StackOverflowError
   Exception
      IllegalAccessException
      IOException
         EOFException
         FileNotFoundException
         InterruptedIOException
         MalformedURLException
      RuntimeException
         ArithmeticException
         ClassCastException
         EmptyStackException
         IndexOutOfBoundsException
            ArrayIndexOutOfBoundsException
            StringIndexOutOfBoundsException
         NegativeArraySizeException
         NullPointerException
         SecurityException
```

Figure 16.1   Some of the exceptions issued in the standard library.

16.5   THROWING EXCEPTIONS

A method that will in some situations throw an exception must declare so in the method heading. For example, suppose one is developing a stack abstraction (see Chapter 19) making use of an array. Popping from an empty stack might be a condition that would trigger an exception. To throw an exception, a new value is created (using the new operator). This value must be a subclass of Throwable.

```
class Stack {
   private int index;
   private Vector values;
   .
   .
   .
```

```
Object pop( ) throws Exception {
    if (index < 0)
        throw new Exception("pop on empty stack");
    Object result = values.elementAt(index);
    index--;
    return result;
    }
}
```

It is possible to convey more precise information by first creating a subclass of Exception, then throwing an instance of this class. The class Exception has two constructor forms, and subclasses generally follow the same pattern.

```
class StackUnderflowException extends Exception {
    StackUnderflowException ( ) { super( ); }
    StackUnderflowException (String gripe) { super(gripe); }
}

class Stack {
    private int index;
    private Vector values;
        .
        .
        .

    Object pop( ) throws StackUnderflowException {
        if (index < 0)
            throw new StackUnderflowException( );
        Object result = values.elementAt(index);
        index--;
        return result;
    }
}
```

16.6   PASSING ON EXCEPTIONS

Occasionally it is useful for a method not to handle an exceptional condition and simply to pass the exception back to the caller. This can be accomplished by simply adding the exception type to the method header. An example occurs in the concordance program examined in Chapter 19.

```
class Concordance {

    public void readLines (DataInputStream input) throws IOException {
        String delims = " \t\n.,!?;:";
```

```
       for (int line = 1; true; line++ ) {
          String text = input.readLine( );
          if (text == null) return;
          text = text.toLowerCase( );
          Enumeration e = new StringTokenizer(text, delims);
          while (e.hasMoreElements( ))
             enterWord ((String) e.nextElement( ), new Integer(line));
          }
       }
   .
   .
   .
}
```

Here the IOException could be thrown by the method readLine. However, this method really had no better way of dealing with this particular error than did the readLine routine itself. Thus, the error is simply passed back to the caller of readLines, who could take the appropriate action.

16.7 CHAPTER SUMMARY

The exception-handling mechanism in Java is a powerful technique for increasing the reliability and robustness of Java programs. Exceptions handle unexpected conditions that can disrupt the normal flow of control in the execution of a program. By properly declaring and catching exception, programmers are provided with a way to recover gracefully from potentially error-producing situations.

STUDY QUESTIONS

1. What is an exception?

2. Before exceptions were part of programming languages, a common technique used to indicate errors was to have a function return a special value, such as a null pointer. How is the exception mechanism an improvement over this technique?

3. In what ways is a catch clause similar to a procedure? In what ways is it different?

4. What is the difference between the termination and resumptive models of exception handling?

5. What is the difference between exceptions formed as subclasses of Error, and those that are subclasses of Exception?

17 Utility Classes

The Java library provides a number of small utility classes that are useful in a wide variety of situations. In this chapter we will consider several of these, including Point, Dimension, Date, Math, Random, Toolkit, and the data field named System. In addition, we will consider strings and their related classes.

17.1 POINT

A Point represents a location in two-dimensional space. The point is described by a pair of integer values, called the x and y values. Points are used in conjunction with a number of the AWT painting operations and with layout managers. An important feature to remember is that in the AWT coordinate system, the y coordinates increase as locations move downward, rather than decreasing as is true in classical geometry.

The following summarizes the characteristics of the class Point:

```
class Point {
        // constructor
    public Point (int x, int y)

        // public accessible data fields
    public int x
    public int y

        // operations
    public void move (int x, int y) // move to given location
    public void translate (int x, int y) // change by offset
    public boolean equals (Object p) // compare two points
    public String toString ( ) // convert to string
}
```

17.2 DIMENSION

A dimension is used to represent a rectangular size. Dimensions are characterized by a width and a height. Dimensions are used in many AWT methods and returned as the result of methods that need to characterize a size. The following summarizes the features of the class Dimension:

```
class Dimension {
    // constructors
  public Dimension ()
  public Dimension (int w, int h)
  public Dimension (Dimension d) // make copy

    // public accessible data fields
  public int width
  public int height

    // operations
  public String toString()
}
```

17.3 DATE

The class Date is used to represent both data and time values. Two dates can be compared to determine if one comes after the other. Once set, any of the fields in a date can be changed. The following summarizes the methods provided by the class Date:

```
class Date {
    // constructors
  public Date () // return current date and time
  public Date (int year, int month, int day)
  public Date (int year, int month, int day, int hours,
    int minutes)
  public Date (int year, int month, int day,
    int hours, int minutes, int seconds)

    // field access methods
  public int getDate () // returns day of month, 1-31
  public int getDay () // returns day of week, 0-6
  public int getHours () // returns hour, 0-23
  public int getMinutes () // returns minute of hour, 0-59
  public int getMonth () // returns month of year, 0-11
  public int getSeconds () // returns second of minute 0-59
  public int getYear () // returns year number - 1900
```

```
public int getTimesoneOffset ( ) // returns offset from GMT

    // epoch methods
public long getTime ( ) // returns milliseconds since epoch
public void setTime (long lval) // set time from epoch

    // field setting methods
public void setDate (int date)
public void setHours (int hour)
public void setMinutes (int minutes)
public void setMonth (int month)
public void setSeconds (int seconds)
public void setYear ( )

    // comparison methods
public boolean after (Date day)
public boolean before (Date day)
public boolean equals (Object day)

    // output
public String toString ( )
}
```

When provided with no constructors, the class Date returns the current time and day. Otherwise, the date is set from the argument values given. The year value is given as the year minus 1900, that is, 97 represents 1997, and 112 represents 2012.

Notice that the method equals overrides the similarly named method inherited from class Object. Thus, the argument to this method must be simply Object. However, the methods after and before, which are defined here for the first time, can be restricted to working only with Date objects.

17.3.1 *After the Epoch*

Recent dates and times can be compactly represented by a single long value that represents the number of milliseconds since January 1, 1970, which is termed the start of the *epoch*. This quantity is returned by the method getTime. Most often these values are used in pairs, to obtain the amount of time used to perform a certain operation:

```
Date start = new Date( ); // starting time

int j = 0;
for (int i = 0; i < 100000; i++)
    j = j + 1;
```

```
Date end = new Date( ); // ending time
System.out.println("That took " + (end.getTime( )
    - start.getTime( )) + " milliseconds");
```

Epoch values for dates prior to January 1, 1970 are returned as negative numbers.

17.4 MATH

The class Math provides a number of constants, as well as useful mathematical functions. All values and functions are declared as static. Thus, these elements are accessible without creating an instance of the class. The class can be summarized as follows:

```
final class Math {
    // constants
    public static final double E   // 2.71828 ...
    public static final double PI  // 3.1415926 ...

    // trigonometric operations, angles in radians
    public static double sin (double num)
    public static double cos (double num)
    public static double tan (double num)
    public static double asin (double num)
    public static double acos (double num)
    public static double atan (double num)
    public static double atan2 (double s, double c)

    // rounding operations
    public static double ceil (double num)
    public static double floor (double num)
    public static double rint (double num)
    public static int round (float num)
    public static long round (double num)

    // exponential and powers
    public static double exp (double y) // e raised to x
    public static double pow (double x, double y) // x raised to y
    public static double log (double x) // log base e
    public static double sqrt (double x) // x raised to 1/2

    // other operations
    public static int abs (int num)
    public static long abs (long num)
```

```
      public static float abs (float num)
      public static double abs (double num)
      public static int max (int x, int y)
      public static float max (float x, float y)
      public static double max (double x, double y)
      public static int min (int x, int y)
      public static float min (float x, float y)
      public static double min (double x, double y)
      public static double random ( ) // value between 0 and 1
   }
```

The method random( ) returns a value that is larger than or equal to 0.0, and strictly smaller than 1.0, uniformly distributed over the range. The following, for example, could be used to return a random number between 1 and 10 (inclusive of both endpoints):

```
   int val = (int) Math.floor(Math.random( ) * 10 + 1);
```

More extensive random number operations are provided by class Random.

17.5   RANDOM

The function Math.random( ) can be used to generate random floating-point values larger than or equal to 0.0 and smaller than 1.0 with a uniform distribution. The class Random provides more general facilities, allowing not only the generation of random integers, but also the ability to reset the random number generator with a *seed* value. This latter feature provides a way to recreate the same random sequence of values many times, a property that is often useful in testing programs, as well as other situations. The facilities provided by Random can be summarized as follows:

```
   class Random {
         // constructors
      public Random ( )
      public Random (long seed)

         // operations
      public void setSeed (long seed)
      public double nextDouble ( )
      public float nextFloat ( )

         // integer value, can be either positive or negative
      public int nextInt ( )
      public long nextLong ( )
```

```
    // alternative distribution
  public double nextGaussian ( )
}
```

All methods use a uniform distribution, with the exception of nextGaussian, which uses a Gaussian distribution. Other distributions can often be constructed from these. The following function, for example, takes as argument an integer array of weights and computes a random number with weighted distribution. It sums the array of weights, computes a random integer between 0 and the sum, then locates the integer in the array of weights:

```
static public int weightedDistribution (int [ ] weights) {
    int sum = 0; // compute sum of weights
    for (int i = 0; i < weights.length; i++)
      sum += weights[i];
      // compute random value less than sum
    int val = (int) Math.floor(Math.random( ) * sum + 1);
      // find point in distribution
    for (int i = 0; i < weights.length; i++) {
      val -= weights[i];
      if (val < 0)
        return i;
    }
    return 0; // should never happen
}
```

Given an array of weights (1, 3, 2), for example, the value 0 would be returned 1/6 of the time, the value 1 returned 1/2 of the time, and the value 2 returned 1/3 of the time.

17.6 TOOLKIT

The class Toolkit is mostly used to create the peer objects used in providing the device independent aspects of the AWT (see Section 15.11). However, in addition to creating the windows, buttons, menus, and other features of a graphical interface, the class also provides a few utilities useful to the programmer.

Toolkit is an abstract class, specialized for each type of platform on which a Java program can be executed. The implementation of Toolkit appropriate to the current environment is found by executing the method Toolkit.getDefaultToolkit( ).

The method getFontList( ) returns an array of string values, containing the names of the fonts available on the current system.

The method getImage( ) takes as argument either a string or a URL (see Section 21.4.1). If a string argument is used it should contain the name of a file. The image is loaded from the file or the URL address, and returned as a value of type Image.

The methods getScreenSize( ) and getScreenResolution( ) together return the size of the screen. The first returns the number of pixels in the screen, both height and width in a value of type Dimension. The second returns the number of dots per inch. Dividing one by the other will yield the physical size of the screen.

17.7 System

The class System, and the instance data field of the same name provided by class Frame, give access to several systemwide resources. The most commonly used values are the input and output streams for the standard input, standard output and error output. These are found at System.in, System.out, and System.err, respectively.

The function System.exit(int) immediately halts the currently running program, yielding to the operating system the integer status value given in the argument.

The method currentTimeMillis( ) returns the current time in milliseconds. The value is returned as a signed long value, representing the number of milliseconds since January 1, 1970 (see Section 17.3.1). Since the value is returned as a long, overflow will occur sometime in the year 292280995.

17.8 Strings and Related Classes

The handling of strings in Java is similar enough to the handling of strings in other languages to seem natural to the programmer learning the language, yet sufficiently different in subtle points to be a potential source of trouble. In this chapter we will describe strings, string buffers, string tokenizers, and related classes.

The most important fact to remember is that in Java a String is an immutable value; it cannot be changed. One should think of a string as a constant, like a double-precision value. Just as a variable declared as holding a double can be assigned a new value, a variable assigned as holding a String can be assigned a new string, but this is not the same as changing the string value. A second class, StringBuffer, is closer, for example, to the C concept of a string as simply an array of character values. A string buffer can be subscripted, and individual elements modified. The following shows, for example, how to change *hope* into *cope* in both C and in Java.

C version	*Java version*
```char * str = "hope";```	```String str = "hope";```
```str[0] = 'c';```	```StringBuffer strbuf(str);```
	```strbuf.setCharAt(0, 'c');```

17.8.1   *Operations on Strings*

The most common way to create a string is with a literal:

```
String name = "John Smith";
```

The various constructors for string also allow a string to be created from another string, from an array of characters or bytes, or from a string buffer:

```
char data[ ] = {'q','e','d'};
String quod = new String(data);
    // quod erat demonstrandum
```

The addition operator, +, is overloaded with a new meaning when either the left or the right argument is a string. In this case, the nonstring argument (if any) is converted into a string and a string catenation is performed. This is most often used to produce formatted output:

```
System.out.println(" The answer is: " + answer);
```

Note that the addition operator groups left to right, so that the meaning of the addition in the following two expressions is very different:

```
System.out.println("Catch-" + 2 + 2); // catch-22
System.out.println(2 + 2 + "warned"); // be forewarned
```

The String class defines a number of methods for returning portions of a string, converting values to a string, and comparing strings. These can be summarized as follows:

```
final class String { // declared final so it cannot be subclassed

        // constructors
    public String (String src)
    public String (char [ ] charArray)
    public String (byte [ ] byteArray)
    public String (StringBuffer buffer);

        // methods for creating new strings
        // catenate string with argument string
    public String concat (String str)
        // replace old characters with new
    public String replace (char oldChar, char newChar)
        // return subportion of string
    public String substring (int offset)
    public String substring (int offset, int endIndex)
        // convert case of all letters
    public String toLowerCase ( )
```

```
        public String toUpperCase ( )
            // return reference of current string
        public String toString ( )
            // trim leading and trailing whitespace
        public String trim ( )
            // create string from primitive data type
        public static String valueOf (boolean bool)
        public static String valueOf (char ch)
        public static String valueOf (char [ ]  charArray)
        public static String valueOf (int i)
        public static String valueOf (long l)
        public static String valueOf (float f)
        public static String valueOf (double d)
        public static String valueOf (Object obj)


            // comparison methods
            // compare ordering, return negative, zero or positive
        public int compareTo (String str)
            // compare for equality
        public boolean equals (Object obj)
        public boolean equalsIgnoreCase (String str)
            // test front or end of string
        public boolean endsWith (String str)
        public boolean startsWith (String str)
            // find first occurrence of char or string
        public int indexOf (char c)
        public int indexOf (char c, int startingOffset)
        public int indexOf (String str, int startingOffset)
        public int lastIndexOf (char c)
        public int lastIndexOf (char c, int startingOffset)
        public int lastIndexOf (String str, int startingOffset)
    }
```

There are a few subtle points that can trap the unwary programmer. Note that the identity operator, ==, tests whether two variables refer to exactly the same value. This is not the same as testing whether two string values have exactly the same character representation. In general, one should always use equals( ) to test the equality of objects, including strings, and not use the == operator. Because equals overrides the method inherited from Object, the argument must be an Object and not a String. A string value will always return false when compared to a nonstring. The method equalsIgnoreCase tests whether two values are the same, ignoring uppercase and lowercase distinctions.

The method compareTo( ) returns an integer result. This value is negative if the current string is lexicographically smaller than the argument, zero if they are equal, and positive if the string is larger than the argument. The exact integer value returned is implementation dependent and should not be counted upon in any program.

The static method String.valueOf (Object obj) is a good example of a polymorphic function. The argument can be any type of object, including a null object. If it is not null, the method toString is used to convert the object into a string value:

```
final class String {
    .
    .
    .
    public static String valueOf (Object obj) {
        if (obj == null)
            return "null";
        else
            return obj.toString();
    }
    .
    .
    .
}
```

The method toString is defined in class Object (where it returns the class name of the receiver as a string), and redefined in many classes. The value yielded by toString(), and hence by valueOf(), will be whatever method is appropriate for the dynamic, run-time type of the argument.

Because String.valueOf returns a legal result regardless whether or not the argument is null, it is a safer alternative to the use of toString directly:

```
Shape aShape = null;
    .
    .
    .
String a = String.valueOf(aShape); // will return "null" as string
String b = aShape.toString(); // will generate null value exception
```

This property of the == operator can be used to demonstrate one subtle difference between creating a new string using the String constructor, and creating a string using the valueOf operator. One case generates a copy of the original string, while the other simply returns a reference to the original.

```
String one = "One";
String two = new String(one);
String three = String.valueOf(one);
System.out.println(" is one == two " + (one == two));
    // returns false
System.out.println(" is one == three " + (one == three));
    // returns true
```

17.8.2   *String Buffers*

A StringBuffer is similar to the C language concept of a string as an array of character values. A string buffer, like a vector, has a buffer of positions that may be larger than the number of character values it currently holds. This makes the representation useful when a sequence of insertion operations must be performed on the same string value. The methods provided by class StringBuffer can be described as follows:

```
final class StringBuffer {
     // constructors
   public StringBuffer (int capacity) // initially null string
   public StringBuffer (String str)

       // methods that change contents, return reference to ourselves
   public StringBuffer append (boolean bool)
      ... // and all other primitive data types
   public StringBuffer insert (int offset, boolean bool)
      ... // and all other primitive data types
   public StringBuffer reverse ()
   public void setCharAt (int index, char c)

       // methods to access values
   public char charAt (int index);

       // misc methods
   public int length ()
   public void setLength (int length)
   public void ensureCapacity ()
   public String toString ()
}
```

Note that the methods append, insert, and reverse both change the current string buffer and return a reference to the updated string buffer. This is different from the transformation methods in class String, which leave the receiver string unchanged but return a new string in which the transformations have been applied.

The append operator is used internally by the Java compiler to implement the + operator. A statement such as:

```
System.out.println("answer: " + answer);
```

is compiled as if it were written:

```
System.out.println(new StringBuffer("answer: ").append(answer)
   .toString());
```

17.8.3 *String Tokenizers*

The class StringTokenizer is useful for breaking a string into a sequence of *tokens*. Tokens are defined by a set of delimiter characters. Common delimiters include spaces, tabs, and punctuation such as periods or commas. The class StringTokenizer implements the Enumeration protocol (see Section 19.2), and can therefore be manipulated in an enumeration-style loop.

The methods provided by StringTokenizer can be described as follows:

```
class StringTokenizer implements Enumeration {
    // constructors
  public StringTokenizer (String str)
  public StringTokenizer (String str, String delims)
  public StringTokenizer (String str, String delims,
      boolean returnDelims)

    // enumeration protocol
  public boolean hasMoreElements ()
  public Object nextElement ()
  public String nextToken ()

    // return number of remaining tokens
  public int countTokens ()
}
```

The enumeration protocol requires that the method nextElement() return a value of type Object. In order to avoid the consequent casting of this value to a String, the equivalent method nextToken() can be used instead. The concordance program to be described in Section 19.7.1 will illustrate the use of a string tokenizer in breaking a line into a sequence of words:

```
class Concordance {
    public void readLines (DataInputStream input) throws IOException
{
        String delims = " \t\n.,!?;:";
        for (int line = 1; true; line++ ) {
            String text = input.readLine();
            if (text == null) return;
            text = text.toLowerCase();
            Enumeration e = new StringTokenizer(text, delims);
            while (e.hasMoreElements())
                enterWord ((String) e.nextElement(), new Integer(line));
        }
    }
}
```

The class StreamTokenizer (Section 14.1.3) provides a similar facility to breaking an input stream into tokens.

17.8.4   *Parsing String Values*

A StringTokenizer provides one method for breaking a string into component parts, resulting in a sequence of string tokens. If the string tokens represent primitive data values, the programmer requires a method to change the string representation into the primitive value. This functionality is provided by the wrapper classes, Boolean, Integer, Double, Float, and Long. One form of the constructor in each of these classes takes a String as argument and parses the string to ascertain the underlying value. The original value can then be obtained from the wrapper class, as shown in the following example:

```
String dstr = "23.7";
Double dwrap = new Double(dstr); // parse the string
double dval = dwrap.doubleValue( );
```

The wrapper classes also provide the reverse; that is, a way to change a primitive value into a string. Often there are a variety of different formats available. These facilities are summarized in Table 17.1.

Most of the conversion methods will throw a NumberFormatException if the characters do not represent a value in the correct format.

Table 17.1

Class	Conversion from string	Conversion to string
Boolean	new Boolean(str)	toString( )
	Boolean.valueOf(Boolean bval)	
Double	new Double(str)	toString( )
	Double.valueOf(double dval)	
Float	new Float(str)	toString( )
	Float.valueOf(Float fval)	
Integer	new Integer(str)	toString( )
	Integer.parseInt(String str, int radix)	toBinaryString( )
	Integer.valueOf(int ival)	toOcatalString( )
		toHexString( )

17.9   CHAPTER SUMMARY

The Java run-time system provides a number of useful utility classes. In this chapter we have explored several of these. A Point represents a location in a two-dimensional space, described by a pair of integer coordinates. A Dimension has the same representation—a pair of integer values—but is used to represent a two-dimensional size (height and width). A Date represents a calendar date and time value. The class Math provides access to a number of mathematical constants and useful functions. The Toolkit provides the means for accessing fonts, and retrieving images over a network. The class System provides access to standard input and output areas.

A String in the Java language is an immutable (constant) value. The String data type provides a number of high-level operations. A related class, StringBuffer, permits changes to the individual fields in a string. The class StringTokenizer can be used to break a string into individual parts.

STUDY QUESTIONS

1. What type of values does a Point represent?

2. What type of values does a Dimension represent?

3. Both points and dimensions have the same internal representation; a pair of integer data values. What makes them different?

4. What type of values does a Date represent?

5. Write a Java expression that prints the current day of the month and hour.

6. What is the start of the epoch?

7. Why are data fields and constants in class Math declared as static?

8. How is a String different from a StringBuffer?

18 Understanding Graphics

The Java language provides one of the richest collections of graphical commands of any general purpose programming language. In this chapter we will explain some of the basic aspects of the classes associated with graphical operations in Java. Topics discussed include colors, fonts, images, and animation.

18.1 Color

The class Color is used to represent a color value. We know from optics that all colors can be formed by combinations of red, green, and blue. Color televisions use this principle, displaying colors as combinations of red, green, and blue dots. In order to represent colors in a computer more easily, each of the three amounts of red, green, and blue is represented by an integer value between 0 and 255. (There is nothing magic about the value 255; it was simply chosen so that each quantity could be stored in an eight-bit byte.) For each quantity, the larger the value, the brighter the component. A value of (0,0,0) is therefore black, while a value of (255, 255, 255) is white.[1] While in theory this encoding can represent 2^{512} different colors ($2^8 \times 2^8 \times 2^8$), in practice most display devices can handle only a limited range. When the exact color is unavailable, the actual color produced by a display device will usually be the closest matching color.

The Java library class Color allows colors to be specified using three integer values. The class also defines predefined constants for a number of commonly used colors. These are described in Table 18.1. The constructor for color takes as

---

[1] There is an alternative system that represents each color by a triple of floating-point values that represent the Hue, Saturation, and Brightness of the color. The HSB system is not used as much as the RGB system and will not be described here. The class Color provides methods for converting between the two systems.

Table 18.1   Methods for Class Color.

Predefined Colors

Color.black	Color.magenta
Color.blue	Color.orange
Color.cyan	Color.pink
Color.darkGray	Color.red
Color.gray	Color.white
Color.green	Color.yellow
Color.lightGray	

Description of Methods in Class Color

new Color (int, int, int)	constructor
brighter()	create brighter version of color
darker()	create darker version of color
getBlue()	return blue component of color
getGreen()	return green component of color
getRed()	return red component of color
toString()	return string representation of color

argument the three integer values representing the red, green, and blue components. These values can subsequently be retrieved from a color using the methods getRed, getGreen, and getBlue. The methods brighter and darker return brighter and darker versions of the current color. Finally, the method toString returns a string representation of the current color. A program that illustrates the use of many of the features of class Color is described in Section 13.5.

18.2   RECTANGLES

There are two classes in the Java library used for manipulating polygon shapes. The class Rectangle represents a rectangular area on a two-dimensional plane. The class Polygon represents more general polygon shapes.

We have used the class Rectangle already in the Cannon World program described in Chapter 6. In that program, every graphical object, each ball as well as each target, was placed on top of a rectangle that represented the location of the item. The application used the fact that a rectangle not only records a position on the two-dimensional surface but also can be easily moved to a new position and can tell whether or not it intersects with another rectangle.

A new rectangle can be created in a variety of ways. If no arguments are provided with the constructor, then an empty rectangle whose northwest corner is the origin is created. If two integers are specified, they are taken to be a width and height for a rectangle with the northwest corner at the origin. If four integer arguments are specified, the first two are the locations of the northwest corner, and the remaining arguments are the width and height.

```
Rectangle r = new Rectangle ();
Rectangle rTwo = new Rectangle (3, 4); \\ width 3, height 4
Rectangle rThree = new Rectangle (7, 6, 3, 4); \\ corner 7,6
```

Operations that test the state of a rectangle can be summarized as follows:

r.equals (rTwo)	Tell whether two rectangles are equal
r.inside (int, int)	Tell whether a point is inside the rectangle
r.intersects (rTwo)	Tell whether two rectangles intersect
r.isEmpty( )	Tell whether rectangle has nonempty extent

The size of a rectangle can be changed in a variety of ways. The add operation takes two integers that represent a point, and increases the size of the rectangle until it includes the point. The union operation does the same with another Rectangle argument, returning the smallest rectangle that encloses both. The grow operation takes two integer arguments and moves each of the horizontal sizes by the first argument amount and each of the vertical sides by the second, which can be either positive or negative. The method intersection calculates the intersection of two rectangles. The setLocation method moves a rectangle to a given location, while the translate method moves a rectangle by a given amount. The setSize method sets a rectangle size. Both the size and location of a rectangle can be changed by the function reshape, which takes four integer arguments in the same form as the constructor.

18.2.1   *Rectangle Sample Program*

A sample program, shown in Figure 18.1, illustrates the use of many Rectangle methods. Two rectangles are initially placed on the window. In each step all rectangles are either resized or moved, and a test is performed to see if any two rectangles intersect. If so, a new rectangle is generated with the same size as their intersection.

The method to move rectangles generates two random numbers. Using these, the rectangle is either changed in size or moved. Tests are performed to ensure the rectangle does not become negative in size or move off the board.

```
private void moveAllRectangles() {
    for (Enumeration e = rects.elements(); e.hasMoreElements(); ) {
        Rectangle r = (Rectangle) e.nextElement();
        int i = rand(5);
        int j = rand(5);
```

```
class RectTest extends Frame {
   public static void main (String [ ] args)
      { Frame window = new RectTest( ); window.show( ); }

   private Vector rects = new Vector( );
   private Random rnd = new Random( );
   private static int FrameWidth = 400;
   private static int FrameHeight = 400;

   public RectTest ( ) {
      setSize (400, 400);
      setTitle ("Rectangle test");
      rects.addElement (new Rectangle(4, 5));
      rects.addElement (new Rectangle(100, 100, 6, 7));
      }

   public void paint (Graphics g) {
      g.setColor(Color.green);
      for (Enumeration e = rects.elements( ); e.hasMoreElements( ); ) {
         Rectangle r = (Rectangle) e.nextElement( );
         g.fillRect (r.x, r.y, r.width, r.height);
         }
      moveAllRectangles( );
      spawnNewRectangles( );
      repaint( );
      }

   private int rand (int max) { return rnd.nextInt( ) % max; }

   private void moveAllRectangles( ) { ... }

   private void spawnNewRectangles( ) { ... }
}
```

Figure 18.1   The rectangle example program.

```
if ((i + j) % 5 == 0) {
   r.grow (i, j);
   if (r.height < 0)
      r.setSize (r.width, - r.height);
   if (r.width < 0)
      r.setSize (- r.width, r.height);
   }
else {
```

```
                r.translate (i, j);
                if (r.x < 0)
                    r.setLocation (r.x + FrameWidth, r.y);
                if (r.y < 0)
                    r.setLocation (r.x, r.y + FrameWidth);
                if (r.x > FrameWidth)
                    r.setLocation (r.x - FrameWidth, r.y);
                if (r.y > FrameWidth)
                    r.setLocation (r.x, r.y - FrameWidth);
            }
        }
    }
```

The routine to test for intersections uses a doubly nested enumeration loop. If it locates two intersecting rectangles, a new rectangle is created and placed in the upper corner. Only one new rectangle is created in each move, in order to slow the process of filling the window.

```
private void spawnNewRectangles() {
    for (Enumeration e = rects.elements(); e.hasMoreElements(); ) {
        Rectangle r1 = (Rectangle) e.nextElement();
        for (Enumeration f = rects.elements(); f.hasMoreElements(); )
            {
            Rectangle r2 = (Rectangle) f.nextElement();
            if (r1.intersects(r2) && ! r1.equals(r2)) {
                Rectangle nr = r1.intersection(r2);
                nr.setLocation (0, 0);
                rects.addElement(nr);
                return;
                }
            }
        }
    }
```

18.3   FONTS

A Font object describes the characteristics used to display printed text. Features of a font that the programmer can modify are the style, size, and font family (or logical name).

The logical font name describes the family of font styles being used. There are six recognized logical font names, Dialog, Helvetica, TimesRoman, Courier, DialogInput, and Symbol. The last is used to represent nonalphabetic symbols and is seldom used. Courier is a font with fixed-width characters, much like a typewriter. Helvetica and Times Roman are variable-width fonts, which are the type

Figure 18.2   Example text printed in different fonts.

normally used for printed text. An example of text printed in each of the first five fonts is shown in Figure 18.2.

A font style describes the thickness and slant of the characters. In the Java library there are two characteristics that describe a style. These are the Bold attribute and the Italic attribute. Each is represented by an integer value, which can be combined. Thus, there are four different representations for each font family: plain (neither bold nor italic), bold, italic, and both bold and italic.

A font point size represents the size of the individual characters. Points are units used in typesetting. One point is approximately 1/72 of an inch.

The following chart describes the most commonly used methods recognized by instances of class Font.

Font(String name, int style, int size)	Construct new font
Font.PLAIN	Constant used to describe plain fonts
Font.BOLD	Constant used to describe bold fonts
Font.ITALIC	Constant used to describe italic fonts
getName( )	Return logical name
getSize( )	Return point size
getStyle( )	Return style characteristics
isBold( )	Determine if font is bold
isItalic( )	Determine if font is italic
isPlain( )	Determine if font is plain
toString( )	Return string representation of font

An instance of class Font can be created by providing the logical font name, a style, and a size. The name *must* be one of the six names recognized family names (Dialog, Helvetica, TimesRoman, Courier, DialogInput, and Symbol). The style is formed using the class constants. A font that is both bold and italic can be created by adding the two values Font.BOLD and Font.ITALIC. The size can be any integer value, although not all sizes can be represented by all font families on any particular output device. In general, the size used in a display will be the closest available size to the one specified.

18.3.1   *Font Metrics*

A separate class, FontMetrics, is occasionally needed to get more detailed information about a font or about a string printed in a given font. For example, a font metric can be used to determine the width (in pixels) of a text that is to be printed in a particular font. Font metrics is an abstract class, and therefore you cannot directly construct instances of the class. The most common way to access a font metric object is by means of the method getFontMetrics provided by an object of type Graphics, as in the following example:

```
public void paint (Graphics g) {
    .
    .
    .
    g.setFont (aFont);
    FontMetric fm = g.getFontMetrics();
    .
    .
    .
}
```

To determine the width of an individual character or a string the methods fm.charWidth(char) or fm.stringWidth(String) can be used. The result is described in pixel units. Various other characteristics of a font are accessible using a font metric, for example fm.getHeight() will return the height (maximum character size) of the font. There are other methods. However these are rarely used.

18.3.2   *Font Example Program*

A small test program will illustrate both the use of methods in class Font and the way to program using checkboxes. The application will have a bank of six checkboxes on the bottom of the window, corresponding to the six logical font family names. Two buttons on the right (the east) will set either bold, or italic, or both, while a text edit field will allow the size to be set. An example text that illustrates the selected characteristics is then displayed in the middle of the application window. The main program is shown in Figure 18.3. The two banks of checkboxes are created by the two routines makeStyles and makeNames.

```
class FontTest extends Frame {
   static public void main (String [ ] args)
      { Frame window = new FontTest( ); window.show( ); }

   private int style = 0;
   private int size = 15;
   private String fontName = "Helvetica";

   public FontTest ( ) {
      setTitle("Font Test"); setSize(600, 150);
      add("East", makeStyles( ));
      add("South", makeNames( ));
      }

   private void display ( ) { repaint( ); }

   public void paint (Graphics g) {
      Font f = new Font(fontName, style, size);
      g.setFont(f);
      FontMetrics fm = g.getFontMetrics( );
      g.drawString(f.toString( ), 5, 10 + 2 * fm.getHeight( ));
      }

   private Panel makeStyles( ) { ... }

   private class StyleBox extends Checkbox implements ItemListener ...

   private class SizeBox extends TextField implements ActionListener ...

   private class NameBox extends Checkbox implements ItemListener ...

   private Panel makeNames( ) { ... }
}
```

Figure 18.3   The FontTest program.

The method makeStyles creates a grid layout of four horizontal panels. The first two are filled by instances of a class StyleBox that will allow a style to be set. The third is a SizeBox that will set the size of the example text. The final element is a quit button using the class ButtonAdapter defined earlier in Chapter 13.

```
private Panel makeStyles( ) {
   Panel p = new Panel( );
   p.setLayout(new GridLayout(4,1));
```

```
    p.add (new StyleBox(Font.ITALIC, "italic"));
    p.add (new StyleBox(Font.BOLD, "bold"));
    p.add (new SizeBox( ));
    p.add (new ButtonAdapter("Quit"){
       public void pressed( ){System.exit(0);}});
    return p;
    }
```

A StyleBox uses a technique we have seen earlier in Chapter 13. The class both extends the library class Checkbox and implements the class ItemListener. Thus, the class can encapsulate within itself both the creation of a Checkbox item and the task of listening when the Checkbox has been selected. When each box is selected it either turns on or off the given modifier bits, depending upon the state of the box. Notice that when checkboxes are created in this fashion, they are independent of each other, and can be set or unset individually. (For example, both the bold and italic checkbox can be set, in order to display bold italic output.)

```
private class StyleBox extends Checkbox implements ItemListener {
   private int modifiers;

   public StyleBox (int m, String name)
      { super (name);
      addItemListener (this); modifiers = m; }

   public void itemStateChanged (ItemEvent e) {
      if (getState( ))
         style |= modifiers; // turn on modifiers
      else
         style &= ~ modifiers; // turn off modifiers
      display( );
      }
}
```

A SizeBox is a type of TextField, that when edited changes the size value in the application class.

```
private class SizeBox extends TextField implements ActionListener {
   public SizeBox () { super ("" + size); addActionListener(this); }

   public void actionPerformed (ActionEvent e) {
      String sz = getText( );
      size = (new Integer(sz)).intValue( );
      display( );
      }
   }
```

The method makeNames( ) illustrates the creation of a different type of checkbox. In this form, only one of the collection can be set at any one time. Setting one item will automatically unset all others. Such a group is sometimes referred to as *radio buttons*, as they operate in a fashion similar to the buttons on a car radio. To create a radio button collection, a CheckBoxGroup is created. This checkbox group is then passed with the constructor to each checkbox that will be part of the group.

```
private class NameBox extends Checkbox implements ItemListener {
    public NameBox (String name, CheckboxGroup cg)
        { super(name, cg, false); addItemListener(this); }

    public void itemStateChanged (ItemEvent e)
        { fontName = getLabel( ); display( ); }
    }

private Panel makeNames( ) {
    Panel p = new Panel( );
    p.setLayout(new GridLayout(1,6));
    CheckboxGroup cg = new CheckboxGroup( );
    p.add (new NameBox("Courier", cg));
    p.add (new NameBox("Dialog", cg));
    p.add (new NameBox("DialogInput", cg));
    p.add (new NameBox("Helvetica", cg));
    p.add (new NameBox("TimesRoman", cg));
    p.add (new NameBox("Symbol", cg));
    return p;
    }
```

When any button is pressed, the fontName field will be changed, and the display method activated.

18.4   IMAGES

An image is really nothing more than a two-dimensional collection of pixel values. Most commonly images are created by some video device, such as a digital camera, and stored in a file in a standard format, such as JPEG or GIF. A picture stored in such a format can be read into a Java program by first creating a URL (see Section 21.4.1), then using the toolbox routine getImage. The following program illustrates this technique. The first command-line argument is assumed to be a URL for a file stored in one of the standard formats. This image is read from the file and displayed as the value of the application window.

```
import java.awt.*;
import java.net.*;

class ImageTest extends Frame {
    public static void main (String [ ] args) {
        Frame world = new ImageTest (args[0]);
        world.show( );
        }

    private Image image = null;

    public ImageTest (String fileName) {
        setSize (300, 300);
        setTitle ("Image Test");
        try { // read image from URL given in argument
            URL imageAddress = new URL (fileName);
            image = getToolkit( ).getImage(imageAddress);
            } catch (Exception e) { image = null; }
        }

    public void paint (Graphics g) {
        if (image != null)
            g.drawImage (image, 0, 0, this);
        }
    }
```

18.4.1   *Animation*

Animation is simply the process of displaying a sequence of still pictures one after another. Just as with a movie, the eye is fooled into linking the pictures together, giving the appearance of smooth motion. The simplest animation program is shown below. Here a series of GIF files is read into an array of images. The paint routine selects one of these for display, then updates an index value so that the next image in sequence will be selected by the following display. Calling repaint ensures that the next image will then be displayed.

```
class AnimationTest extends Frame {

    public static void main (String [ ] args) {
        Frame world = new AnimationTest ( );
        world.show( );
        }

    private Image [ ] imageArray;
```

```
    private int index = 0;

    public AnimationTest () {
        setSize(300, 300);
        setTitle("Simple Animation");
        imageArray = new Image [ 17 ];
        for (int i = 0; i < 17; i++) {
            String name = "T" + (i+1) + ".gif";
            try {
                URL address = new URL (name);
                imageArray[i] = getToolkit().getImage(address);
            } catch (Exception e) { imageArray[i] = null; }
        }
    }

    public void paint (Graphics g) {
        if (imageArray[index] != null)
            g.drawImage(imageArray[index++], 0, 0, this);
        if (index >= imageArray.length)
            index = 0;
        try {
            Thread.sleep(200);
        } catch (Exception e) { }
        repaint();
    }
}
```

In order to slow down the animation, the paint routine will sleep for 200 milliseconds after drawing the image. On some platforms the animation will show an annoying flicker. This is because the procedure update, called by repaint, will redraw the screen in the background color before calling paint. This can sometimes be eliminated by simply overriding the method update to avoid redrawing the background:

```
    // override update to simply paint window
public void update (Graphics g) {
    paint(g);
}
```

18.5   GRAPHICS CONTEXTS

As we have seen in almost all of our example programs, the majority of graphics in Java are generated using an object of class Graphics. Such an object is termed the *graphics context*. As we noted in Chapter 6, graphics contexts maintain a

Table 18.2 Operations Provided by Graphics Context.

clearRect	Clear a rectangular region
copyArea	Copy a rectangular region to another location
draw3DRect	Paint a three-dimensional rectangle
drawArc	Draw elliptical arc
drawBytes	Display bytes as text
drawChars	Display characters as text
drawImage	Display pixel image
drawLine	Draw a line from one point to another
drawOval	Draw oval outline
drawPolygon	Draw polygon outline
drawRect	Draw rectangle
drawRoundRect	Draw rounded rectangle
drawString	Draw string at given location
fillArc	Paint a filled elliptical arc
fillOval	Paint a filled oval shape
fillRect	Paint a filled rectangular area
fillRoundRect	Paint a filled rounded rectangular area
getColor	Retrieve the current foreground color
getFont	Retrieve the font used to print text
getFontMetrics	Retrieve font metrics object for current font
setColor	Set the current foreground color
setFont	Set the font for future printing operations
setPaintMode	Set drawing to paint mode
setXORMode	Set drawing to XOR mode

coordinate system in which the 0,0 location is the upper left corner, and values increase as they move down and to the right. Graphics contexts also maintain both a foreground and a background color, in a fashion we have already seen used with windows. Table 18.2 summarizes the most commonly used method provided by class Graphics. We have used many of these in our earlier case studies.

Drawing operations in graphics contexts can be performed in one of two different *modes*. The common mode is *paint* mode, established by calling the method setPaintMode. An alternative is XOR mode. The unique property of XOR mode is that if the same object is drawn twice, the second drawing command *erases* the object, restoring the image to the state it has prior to the first command. This property is similar to the logical exclusive-or (XOR) command, hence the name. The common use for this property is to draw cursors, or other graphics images that track the position of the mouse as it moves across a window. We will see an example of this in the program described in the next section.

18.6   A Simple Painting Program

An example program will illustrate the use of many of the graphics context commands. The program will also show how one can create a static image that can be generated as a sequence of graphical commands, rather than all at one time.

The window for the application (Figure 18.4) has a row of buttons across the top. Pressing one of these buttons selects the type of figure to be drawn. Pressing the mouse in the canvas window then begins a drawing operation. As the mouse moves while still being pressed, a "ghost" image of the figure tracks the mouse location. When the mouse is released, the selected figure is drawn.

The source code for the painting application is shown in Figure 18.5. A Panel is used to hold the three buttons. The buttons themselves are defined as subclasses of an inner class Shape, which will do double duty as both a button listener class, and a recording of the currently selected shape. When pressed, the button will simply save its value in the variable currentShape. In addition to

Figure 18.4 Window for painting application.

```
class Paint extends Frame {
   public static void main (String [ ] args)
      { Frame world = new Paint( ); world.show( ); }

   private Image image = null;
   private Shape currentShape = null;

   public Paint ( ) {
      setTitle("Paint");
      setSize(400, 300);

         // create panel of buttons
      Panel p = new Panel( );
      p.setLayout(new GridLayout(1,3));
      p.add(new Rectangle( ));
      p.add(new Oval( ));
      p.add(new Line( ));
      add("North", p);
         // add mouse event listener
      MouseKeeper k = new MouseKeeper( );
      addMouseListener(k);
      addMouseMotionListener(k);
      }

   public void paint (Graphics g) {
      if (image == null) // will happen only once
         image = createImage(400, 300);
      if (image != null)
         g.drawImage(image, 0, 0, this);
      }

   private abstract class Shape
      extends Button implements ActionListener { ... }
   private class Rectangle extends Shape { ... }
   private class Oval extends Shape { ... }
   private class Line extends Shape { ... }

   private class MouseKeeper
      extends MouseAdapter implements MouseMotionListener { ... }
}
```

Figure 18.5   Source for painting application.

representing a button, each shape will know how to draw itself in a rectangular region (Figure 18.6). The class Shape, as well as the drawing method, have been declared abstract. This means that it is not possible to create an instance of the class without first subclassing. Furthermore, each subclass *must* implement the method draw.

The first time the application is asked to draw its window, it copies the Image associated with the application component into a variable named image. Thereafter, to render the application window it is only necessary to draw the contents of this image.

Most applications that interact with the mouse need to recognize the mouse moving down. Of these, a few (such as the current application) need to differentiate between the mouse going down and the mouse going up. Fewer still need also to track the position of the mouse as it is moving. Because the latter action is relatively infrequent, the Java event library separates this task into a different listener. A MouseListener tracks only mouse presses and releases. A MouseMotionListener also tracks mouse movements, either while pressed or not. The mouse class we created for this class implements both interfaces, by extending the MouseAdapter, and implementing the MouseMotionListener interface (Figure 18.7, on page 298).

When the mouse is first pressed, the location of the mouse press is saved in a pair of local integer variables. A second pair of integer variables records the new location and is initially the same as the source location. As the mouse moves, the method mouseDragged is repeatedly executed. This method sets the graphical display mode to XOR, then repaints the current shape using the old coordinate locations. The effect will be the *erase* of the previous image. The end point locations are then set to the current mouse position and the shape redrawn. The effect is that the shape is continually erased and redrawn as the mouse is moved. When the mouse is finally released, the method mouseReleased is executed. This erases the old image one last time, changes the mode to paint, and draws the shape in its final location.

18.7   CHAPTER SUMMARY

A Java run-time library provides a rich collection of classes that can be used to manipulate graphical images. In this chapter we have investigated several of these. A Color represents a color value. Colors are specified by a trio of integer values, representing the amount of red, green and blue in the color. A Rectangle represents a rectangular region of the plane. A Font describes the characteristics of a printed letter. An Image is a picture composed of pixel values. A succession of images can be displayed one after the other in an animation. A Graphics object provides the tools necessary to perform simple graphical operations, such as drawing a line or oval.

```
private abstract class Shape
     extends Button implements ActionListener {

   public Shape (String name) {
      super(name);
      addActionListener (this);
      }

   public abstract void draw (Graphics g, int a, int b, int c, int d);

   public void actionPerformed (ActionEvent e)
      { currentShape = this; }
}

private class Rectangle extends Shape {

   public Rectangle () { super("Rectangle"); }

   public void draw (Graphics g, int a, int b, int c, int d) {
      int w = c - a; // width
      int h = d - b; // height
      g.drawRect(a, b, w, h);
      }
}

private class Oval extends Shape {
   public Oval () { super("Oval"); }

   public void draw (Graphics g, int a, int b, int c, int d) {
      int w = c - a; int h = d - b;
      g.drawOval(a, b, w, h);
      }
}

private class Line extends Shape {
   public Line () { super("Line"); }

   public void draw (Graphics g, int a, int b, int c, int d)
      { g.drawLine(a, b, c, d); }
}
```

Figure 18.6   Shape subclasses.

```
private class MouseKeeper
        extends MouseAdapter implements MouseMotionListener {
    private int startx, starty; // upper right corner
    private int lastx, lasty; // current position

    public void mousePressed (MouseEvent e) {
        lastx = startx = e.getX( );
        lasty = starty = e.getY( );
        }

    private void drawShape (Graphics g) {
        if (currentShape != null)
            currentShape.draw(g, startx, starty, lastx, lasty);
        }

    public void mouseDragged (MouseEvent e) {
        Graphics g = image.getGraphics( );
        g.setXORMode(Color.white);
            // erase old image
        drawShape(g);
            // draw new rectangle
        lastx = e.getX( ); lasty = e.getY( );
        drawShape(g); repaint( );
    }

    public void mouseReleased (MouseEvent e) {
        Graphics g = image.getGraphics( );
            // erase old image
        g.setXORMode(Color.white);
        drawShape(g);
            // now paint new image
        g.setPaintMode( );
        lastx = e.getX( ); lasty = e.getY( );
        drawShape(g); repaint( );
    }

    public void mouseMoved (MouseEvent e) { }
}
```

Figure 18.7 The mouse listener for the painting application.

Study Questions

1. What do the three integer values in a color represent?

2. What are the predefined colors available to the Java run-time system?

3. How does one tell whether or not a point is found inside a rectangle?

4. What are the style modifiers used with a value of type Font?

5. What is an animation? How can an animation be produced in Java?

6. How is a MouseMotionListener different from a MouseActionListener?

Exercises

1. Add buttons to the painting program described in Section 18.6 to create filled rectangles and ovals, as well as the outline rectangles and ovals it currently produces.

2. Add a panel with three sliders for selecting colors, similar to the panel described in Chapter 13. Use the colors selected by these sliders for the fill color in the figures you added in the previous question.

3. By adding a KeyListener object, add the ability to enter text and have it displayed at the current mouse location.

4. Add menu items to change the font and style of text values.

19 Collection Classes

Collections are classes designed for holding groups of objects. Almost all non-trivial programs need to maintain one or more collections of objects. Although the Java library provides only a few different forms of collection, the features provided by these classes are very general, making them applicable to a wide variety of problems. In this chapter we will first describe some of the basic concepts common to the collection classes, then summarize the basic collections provided by Java, and finally describe a few container types that are not provided by the standard library, but which can be easily constructed by the programmer.

19.1 ELEMENT TYPES AND PRIMITIVE VALUE WRAPPERS

With the exception of the array data type, all the collections provided by the Java library maintain their values in variables of type Object. There are two important consequences of this feature:

- Since primitive types, such as integers, Booleans, characters, and floating-point values, are not subclasses of Object, they cannot be directly stored in these collections.

- When values are removed from the collection, they must be cast back to their original type.

One way to circumvent the first restriction is through the use of *wrapper classes*. A wrapper class maintains a primitive data value but is itself an object and can thus be stored in a container. Methods are typically provided both to construct an instance of the wrapper class from a primitive value, and to recover the original value from the wrapper. The following, for example, stores two integers into instances of class Integer, then recovers the original values so that an arithmetic operation can be performed:

```
Integer a = new Integer(12);
Integer b = new Integer(3);
    // must recover the int values to do arithmetic
int c = a.intValue( ) * b.intValue( );
```

In addition, many wrapper classes provide other useful functionality, such as the ability to parse string values. A common way to convert a string containing an integer value literal into an int, for example, is to use an Integer as a middle step:

```
String text = "123"; // example string value
Integer val = new Integer(text); // first convert to Integer
int ival = val.intValue( ); // then convert Integer to int
```

Table 19.1 summarizes the most common wrapper classes and a few of their more useful behaviors.

Table 19.1   Wrapper Classes and Selected Behaviors.

Integer Wrapper	
new Integer(int value)	Build Integer from int
Integer(String value)	Parse integer in String
intValue( )	Value of Integer as int
toString( )	Return decimal string representation of Integer
toBinaryString( )	Return binary representation
toOctalString( )	Return octal representation
toHexString( )	Return hex representation
Character Wrapper	
new Character(char value)	Convert char to Character
charValue( )	Return char value of Character
isLetter( )	Determine if character is letter
isDigit( )	True if character is digit
Boolean Wrapper	
new Boolean (boolean value)	Convert boolean to Boolean
booleanValue ( )	Retrieve boolean value from Boolean
toString( )	Generate string representation of boolean
Double Wrapper	
new Double(double)	Convert double to Double
new Double(String)	Construct Double from string
doubleValue( )	Return double value of Double

19.2 ENUMERATORS

All collections can be envisioned as a linear sequence of elements. However, the particular means used to access each element differs from one collection type to another. For example, a vector is indexed using an integer position key, whereas a hash table can use any type of object as a key. It is frequently desirable to abstract away these differences and access the elements of the collection in sequence without regard to the technique used to obtain the underlying values. This facility is provided by the Enumeration interface and its various implementations. The Enumeration interface specifies two methods:

hasMoreElements()   A Boolean value that indicates whether

or not there are any more elements to be enumerated

nextElement()   Retrieves the next element in the enumeration

These two operations are used together to form a loop. The following code, for example, shows how all the elements of a hash table could be printed:

```
for (Enumeration e = htab.elements(); e.hasMoreElements(); ) {
    System.out.println (e.nextElement());
    }
```

The methods hasMoreElements() and nextElement should always be invoked in tandem. That is, nextElement should never be invoked unless hasMoreElements has first determined that there is another element, and nextElement should never be invoked twice without an intervening call on hasMoreElements. If it is necessary to refer more than once to the value returned by nextElement, the result of the nextElement call should be assigned to a local variable:

```
for (Enumeration e = htab.elements(); e.hasMoreElements(); ) {
    Object value = e.nextElement();
    if (value.equals(Test))
        System.out.println ("found object " + value);
    }
```

With the exception of the array, all the collections provided by the Java library provide a function that generates an enumeration. In addition, several other classes that are not necessarily collections also support the enumeration protocol. For example, a StringTokenizer is used to extract words from a string value. The individual words are then accessed using enumeration methods. Section 19.6.1 describes how the programmer can create a new type of enumeration.

19.3   THE ARRAY

The most basic collection form in Java is the array. As noted in earlier chapters, the creation and manipulation of an array value is different in Java than in many other programming languages. The Java language makes a separation between (a) declaring a variable of array type, (b) defining the size of the array and allocating space, and (c) assigning values to the array. In many other languages the first and second tasks are merged. Combining these concepts makes it difficult to, for example, write functions that will operate on arrays of any size. These problems are largely eliminated in Java's approach to arrays.

An array variable is declared by indicating the type of elements the array will contain, and a pair of square brackets that indicate an array is being formed. The following, for example, is from the Solitaire game case study examined in Chapter 9.

```
static public CardPile allPiles [ ];
```

The brackets can be written either after the variable name, or after the type. The following, for example, is an equivalent declaration:

```
static public CardPile [ ] allPiles;
```

Note that the array is the only collection in the Java library that requires the programmer to specify the type of elements that will be held by the container. An important consequence of this is that the array is the *only* collection that can maintain nonobject types, such as integers, Booleans, or characters. Other containers hold their values as instances of class Object, and can therefore only hold primitive values if they are surrounded by wrapper classes (Integer, Double, and so on).

An array *value* is created, as are all values, using the new operator. It is only when the array value is created that the size of the array is specified.

```
allPiles = new CardPile [ 13 ]; // create array of 13 card piles
```

Arrays can also be created as an initialization expression in the original declaration. The initialization expression provides the values for the array, as well as indicating the number of elements.

```
int primes [ ] = {2, 3, 5, 7. 11, 13, 17, 19};
```

Elements of an array are accessed using the subscript operator. This is used both to retrieve the current value held at a given position and to assign a position a new value:

```
primes[3] = primes[2] + 2;
```

Legal index values range from zero to one less than the number of elements held by the array. An attempt to access a value with an out-of-range index value results in an IndexOutOfBoundsException being thrown.

The integer field length describes the number of elements held by an array. The following loop shows this value being used to form a loop to print the elements in an array:

```
for (int i = 0; i < primes.length; i++)
    System.out.println("prime " + i + " is " + primes[i]);
```

Arrays are also *cloneable* (see Section 11.3.1). An array can be copied and assigned to another array value. The clone operation creates a shallow copy.

```
int numbers [ ];
numbers = primes.clone( ); // creates a new array of numbers
```

19.4 THE Vector COLLECTION

The Vector data abstraction is similar to an array of objects. However, it provides a number of high-level operations not supported by the array abstraction. Most importantly, a vector is *expandable*, meaning it grows as necessary as new elements are added to the collection. Thus, the programmer need not know the eventual collection size at the time the vector is created. To use this collection the Vector class must be imported from java.util.Vector. A new vector is created using the new operator.

```
import java.util.Vector;
  .
  .
  .
Vector numbers = new Vector ( );
```

Because objects held by a Vector must be subclasses of Object, a vector can not be used to hold primitive values, such as integers or floats. However, wrapper classes can be used to convert such values into objects.

Table 19.2 summarizes the most useful operations provided by the Vector data abstraction. The class has been carefully designed so that it can be used in a variety of different ways. The following sections describe some of the more common uses.

19.4.1 *Using a* Vector *as an Array*

Unlike an array, a vector is not created with a fixed size. A vector can be given a specific size either by adding the appropriate number of elements (using the

Table 19.2   Operations Provided by the Vector Data Type.

Size Determination	
size( )	Returns number of elements in collection
isEmpty( )	Returns true if collection is empty
capacity( )	Return current capacity of vector
setSize( )	Set size of vector, truncating or expanding as necessary
Element Access	
contains( )	Determines whether a value is in this vector
firstElement( )	Returns first element of collection
lastElement( )	Returns last element of collection
elementAt(index)	Returns element stored at given position
Insertion and Modification	
addElement(value)	Add new value to end of collection
setElementAt(value, index)	Change value at position
insertElementAt(value, index)	Insert value at given index
Removal	
removeElementAt(index)	Remove element at index, reducing size of vector
removeElement(value)	Remove all instances of value
removeAllElements( )	Delete all values from vector
Search	
indexOf(value)	Return index of first occurrence
lastIndexOf(value)	Return index of last occurrence
Miscellaneous	
clone( )	Return shallow copy of vector
toString( )	Return string representation of vector

addElement operation) or by using setSize. In the latter case a null value will be stored in any index locations that have not previously been assigned a value.

```
Vector aVec = new Vector ( ); // create a new vector
aVec.setSize (20); // allocate 20 locations, initially undefined
```

Once sized, the value stored at any position can be accessed using the method elementAt, while positions can be modified using setElementAt. Note that in the latter, the index of the position being modified is the second parameter, while the value to be assigned to the location is the first parameter. The following illustrates how these functions could be used to swap the first and final elements of a vector:

```
Object first = aVec.elementAt(0); // store first position
aVec.setElementAt(aVec.lastElement(), 0); // store last in location 0
aVec.setElementAt(first, aVec.size()-1); // store first at end
```

19.4.2 *Using a* Vector *as a Stack*

A *stack* is a data structure that allows elements to be inserted and removed at one end, and it always removes the last element inserted. A stack of papers on a desk is a good intuitive picture of the stack abstraction.

Although the Java standard library includes a Stack data abstraction (see Section 19.5), it is easy to see how a Vector can be used as a stack. The characteristic operations of a stack are to insert or remove an item from the top of the stack, peek at (but do not remove) the topmost element, or/and test the stack for emptiness. The following shows how each of these can be performed using operations provided by the vector class:

aVec.addElement (value)	Push a value on the stack
aVec.lastElement( )	Peek at the topmost element of the stack
aVec.removeElementAt(aVec.size( ) - 1)	Remove the topmost element of the stack

As will be noted in Section 19.5, the Stack abstraction is slightly more robust, since it will throw more meaningful error indications if an attempt is made to remove an element from an empty stack.

19.4.3 *Using a* Vector *as a Queue*

A *queue* is a data structure that allows elements to be inserted at one end, and removed from the other. In this fashion, the element removed will be the *first* element that was inserted. Thinking about a line of people waiting to enter a theater provides a good intuition.

In a manner analogous to the way that the vector can be used as a stack, the vector operations can also be used to simulate a queue:

aVec.addElement (value)	Push a value on the queue
aVec.firstElement( )	Peek at the first element in the queue
aVec.removeElementAt(0)	Remove the first element of the queue

There is one important difference between this abstraction and the earlier simulation of the stack. In the stack abstraction, all the operations could be performed in constant time, independent of the number of elements being held by the stack.[1] Removing the first element from the queue, on the other hand, *always* results in all elements being moved and therefore always requires time proportional to the number of elements in the collection.

19.4.4 *Using a* Vector *as a Set*

A *set* is usually envisioned as an unordered collection of values. Characteristic operations on a set include testing to see if a value is being held in the set, and adding or removing values from the set. The following shows how these can be implemented using the operations provided by the Vector class:

aVec.contains(value)	See if value is held in set
aVec.addElement(value)	Add new element to set
aVec.removeElement(value)	Remove element from set

The equals method is used to perform comparisons. Comparisons are necessary to determine whether or not a value is held in the collection and whether a value is the element the user wishes to delete. For user-defined data values the equals method can be overridden to provide whatever meaning is appropriate (see Section 11.4).

Operations such as union and intersection of sets can be easily implemented using a loop. The following code, for example, places in setThree the union of the values from setOne and setTwo.

```
Vector setThree = new Vector( );
setThree = setOne.clone( ); // first copy all of set one
    // then add elements from set two not already in set one
for (Enumeration e = setTwo.elements( ); e.hasMoreElements( ); ) {
    Object value = e.nextElement( );
    if (! setThree.contains(value))
        setThree.addElement(value);
    }
```

For sets consisting of positive integer values, the BitSet class (Section 19.6) is often a more efficient alternative.

---

[1] The assertion concerning constant time operation of stack operations is true with one small caveat. An insertion can, in rare occasions, result in a reallocation of the underlying vector buffer and thus require time proportional to the number of elements in the vector. This is usually, however, a rare occurrence.

19.4.5 *Using a* Vector *as a List*

Characteristic operations of a *list* data abstraction give the abilities to insert or remove elements at any location and the ability to find the location of any value.[2]

aVec.firstElement( )	First element
aVec.lastElement( )	Last element
aVec.insertElementAt(value, 0)	Insert to front of list
aVec.addElement(value)	Insert to end of list
aVec.contains(value)	See if value is in collection
aVec.removeElementAt(0)	Remove first element
aVec.removeElementAt(aVec.size( ) - 1)	Remove last element
aVec.indexOf(value)	Find location of element
aVec.removeElementAt(index)	Remove value from middle

Again, this use of the Vector abstraction to simulate a list differs from the classical description of the *list* abstraction in the algorithmic execution time of certain operations. In particular, the insertion or removal from the front of the collection may result in the entire set of values being moved, thereby requiring time proportional to the size of the collection. This is a critical concern only when the size of the collections is large or when this is a frequent operation. A more direct implementation of a list is described in Section 19.9.

19.5 THE STACK COLLECTION

Section 19.4.2 described how a stack could be simulated using a Vector. However, the Java standard library also provides the Stack as a data value. The names of the methods used to operate on this data type are slightly different from the Vector operations described in Section 19.4.2, and the structure is slightly more robust. Stack operations can be described as follows:

Stack aStack = new Stack( )	Create a new stack
aStack.push (value)	Push a value onto the stack
aStack.peek( )	Peek at the topmost element of the stack
aStack.pop( )	Remove the topmost element of the stack
aStack.size( )	Number of elements in the collection

---

[2] The list referred to here is the traditional data abstraction known by that name. The Java library unfortunately uses the class name List to refer to a graphical component that allows the user to select a value from a series of string items.

aStack.empty( )	Test for empty stack
aStack.search(value)	Position of element in stack

The pop operation both removes and returns the topmost element of the stack. Both the pop and the peek operations will throw an EmptyStackException if they are applied to an empty stack.

The search method returns the index of the given element starting from the top of the stack; that is, if the element is found at the top of the stack search will return 0, if found one element down in the stack search will return 1, and so on. Because the Stack data structure is built using inheritance from the Vector class it is also possible to access the values of the stack using their index. However, the positions returned by the search operation do not correspond to the index position. To discover the index position of a value the Vector operation indexOf can be used.

In Chapter 10 we described some of the advantages and disadvantages of creating the stack using inheritance from class Vector.

19.6   THE BitSet COLLECTION

A BitSet is abstractly a set of positive integer values. The BitSet class differs from the other collection classes in that it can only be used to hold integer values. Like an array or a Vector, each element is given an index position. However, the only operations that can be performed on each element are to set, test, or clear the value. A BitSet is a compact way to encode either a collection of positive integer values or a collection of Boolean values (for example, on/off settings).

To create a BitSet the user can specify the number of positions the set will represent. However, like the Vector, the bit set is extensible and will be enlarged automatically if a position outside the range is accessed.

```
// create a BitSet that initially contains 75 elements
BitSet bset = new BitSet(75);
```

The following list summarizes the operations used to set or test an individual position in the bit set:

bset.set (index)	Set a bit position
bset.get (index)	Test a bit position
bset.clear (index)	Clear a bit position

The get method returns a boolean value, which is true if the given bit is set, and false otherwise. Each of these operations will throw an IndexOutOfBoundsException if the index value is smaller than zero.

A BitSet can be combined with another BitSet in a variety of ways:

bset.or(setTwo)	Form bitwise union with argument set
bset.and(setTwo)	Form bitwise intersection with argument set
bset.xor(setTwo)	Form bitwise symmetric difference with argument set

The method toString returns the string representation of the collection. This consists of a comma-separated list of the indices of the bits in the collection that have been set.

19.6.1 *Example Program: Prime Sieve*

A program that will generate a list of prime numbers using the sieve of Eratosthenes can be used to illustrate the manipulation of a bit set. The constructor for the class Sieve (Figure 19.1) takes an integer argument *n*, and creates a bit set of *n* positions. These are initially all set to 1, using the member function set. The sieve algorithm then walks through the list, using get to find the next set value. A loop then walks through the remainder of the collection, throwing out (via the clear( ) member function) values that are multiples of the earlier value. When we are finished, any value not crossed out must be prime.

The remaining two functions illustrate how a new enumeration can be created. The value index will maintain the current "position" in the list, which will change as values are enumerated. The function hasMoreElements loops until a prime value is found, or until the size of the bit set is exceeded. The first results in a true value, the latter a false one. The method nextElement simply makes an object out of the integer value. A small test method is also included in the class, to illustrate how this class could be used.

19.7 THE Dictionary INTERFACE AND THE Hashtable COLLECTION

A *dictionary* is an indexed collection, similar to an array or a Vector. However, unlike array values, the index values need not be integer. Instead, any object type can be used as an index (called a *key*), and any object value can be stored as the element selected by the key. To place a new value into the collection, the user provides both the key and value. To access an element in the collection, the user provides a key, and the associated value is returned.

In the Java library the class Dictionary is an abstract class that defines the behavior of the *dictionary* abstraction but does not provide an implementation. This interface can be described as follows:

dict.get(key)	Retrieve value associated with given key
dict.put(key, value)	Place value into collection with given key
dict.remove(key)	Remove value from collection

```java
import java.util.*;

class Sieve implements Enumeration {
   private BitSet primes;
   private int index = 2;

   public Sieve (int n) {
      primes = new BitSet(n);
         // first set all the bits
      for (int i = 1;  i < n;  i++)
         primes.set(i);
         // then erase all the nonprimes
      for (int i = 2;  i * i < n;  i++)
         if (primes.get(i))
            for (int j = i + i;  j <= n;  j += i)
               primes.clear(j);
      }

   public boolean hasMoreElements () {
      index++;
      int n = primes.size( );
      while (! primes.get(index))
         if (++index > n)
            return false;
      return true;
      }

   public Object nextElement( ) { return new Integer(index); }

      // test program for prime sieve algorithm
   public static void main (String [ ] args) {
      Sieve p = new Sieve(100);
      while (p.hasMoreElements( ))
         System.out.println(p.nextElement( ));
      }
}
```

Figure 19.1   Prime Sieve program.

dict.isEmpty( )	See if collection is empty
dict.size( )	Return number of elements in collection
dict.elements( )	Return enumeration for collection values
dict.keys( )	Return enumeration of collection keys

The get method will return null if the given value is not found in the collection. Otherwise, the value is returned as an Object, which must then be cast into the appropriate type. The remove method returns the value of the association being deleted, again returning null if the key is not a legal index element. There are two enumeration generating methods, one to return an enumeration of keys and one to return an enumeration of values.

The class Hashtable provides an implementation of the Dictionary operations. A hash table can be envisioned as an array of collections called *buckets*. To add an element to the collection, an integer value, called the *hash value*, is first computed for the given key. The method hashCode is used for this purpose. This method is defined in class Object and is therefore common to all object values. It is overridden in various classes to provide alternative algorithms. Using this integer, one of the buckets is selected and the key/value pair inserted into the corresponding collection.

In addition to the methods matching the Dictionary specification, the hash table provides the method clear( ), which removes all values from the container, contains(value), which determines whether an element is contained in the collection, and containsKey(key), which tests to see if a given key is in the collection.

The default implementation of the hashCode method, in class Object, should be applicable in almost all situations, just as the default implementation of equals is usually adequate. If a data type that is going to be used as a hash table key overrides the equals method, it is a good idea to override hashCode as well, so that two objects that test equal to each other will also have the same hash value.

19.7.1   *Example Program: A Concordance*

A concordance is a listing of words from a printed text, each word being followed by the lines on which the word appears. A class that will create a concordance will illustrate how the Dictionary data type is used, as well as how different collection classes can be combined with each other.

In the program shown in Figure 19.2, the primary data structure is a dictionary, implemented using the Hashtable class. The keys for this dictionary will be the individual words in the input text. The value associated with each key will be a set of integer values, representing the line numbers on which the word appears. A Vector will be used to represent the set, using the techniques described in Section 19.4.4.

```
import java.util.*;
import java.io.*;

class Concordance {
    private Dictionary dict = new Hashtable( );

    public void readLines (DataInputStream input) throws IOException {
        String delims = " \t\n.,!?;:";
        for (int line = 1; true; line++ ) {
            String text = input.readLine( );
            if (text == null) return;
            text = text.toLowerCase( );
            Enumeration e = new StringTokenizer(text, delims);
            while (e.hasMoreElements( ))
                enterWord ((String) e.nextElement( ), new Integer(line));
        }
    }

    public void generateOutput (PrintStream output) {
        Enumeration e = dict.keys( );
        while (e.hasMoreElements( ) ) {
            String word = (String) e.nextElement( );
            Vector set = (Vector) dict.get(word);
            output.print (word + ": ");
            Enumeration f = set.elements( );
            while (f.hasMoreElements( ))
                output.print (f.nextElement( ) + " ");
            output.println (" ");
        }
    }

    private void enterWord (String word, Integer line) {
        Vector set = (Vector) dict.get(word);
        if (set == null) { // word not in collection
            set = new Vector( ); // make new set
            dict.put (word, set);
        }
        if (! set.contains(line)) set.addElement(line);
    }
}
```

Figure 19.2   The class Concordance.

The method readLines reads the input line by line, maintaining a counter to indicate the line number. The method readLine, provided by the class DataInput-Stream, returns a null value when end of input is encountered, at which time the method returns. (This method is also the potential source for the IOException, which can be thrown if an error occurs during the read operation. In our program we simply pass this exception back to the caller). Otherwise, the text is converted to lowercase, using the method toLowerCase provided by the String class; then a StringTokenizer is created to split the text into individual words. A StringTokenizer is a form of Enumeration, and so an enumeration loop is used to enter each word into the concordance.

The private method enterWord is used to place each new word in the concordance. First, the value associated with the key (the word) is determined. Here the program handles the first of two exceptional conditions that might arise. If this is the first time the word has been seen, there will be no entry in the dictionary, and so the result of calling get will be a null value. In this case a new and empty Vector is created and is inserted into the dictionary using the word as key. Using the Vector in the fashion of a set, the method contains is invoked to determine if the line has already been placed in the collection. (This is the second exceptional condition, which will occur if the same word appears two or more times on one line.) If not, the line is then added to the list.

Finally, once all the input has been processed, the method generateOutput is used to create the printed report. This method uses a doubly nested enumeration loop. The first loop enumerates the keys of the Dictionary, generated by the keys method. The value associated with each key is a set, represented by a Vector. A second loop, using the enumerator produced by the elements method, then prints the values held by the vector.

An easy way to test the program is to use the system resources System.in and System.out as the input and output containers, as in the following:

```
static public void main (String [ ] args) {
    Concordance c = new Concordance( );
    try {
       c.readLines(new DataInputStream(System.in));
    } catch (IOException e) { return; }
    c.generateOutput (System.out);
}
```

19.7.2   *Properties*

The Java run-time system maintains a special type of hash table, termed the *properties list*. The class Properties, a subclass of Hashtable, holds a collection of string key/value pairs. These represent values that describe the current executing environment, such as the user name, operating system name, home directory, and so on. The following program can be used to see the range of properties available to a running Java program:

```
public static void main (String [ ] args) {
    Dictionary props = System.getProperties( );
    Enumeration e = props.keys( );
    while (e.hasMoreElements( )) {
        Object key = e.nextElement( );
        Object value = props.get(key);
        System.out.println("property " + key + " value " + value);
        }
    }
```

19.8   WHY ARE THERE NO ORDERED COLLECTIONS?

If one considers the "classic" data abstractions found in most data structures textbooks, a notable omission from the Java library are data structures that maintain values in sequence. Examples of such abstractions are ordered lists, ordered vectors, or binary trees. Indeed, there is not even any mechanism provided in the Java library to sort a vector of values. Rather than being caused by oversight, this omission reflects some fundamental properties of the Java language.

All of the Java collections maintain their values in variables of type Object. The class Object does not define any ordering relation. Indeed, the only elements that can be compared using the < operator are the primitive numeric types (integer, long, double, and so on). One could imagine defining in class Object a method lessThan(Object), similar to the method equals(Object). However, while there is a clear default interpretation for the equality operator (namely, object identity), it is difficult to imagine a similar meaning for the relational operator that would be applicable to all objects. Certainly it could not provide a total ordering on all objects. What, for example, would be the result of comparing the String "abc" and the integer 37? In short, ordered collections are not found in the Java library because there is no obvious general mechanism to define what it means to order two values.

One could imagine that an alternative to placing the method lessThan in class Object would be to create an Ordered interface, such as the following:

```
interface Ordered {
    public boolean compare (Ordered arg);
    }
```

One could then create a collection in which all values need to implement the Ordered interface, rather than simply being Object. However, there are two major objections to this technique. The first is that since the argument is only known to be an object that implements the Ordered interface, one must still decide how to compare objects of different types (a Triangle and an Orange, for example). The second problem is that restricting the type of objects the collection can maintain to only those values that implement the Ordered relation severely limits the utility of the classes.

Another possibility is to imagine an interface for an object that is used to create comparisons. That is, the object takes both values as arguments, and returns their ordering. Such an interface could be written as follows:

```
interface ComparisonObject {
    public boolean Compare (Object one, Object two);
}
```

To manipulate an ordered collection, one would then create an implementation of this interface for the desired elements. The following, for example, would be a comparison class for Integer objects:

```
class IntegerComparison implements ComparisonObject {
    public boolean Compare (Object one, Object two) {
        if ((one instanceof Integer) && (two instanceof Integer)) {
            Integer ione = (Integer) one;
            Integer itwo = (Integer) two;
            return ione.intValue() < itwo.intValue();
        }
        return false;
    }
}
```

The following program illustrates how such an object could be used. The static method sort is an implementation of the insertion sort algorithm. The main method creates a vector of integer values, then creates a comparison object to be passed as argument to the sort algorithm. The sorting algorithm orders the elements in place, using the comparison object to determine the relative placement of values.

```
class VectorSort {
    public static void sort (Vector v, ComparisonObject test) {
            // order a vector using insertion sort
        int n = v.size();
        for (int top = 1; top < n; top++) {
            for (int j = top-1; j >= 0 &&
                test.Compare(v.elementAt(j+1), v.elementAt(j)); j--) {
                    // swap the elements
                Object temp = v.elementAt(j+1);
                v.setElementAt(v.elementAt(j), j+1);
```

```
                    v.setElementAt(temp, j);
                }
            }

        }

        public static void main (String [ ] args) {
            Vector v = new Vector( );
            Random r = new Random( );
            for (int i = 0; i < 10; i++)
                v.addElement(new Integer(r.nextInt( )));

                // sort the vector
            sort (v, new IntegerComparison( ));

            for (Enumeration e = v.elements( ); e.hasMoreElements( ); )
                System.out.println(e.nextElement( ));
        }
    }
```

19.9 BUILDING YOUR OWN CONTAINERS

Even though the containers in the Java library are flexible, they cannot handle
all situations in which a collection class is needed. It is therefore sometimes
necessary to create new collection classes. To see how this can be done we will
create a class that implements the idea of a linked list. The major advantage of
the linked list over a vector is that insertions or removals to the beginning or the
middle of a linked list can be performed very rapidly (technically, in constant
time). In the vector these operations require the movement of all the elements in
the collection and can therefore be much more costly if the collection is large.

The LinkedList class abstraction is shown in Figure 19.3.[3] The actual values
are stored in instances of class Link, which is a nested inner class. In addition to
a value, links maintain references to the previous and next element in the list. A
private internal value firstLink will reference the first link. A link with an empty
value is used to mark the end of the list. The private internal value lastLink points
to this value.

Values can be inserted either to the front or the back of the list. An enumeration value can also be used to insert new elements into the middle of a list.
The value is inserted immediately before the element referred to by the enumera-

---

[3] It would have been preferable to call this class List. However, as we noted in an earlier footnote, the
Java library already has a List class, which implements a graphical component used for selecting one string
item out of many alternatives.

```java
class LinkedList {
   private Link firstLink;
   private Link lastLink;
   private int  count = 0;

   public LinkedList ()
      { firstLink = lastLink = new Link(null, null, null); }

   private class Link { ... }

   private class ListEnumeration implements Enumeration { ... }

   public boolean isEmpty () { return firstLink == lastLink; }

   public int size () { return count; }

   public Object firstElement () { return firstLink.value; }

   public Object lastElement () { return lastLink.prev.value; }

   public void addFront (Object newValue) { firstLink.insert(newValue); }

   public void addBack (Object newValue) { lastLink.insert(newValue); }

   public void addElement (Enumeration e, Object newValue) {
      ListEnumeration le = (ListEnumeration) e;
      le.link.insert (newValue);
   }

   public Object removeFront () { return firstLink.remove(); }

   public Object removeBack () { return lastLink.prev.remove(); }

   public Object removeElement (Enumeration e) {
      ListEnumeration le = (ListEnumeration) e;
      return le.link.remove ();
   }

   public Enumeration elements () { return new ListEnumeration(); }
}
```

Figure 19.3   The LinkedList class.

```
class LinkedList {
    private class Link {
        public Object value;
        public Link next;
        public Link prev;

        public Link (Object v, Link n, Link p)
            { value = v; next = n; prev = p; }

        public void insert (Object newValue) {
            Link newNode = new Link (newValue, this, prev);
            count++;
            if (prev == null) firstLink = newNode;
            else prev.next = newNode;
            prev = newNode;
        }

        public Object remove () {
            if (next == null)
                return null; // cannot remove last element
            count--;
            next.prev = prev;
            if (prev == null) firstLink = next;
            else prev.next = next;
            return value;
        }
    }

    private class ListEnumeration implements Enumeration {
        public Link link = null;

        public boolean hasMoreElements () {
            if (link == null) link = firstLink;
            else link = link.next;
            return link.next != null; }

        public Object nextElement () { return link.value; }
    }
    .
    .
    .
}
```

Figure 19.4   The inner classes in LinkedList.

tion. All three methods make use of a common insertion routine provided by the inner class Link. This method is also used to maintain the count of the number of elements in the list. The classes Link and ListEnumeration are shown in Figure 19.4.

The class ListEnumeration implements the Enumeration protocol and is used for iterating over list elements. Note that the Enumeration protocol assumes that the methods hasMoreElements and nextElement will work in tandem and does not specify which of the two will actually advance the internal reference to the next element. Implementations of the Enumeration protocol use a variety of different schemes. This is why, for example, one should never invoke nextElement twice without an intervening call on hasMoreElements. In the LinkedList class, however, we assume that having examined the current value (the value yielded by nextElement) the programmer may wish to either insert a new value or remove the current value. Thus, in this case the task of advancing to the next value is given to the method hasMoreElements.

19.10 CHAPTER SUMMARY

In this chapter we have described the classes in the Java library that are used to hold collections of values. The simplest collection is the array. An array is a linear, indexed homogenous collection. A difficulty with the array is that the size of an array is fixed at the time the array is created. The Vector class overcomes this restriction, growing as necessary as new values are added to the collection. Vectors can be used to represent sets, queues, and lists of values. The Stack datatype is a specialization of the vector used when values are added and removed from the collection in a strict first-in, first-out fashion. A BitSet is a set of positive integer values. A Dictionary is an interface that describes a collection of key and value pairs. The HashTable is one possible implementation of the Dictionary interface.

The lack of any ordered collections is a reflection of the problem that there is, in general, no way to construct an ordering among all Java values.

The chapter concludes by showing how new collection classes can be created, using as an example a Linked List container.

STUDY QUESTIONS

1. What are collection classes used for?

2. Because the standard library collection classes maintain their values as an Object, what must be done to a value when it is removed from a collection?

3. What is a wrapper class?

4. What is an enumerator?

5. What is the protocol for the class Enumerator? How are these methods combined to form a loop?

6. How is the Java array different from arrays in other languages?

7. What does it mean to say that the Vector data type is expandable?

8. How does the use of the Stack data type differ from the use of a Vector as a stack?

9. What concept does the class BitSet represent?

10. What is the relationship between the classes Dictionary and Hashtable?

11. Why are there no ordered collections in the Java library?

EXERCISES

1. Assume two sets are implemented using vectors, as described in Section 19.4.4. Write a loop that will place the intersection of the two sets into a third set.

2. Assume two sets are implemented using vectors, as described in Section 19.4.4. Write a loop that will place the symmetric difference of the two sets into a third set. (The symmetric difference is the set of elements that are in one or the other set, but not both.)

3. Add the following methods to the LinkedList class described in Section 19.9:

setElement(Enumeration e, Object v)	Change value at given location
includes(Object v)	Test whether value is in collection
find(Object v)	Return enumeration if value is in collection, or null

4. Modify the LinkedList class of Section 19.9 so that linked lists support the cloneable interface. (The cloneable interface is described in Section 11.3.1.)

5. Write an OrderedList class. This class will be like a linked list, but will maintain a comparison object, as described in Section 19.8. Using this object, elements will be placed in sequence as they are inserted into the container.

20 Multiple Threads of Execution

Most users of a computer are familiar with the idea of *multitasking*. A user of a multitasking computer might be editing a spreadsheet, for example, at the same time the computer is printing a report or receiving a fax. The computer appears to be doing more than one activity at the same time. Whether this is actually true depends upon the hardware involved. Unless you are using a machine with multiple processors, in fact what is actually occurring is that the operating system is rapidly cycling between the different activities, allowing each to execute for a small amount of time.

Multithreading is the same concept applied to an individual program. Each program is giving the ability to execute a number of tasks at the same time. Each of these computational tasks is called a *thread*. Unlike separate computer applications, multiple threads exist in the same executing environment (technically speaking, we say they have the same *context*). This means they share the same data variables, access the same procedures, and so on. As with multithreading, this parallel behavior is usually just a charade; in fact the operating system is still executing only one thread at any one time and is cycling among all the different threads to give each an equal share.

20.1 CREATING THREADS

Recall the BallWorld application from Chapter 5 (Figure 5.2). This program created a bouncing ball, then moved the ball around on the window 2000 times before halting. You may recall that this is *all* the program did. It did not allow any sort of user interaction, and if you tried to stop the program before 2000 steps you could not.

In practice it is desirable to have programs that are more user friendly. Part of this is being able to interact with an application while it is running. One way to do this is to place the execution of the program in a separate thread, leaving the main program thread free to listen for user activity.

In Java, threads are created using the class Thread. There are two common ways that this class is used. One way is to subclass from Thread, and override the method run, which is the class that is executed to perform the task assigned to a thread. We could, for example, modify the BallWorld application (Figure 5.2) and create a bouncing ball thread as follows:

```java
public class ThreadedBallWorld extends Frame {
        .
        .
    private class BallThread extends Thread {
        public void run () {
            while (true) {
                aBall.move();
                if ((aBall.x() < 0) || (aBall.x() > FrameWidth))
                    aBall.setMotion (-aBall.xMotion(), aBall.yMotion());
                if ((aBall.y() < 0) || (aBall.y() > FrameHeight))
                    aBall.setMotion (aBall.xMotion(), -aBall.yMotion());
                repaint();
                try {
                    sleep(50);
                    } catch (InterruptedException e) { }
            }
        }
    }
        .
        .
}
```

When started, the thread continually moves the ball, changing the direction of motion when the sides of the window are hit. Each time the ball moves the window is repainted, and the thread "sleeps" for 50 milliseconds.

The revised ball world application is shown in Figure 20.1. In the constructor for the application ThreadedBallWorld a Ball is created, and then a BallThread is produced to control the movement of the ball. Execution of the new thread is initiated by the call to start for the thread object. To illustrate that the user can now interact with the application as the ball moves, we have added a mouse listener object. When the mouse is clicked in the application window, the ball is moved to the mouse location.

Platforms differ on how they assign time to threads. On some systems threads are run until they sleep or until they yield to another thread. On other systems threads are given a fixed amount of time to execute, then halted automatically if they have not yet given up control when their time unit is finished. In order to provide maximum portability, threads should either sleep occasionally (as is

```
public class ThreadedBallWorld extends Frame {

    public static void main (String [ ] args)
    { ThreadedBallWorld world = new ThreadedBallWorld (Color.red);
       world.show ( ); }

    private static final int FrameWidth = 600;
    private static final int FrameHeight = 400;
    private Ball aBall;
    private int counter = 0;

    private ThreadedBallWorld (Color ballColor) {
        // constructor for new ball world
           // resize our frame
        setSize (FrameWidth, FrameHeight);
        setTitle ("Ball World");
        addMouseListener (new BallListener( ));

           // initialize object data field
        aBall = new Ball (10, 15, 5);
        aBall.setColor (ballColor);
        aBall.setMotion (3.0, 6.0);
        Thread ballThread = new BallThread( );
        ballThread.start( );
    }

    private class BallThread extends Thread { ... }

    private class BallListener extends MouseAdapter {
        public void mousePressed (MouseEvent e)
           { aBall.moveTo(e.getX( ), e.getY( )); }
        }

    public void paint (Graphics g) { aBall.paint (g); }
}
```

Figure 20.1   BallWorld application using threads.

done here) or periodically invoke the method yield that is inherited from class Thread. Either of these actions will halt the current thread, allowing other threads a chance to perform their actions.

It is sometimes not convenient to create a thread class by subclassing from Thread. For example, it can happen that the thread class is already inheriting from some other class. Since in Java a class can not extend from two classes, the designers of the language have provided an alternative technique. Instead of inheriting from Thread, the action portion of a thread can be declared as implementing the interface Runable. The ball thread could be rewritten in this form as follows:

```
public class ThreadedBallWorld extends Frame {
    .
    .
    .
    private class BallThread implements Runable {
        public void run () {
            while (true) {
                aBall.move();
                if ((aBall.x() < 0) || (aBall.x() > FrameWidth))
                    aBall.setMotion (-aBall.xMotion(), aBall.yMotion());
                if ((aBall.y() < 0) || (aBall.y() > FrameHeight))
                    aBall.setMotion (aBall.xMotion(), -aBall.yMotion());
                repaint();
                try {
                    Thread.sleep(50);
                    } catch (InterruptedException e) { }
            }
        }
    }
    .
    .
    .
}
```

Note the format used for the call on sleep. Because the new class is not tied to Thread, the method sleep is not automatically inherited. Instead, the class name Thread must be explicitly provided in this case.

Starting a thread in this case involves creating two objects. The first is the instance of Runable, which describes the actions to be performed. The second is the Thread object, which understands how to schedule the actions for execution. The Runable object is passed as argument to the Thread, as in the following:

```
Thread ballThread = new Thread(new BallThread());
ballThread.start();
```

20.1.1 Synchronizing Threads

Two or more threads frequently need to share the same data fields. If two threads attempt to modify the same data area, it is possible for erroneous values to be produced. Assume we have two threads that share an integer data field, and assume that they each try to increment the value by 10. Internally an addition statement is divided into several separate steps. For example, the statement:

```
a = a + 10
```

is executed as something similar to the following:

```
push the value of a on a stack
push the value 10 on the stack
add the two values on the stack
pop the top of stack, assign value to a
```

Assume that this same sequence of instructions is performed by two threads, and the original value of a is 50. Assume further that the thread that is running the first process is stopped immediately after the first push instruction above. The first thread will push the value 50 on its stack, then stop temporarily. The second thread will push the value 50 on its stack, increment by 10, then store the resulting value of 60 on its stack. Suppose now the first thread is restarted. It will continue with its actions, pushing 10 on the stack, adding the two values, and assigning the sum, 60, back to a. The end result will be that the value a will ultimately hold 60, not the value 70 that it should have held.

Although it might seem that a problem such as this might be rare, the speed with which computers execute means that a situation such as that described here, if possible at all, is not at all uncommon. Such errors are also exceedingly difficult to uncover, since they occur in such a rare situation. Fortunately, the designers of Java have foreseen this and provided a simple and elegant solution. A method that is declared as synchronized cannot be executed by two processes at the same time. That is, if one thread is executing a synchronized method and a second thread tries to execute any other synchronized thread with the same object, the second thread will be halted until the first thread completes. The solution to the problem just described is therefore to place the increment operation inside a method that is declared as synchronized:

```
public synchronized void increment ( ) {
        // only one thread can execute this
        // at any time
    a = a + 10;
    }
```

We will illustrate the use of a synchronized method in the case study presented in Section 20.2. There are many more advanced features of threads; however, they are generally not needed in most programs and will not be described here.

20.2 CASE STUDY: A TETRIS GAME

An arcade game is a good illustration of the need for multiple threads of control. In a typical arcade game, the user is constantly entering information, and the game itself is constantly moving. In a conventional single-thread programming language, one or the other of these tasks must be selected as the primary structure. Either the main program is a large loop that listens for the user's commands and every now and then moves the game forward, or it is a large loop that moves the elements of the game and every now and then listens for the user's instructions. Either form will end up being clumsy and difficult to debug.

A much more elegant solution is possible in the language Java. Each of these two tasks can be assigned its own process. Each thread is executed in parallel with other threads. One thread is simply listening for the user's commands, while the other thread is charged with moving the pieces. (See Figure 20.2.)

Of course, there must be some sort of communication between the two threads, and this is where most of the complexity in multithreaded programming occurs. In the Tetris game presented here, the communication consists only of one integer value, which maintains the next command to be performed.

In addition to demonstrating multiple threads of control, the Tetris game presented in this section will illustrate how to read keyboard events, and an important technique for preventing flickering in graphical displays.

20.2.1 The Tetris Game Class

Tetris is a popular arcade game. Playing pieces of several different forms fall from the sky and can merge together when they reach the ground. The player can move a piece left or right or rotate a piece as it falls to the ground. The player scores by arranging pieces as they fall so as to form a completely filled row in the ground. Figure 20.3 shows a snapshot of a game in execution.

The primary class for the Tetris game is shown in Figure 20.4. As with all applications, execution begins with a static procedure named main. The main procedure creates an instance of the class Tetris, which is a type of Frame, and places this window on the display using the method show.

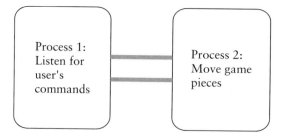

Figure 20.2 A double-thread program.

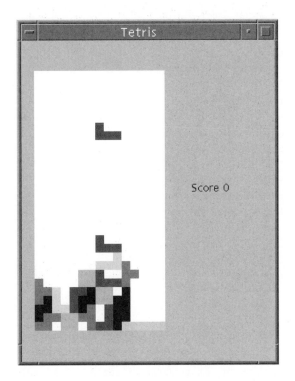

Figure 20.3   Application window for Tetris game.

The constructor for the Tetris class sizes the application window, gives it a name, adds a listener for key presses, then creates and starts the second process. The game playing process will be an instance of a second class, named PieceMover. We will examine the structure of this class shortly. Once created, the thread of execution that will play the game is initiated by the issuing of the command start.

Communication Between Threads

Communication between the two threads of control is accomplished via a single integer variable. This value represents the next command to be executed. This variable is both set and accessed by means of the procedure getcommand. Note that this procedure is declared as synchronized. This means that only one of the two threads can be executing the procedure at any one time. If the other process attempts to execute the procedure, it will be held up until the first process completes. (In truth, the synchronization here is largely unnecessary, since the only penalty for simultaneous access will be that one process may receive an out-of-date value. Nevertheless, the use of the synchronized designation also helps to document the interface between the two routines.)

```
class Tetris extends Frame {

    public static void main(String [ ] args)
       { Tetris world = new Tetris( ); world.show( ); }

       // data fields
    public static final int FrameWidth = 300;
    public static final int FrameHeight = 400;
    private GamePlay player;

    public Tetris ( ) {
       setSize (FrameWidth, FrameHeight);
       setTitle("Tetris");

       addKeyListener (new keyDown( ));
       player = new GamePlay(this);
       player.start( );
    }

       // interface point between two threads
    private int currentCommand = Piece.Down;

    public synchronized int getCommand(int nextCommand) {
       int oldCommand = currentCommand;
       currentCommand = nextCommand;
       return oldCommand;
       }

    private class keyDown extends KeyAdapter { ... }

    public void update (Graphics g)
       { player.paint(sg); }
}
```

Figure 20.4   The Controller class for the Tetris game.

Handing Keyboard Events

Keyboard events are handled in a fashion similar to the mouse click events we
have examined previously. A component maintains a collection of key listeners,
which must each implement the KeyListener interface:

```
interface KeyListener extends EventListener {
    public void keyTyped (KeyEvent e);
```

```
public void keyPressed (KeyEvent e);
public void keyReleased (KeyEvent e);
}
```

As with mouse presses, the programmer can elect to either treat a key press and the key release as independent events, or simply examine one event for both actions. Implementing the KeyListener interface requires defining a procedure for all three methods. As normally one is only interested in one of these, an adapter class, named KeyAdapter, is provided that implements a null procedure for each of the three functions. To create a listener one can inherit from this adapter and redefine the meaning of one of the methods. This is how key presses are handled in our application:

```
class Tetris extends Frame {
    .
    .
    .
    private class keyDown extends KeyAdapter {
        public void keyPressed (KeyEvent e) {
            char key = e.getKeyChar( );
            switch (key) {
                case 'g': player.newGame( ); break;
                case 'j': getCommand(Piece.Left); break;
                case 'k': getCommand(Piece.Rotate); break;
                case 'l': getCommand(Piece.Right); break;
                case 'q': System.exit(0);
            }
        }
    }
    .
    .
    .
}
```

Avoiding Flicker

As the game is being played, the screen is constantly being updated. This update process consists largely of drawing each individual square of the display. If this is done as separate graphical commands, the result can be an annoying flicker. There are several common ways to avoid this. Perhaps one of the easiest is the technique shown here. The method update( ) inherited from class Component normally first redraws the entire screen in the background color, then invokes paint to refresh the screen. If rather than overriding paint, one overrides update, then the redrawing in the background color is avoided.

One often confusing feature to note is that although the update procedure invokes the paint procedure in the class of the player object (namely, the class PieceMover), the resulting actions are not performed by the piece mover thread.

Updating the image is performed by the first thread, and is independent of the piece mover thread, which continues to run on its own.

20.2.2   *The* PieceMover *Thread*

The class PieceMover is shown in Figure 20.5. The fact that the class extends class Thread and the presence of the method named run indicate that this class can potentially be executed as an independent thread.

The constructor for the class will be executed when the instance of PieceMover is created, as in Figure 20.4. The constructor sets the values of local variables, including creating an array of colors for the playing area. The playing area will be 15 elements wide by 30 elements deep. Because we think of the playing area as a graphical object, it will be easier to describe this by placing the horizontal movement first and the vertical movement second.

The thread starting point is a procedure named run. This method will be executed when the thread is started. Note that the method the programmer writes is called run, while the method used to initiate the thread is called start (the call on start in this case appears in Figure 20.4). The start method performs some other actions, such as setting up a schedule for thread execution, before invoking run. In our simple example, the run method will simply repeatedly create and drop playing pieces.

As the playing pieces move, they will indicate the change by altering the colors stored in the color table. Thus, the paint method simply cycles through the table, displaying each color in a small rectangle.

```
public void paint (Graphics g) {
   for (int i = 0; i < 30; i++)
      for (int j = 0; j < 15; j++) {
         g.setColor(table[j][i]);
         g.fillRect(20+10*j, 350-10*i, 10, 10);
         }
   g.setColor (Color.blue);
   g.drawString("Score " + score, 200, 200);
}
```

The heart of the piece movement thread is the function dropPiece. This procedure creates a new piece, selecting the type of piece randomly from among the seven possibilities. If the piece cannot be moved downward once initially created at the top of the scene, the game is over, and the procedure returns false. Otherwise, a loop then reads the commands placed in the buffer shared with the controller, and acts on them, passing the command value to the individual piece for action. After every move the controller is asked to repaint, and control of the processor is yielded, allowing the other process time to execute. When control is returned, the piece movement process still sleeps for 100 milliseconds before reading the next command and moving once more.

```
class PieceMover extends Thread {

   private Tetris controller;
   private Color table[ ][ ];
   private Piece currentPiece;
   private int score = 0;

   public PieceMover (Tetris t) {
      controller = t;
      table = new Color[15][30];
      currentPiece = null;
      newGame( );
      }

      // thread starting point
   public void run ( )
      { while (dropPiece( )) { } }

      // other methods
   public void newGame ( ) {
      for (int i = 0; i  < 30; i++)
         for (int j = 0; j < 15; j++)
            table[j][i] = Color.white;
   }

   public void paint (Graphics g) { ... }

   public boolean dropPiece ( ) { ... }

   private void moveDown (int start) { ... }

   private void checkScore( )  { ... }
}
```

Figure 20.5   The PieceMover class.

```
   private boolean dropPiece ( )
   {
      int piecetype = 1 + (int) (7 * Math.random ( ));
      currentPiece = new Piece (piecetype);
      if (! currentPiece.move (Piece.Down, table))
         return false;
      int command = controller.getCommand (Piece.Down);
```

```
    while (currentPiece.move (command, table)) {
       controller.repaint ( );
       yield ( );
       try {
          sleep (100);
          } catch (InterruptedException e) { }
       command = controller.getCommand (Piece.Down);
       }
    // piece cannot move, check score
    checkScore( );
    return true;
}
```

The while loop terminates when the piece can no longer move. At this point the procedure checkScore is called to determine if any points have been scored. Points are scored by completely filling a row. If such a row is found, the controller is notified that a score has been made, and the entire image is moved downward.

```
private void checkScore( )
{
   for (int i = 0; i < 30; i++) {
      boolean scored = true;
      for (int j = 0; j < 15; j++)
         if (table[j][i] == Color.white)
            scored = false;
      if (scored) {
         score += 10;
         moveDown(i);
         i = i - 1; // check row again
         }
      }
}

private void moveDown (int start)
{
   for (int i = start; i < 30; i++)
      for (int j = 0; j < 15; j++)
         if (i < 29)
            table[j][i] = table[j][i+1];
         else
            table[j][i] = Color.white;
}
```

The procedure moveDown copies the colors from the row above into the current row, copying white values into the topmost row.

20.2.3 *The Game Piece Class*

An individual game piece is composed of a number of blocks. Each block is identified only by an x and y coordinate, maintained in a pair of parallel arrays. A piece also has its own color. The constructor for the class Piece (Figure 20.6) takes an integer that represents the piece type and initializes the locations appropriately. Only the initialization of the "S" shaped piece is shown; the others are all similar.

Other than the constructor, the only publicly accessible procedure for the game piece is the function named move. This function tries to move the piece according to the command given. The function returns false if the command is a move down and the piece cannot move, which indicates that no further actions are possible.

```
class Piece {
    .
    .
    .
    public boolean move (int command, Color [ ][ ] table)
    {
        erase(table);
        boolean canDoIt = false;
        switch (command) {
            case Down: canDoIt = testDown(table); break;
            case Right: canDoIt = testMoveRight(table); break;
            case Left: canDoIt = testMoveLeft(table); break;
            case Rotate: canDoIt = testRotate(table); break;
        }
        if (canDoIt)
            switch (command) {
                case Down: moveDown( ); break;
                case Right: moveRight( ); break;
                case Left: moveLeft( ); break;
                case Rotate: moveRotate( ); break;
            }
        draw(table);
        if (command == Down)
            return canDoIt;
        return true;
    }
}
```

```
class Piece {
        // data fields
    private int x[ ];
    private int y[ ];
    private Color color;
        // moves
    public static final int Down = 1;
    public static final int Left = 2;
    public static final int Rotate = 3;
    public static final int Right = 4;

        // constructor
    public Piece (int type)
    {
        switch(type) {
            case 1: // s shaped piece
                x = new int[4];
                y = new int[4];
                x[0] = 7; y[0] = 29;
                x[1] = 7; y[1] = 28;
                x[2] = 8; y[2] = 28;
                x[3] = 8; y[3] = 27;
                color = Color.green;
                break;
                .
                .
                .
        }
    }
    .
    .
    .
}
```

Figure 20.6 The class Piece.

Erasing and redrawing the piece are performed by transferring colors to the color table:

```
class Piece {
    .
    .
    .
    private void erase (Color [ ][ ] table)
    {
        for (int i = 0; i < x.length; i++)
            table[x[i]][y[i]] = Color.white;
    }
```

```
    private void draw (Color [ ][ ] table)
    {
       for (int i = 0; i < x.length; i++)
          table[x[i]][y[i]] = color;
    }
}
```

Before any command is performed, a test is conducted to see if the spaces the blocks will occupy subsequent to the command are open. The following demonstrates one of these routines; the others are similar. If the target locations are open, the corresponding move routine performs the actual transformation.

```
class Piece {
    .
    .
    .
    private boolean testPosition (int x, int y, Color[ ][ ] table)
    {
       if ((x < 0) || (x > 14))
          return false;
       if ((y < 0) || (y > 29))
          return false;
       if (table[x][y] != Color.white)
          return false;
       return true;
    }

    private boolean testDown (Color [ ][ ] table)
    {
       for (int i = 0; i < x.length; i++)
          if (! testPosition(x[i], y[i]-1, table))
             return false;
       return true;
    }

    private void moveDown ()
    {
       for (int i = 0; i < x.length; i++)
          y[i] = y[i] - 1;
    }
}
```

The only tricky procedure is the rotation. One square, the square at position 1, is designated the square around which rotation will be performed. The differences in coordinates from this square are computed, and the updated coordinates determined.

```
class Piece {
    .
    .
    .
    private boolean testRotate (Color [ ][ ] table)
    {
       for (int i = 0; i < x.length; i++) {
          int dx = x[i] - x[1];
          int dy = y[i] - y[1];
          int nx = x[1] + dy;
          int ny = y[1] - dx;
          if (! testPosition(nx, ny, table))
             return false;
       }
       return true;
    }
}
```

20.3   CHAPTER SUMMARY

Java programs can have several independent sequences of execution, or threads. Each is represented by a different instance of class Thread. Threads share a common execution environment and can communicate with each other through the use of shared data values. Problems involving simultaneous access to these data values can be avoided by declaring methods to be synchronized. Only one thread is permitted to be executing a synchronized method at any one time.

In this chapter we have illustrated the use of threads by describing the implementation of an arcade game, similar to the game of Tetris.

CROSS REFERENCES

The BallWorld case study appears originally in Chapter 5. Placing balls in their own thread of control is also shown in the pinball game application described in Chapter 7.

STUDY QUESTIONS

1. What is the difference between multitasking and multithreading?

2. Describe the two ways to create a new thread.

3. What are the two ways described in this chapter to temporarily halt the execution of a thread?

4. When used in a method heading, what does the keyword synchronized mean?

EXERCISES

1. Add a keyboard listener to the BallWorld application shown in Figure 20.1. When the user types the keys u or d, change the ball direction to move upward or downward, respectively. When the user types q quit the application.

2. Change the mouse down procedure so that when the user presses the mouse a new ball is created and set in motion. To do this you will need to create a collection of ball objects (see Chapter 5). Each new object should execute in its own separate thread.

3. The Tetris game can be made to "speed up" by reducing the amount of time the piece mover sleeps between commands. Change the code so that this time is reduced by 5 milliseconds for every 100 points the user scores.

4. Change the program so that instead of scoring 10 points for each filled row, the player gets additional points for multiple rows scored with the same piece. For example, a second row will get 20 points, a third row 30 points, and a fourth row 40 points.

5. Change the program to score 50 extra points if an entirely filled row is all one color.

21 Applets and Web Programming

As noted in Chapter 2, although Java is a general purpose programming language that can be used to create almost any type of computer program, much of the excitement surrounding Java has been generated by its employment as a language for creating programs intended for execution across the World Wide Web. Programs written for this purpose must follow certain conventions, and they differ slightly from programs designed to be executed directly on a computer, such as the ones we have developed up to now. In this chapter we will examine these differences and see how to create programs for the Web.

21.1 APPLETS AND HTML

Applications written for the World Wide Web are commonly referred to as *applets*. Applets are attached to documents distributed over the World Wide Web. These documents are written using the HyperText Markup Language (HTML) protocol. A Web browser that includes a Java processor will then automatically retrieve and execute the Java program. Two HTML tags are used to describe the applet as part of an HTML document. These are the <applet> tag and the <param> tag. A typical sequence of instructions would be the following:

```
<applet codebase="http://www.sun.com" code=Main width=300
     height=200>
<param name=name1 value="value1">
You do not have a Java enabled browser
</applet>
```

The <applet> tag indicates the address of the Java program. The codebase parameter gives the URL Web address where the Java program will be found, while the code parameter provides the name of the class. The height and width attributes tell the browser how much space to allocate to the applet.

Just as users can pass information into an application using command-line arguments, applets can have information passed into them using the <param> tags. Within an applet the values associated with parameters can be accessed using the method getParameter( ).

Any code other than a <param> tag between the beginning and end of the <applet> tag is displayed only if the program cannot be loaded. Such text can be used to provide the user with alternative information.

21.2 SECURITY ISSUES

Applets are designed to be loaded from a remote computer (the server) and then executed locally. Because most users will execute the applet without examining the code, the potential exists for malicious programmers to develop applets that would do significant damage, for example erasing a hard drive. For this reason, applets are much more restricted than applications in the type of operations they can perform.

1. Applets are not permitted to run any local executable program.

2. Applets cannot read or write to the local computer's file system.

3. Applets can only communicate with the server from which they originate. They are not allowed to communicate with any other host machine.

4. Applets can learn only a very restricted set of facts about the local computer. For example, applets can determine the name and version of the operating system, but not the user's name or e-mail address.

In addition, dialog windows that an applet creates are normally labeled with a special text, so the user knows they were created by a Java applet and are not part of the browser application.

21.3 APPLETS AND APPLICATIONS

All the applications created prior to this chapter that made use of graphical resources have been formed as subclasses of class Frame. This class provided the necessary underpinnings for creating and managing windows, graphical operations, events, and the other aspects of a standalone application.

A program that is intended to run on the Web has a slightly different structure. Rather than subclassing from Frame, such a program is subclassed from Applet. Just as Frame provides the structure necessary to run a program as an application, the class Applet provides the necessary structure and resources needed to run a program on the Web. The class Applet is a subclass of Panel (see Section 13.4) and thus inherits all the graphical component attributes of that class.

Rather than starting execution with a static function named main, as applications do, applets start execution at a function named init, which is defined in class Applet but can be overridden by users. The procedure init is one of four routines defined in Applet that is available for overriding by users. These four can be described as follows:

init( )   Invoked when an applet is first loaded; for example, when a Web page containing the applet is first encountered. This method should be used for one-time initialization. This is similar to the code that would normally be found in the constructor for an application.

start( )   Called to begin execution of the applet. Called again each time the Web page containing the applet is exposed. This can be used for further initialization or for restarting the applet when the page on which it appears is made visible after being covered.

stop( )   Called when a Web page containing an applet is hidden. Applets that do extensive calculations should halt themselves when the page on which they are located becomes covered, so as to not occupy system resources.

destroy( )   Called when the applet is about to be terminated. Should halt the application and free any resources being used.

For example, suppose a Web page containing an applet as well as several other links is loaded. The applet will first invoke init( ), then start( ). If the user clicks on one of the links, the Web page holding the applet is overwritten, but it is still available for the user to return to. The method stop( ) will be invoked to temporarily halt the applet. When the user returns to the Web page, the method start( ), but not init( ), will once again be executed. This can happen many times before the user finally exits altogether the page containing the applet, at which time the method exit( ) will be called.

Figure 21.1 shows portions of the painting application described in Section 18.6, now written as an applet rather than as an application. In place of the main procedure, the applet contains an init procedure. The init takes the place both of main and of the constructor for the application class. Other aspects of the applet are the same. Because an applet is a subclass of Panel, events are handled in exactly the same fashion as other graphical components. Similarly, an applet repaints the window in exactly the same fashion as an application. Because an applet is a panel, it is possible to embed components and construct a complex graphical interface (see Chapter 13). Note, however, that the default layout manager for an Applet is a flow layout rather than the border layout that is default to applications.

```
import java.applet.*;
import java.awt.*;
import java.awt.event.*;

public class PaintApplet extends Applet {

    private Image image = null;
    private Shape currentShape = null;

    public void init () {
            // change our layout manager
        setLayout(new BorderLayout());
            // create panel for buttons
        Panel p = new Panel();
        p.setLayout(new GridLayout(1,3));
        p.add(new Rectangle());
        p.add(new Oval());
        p.add(new Line());
        add("North", p);
        MouseKeeper k = new MouseKeeper();
        addMouseListener(k);
        addMouseMotionListener(k);
        }
    .
    .
    .
}
```

Figure 21.1   Painting program written as applet.

21.4   OBTAINING RESOURCES USING AN APPLET

The class applet provides a number of methods that can be used to load resources from the server machine. The method getImage(URL), for example, takes a URL and retrieves the image stored in the given location. The URL must specify a file in jpeg or gif format. The method getAudioClip(URL) similarly returns an audio object from the given location. The audioClip can subsequently be asked to play itself. A shorthand method play(URL) combines these two features.

The method getCodeBase() returns the URL for the codebase specified for the applet (see the earlier discussion on HTML tags). Since Java programs are often stored in the same location as associated documents, such as gif files, this can be useful in forming URL addresses for related resources.

The method getParameter() takes as argument a String, and returns the associated value (again, as a string) if the user provided a parameter of the given name using a <param> tag. A null value is returned if no such parameter was provided.

21.4.1   *Universal Resource Locators*

Resources, such as Java programs, gif files, or data files are specified using a universal resource locator, or URL. A URL consists of several parts, including a protocol, a host computer name, and a file name. The following example shows these parts:

http://www.mymachine.org/fileName.html

URLs can be created using the class URL. The address is formed using a string, or using a previous URL and a string. The latter form, for example, can be used to retrieve several files that reside in the same directory. The directory is first specified as a URL, then each file is specified as a URL with the file name added to the previous URL address. The constructor for the class URL will throw an exception called MalformedURLException if the associated object cannot be accessed across the Internet.

The class URL provides a method openStream, which returns an inputStream value (see Chapter 14). Once you have created a URL object, you can use this method to read from the URL using the normal InputStream methods. In this way, reading from a URL is as easy as reading from a file or any other type of input stream. The following program reads and displays the contents of a Web page. The URL for the Web page is taken from the command-line argument.

```java
import java.net.*;
import java.io.*;

class ReadURL {
   public static void main (String [ ] args) {
      try {
         URL address = new URL(args[0]);
         DataInputStream in =
            new DataInputStream(address.openStream( ));
         String line = in.readLine( );
         while (line != null) {
            System.out.println(line);
            line = in.readLine( );
            }
         in.close( );
         }
      catch (Exception e)
      { System.out.println("got exception " + e); }
      }
   }
```

If you run the program, you should see the HTML commands and textual content displayed for the Web page given as argument.

21.4.2 *Loading a New Web Page*

Applets used with Web browsers can instruct the browser to load a new page. This feature is frequently used to simulate links or buttons on a Web page, or to implement image maps. The method appletContext.showDocument(URL) takes a URL as argument, then instructs the Web browser to display the indicated page.

21.5 COMBINING APPLICATIONS AND APPLETS

The class Applet pays no attention to any static methods that may be contained within the class definition. We can use this fact to create a class that can be executed both as an applet and as an application. The key idea is that an Applet is a panel. We can nest within the applet class an inner class that creates the Frame necessary for an application. The only component of the window created for this frame will be the panel constructed by the applet. The main program, which is ignored by the applet, will when executed as an application create an instance of the applet. The applet can then create an instance of Frame for the application, placing itself in the center of the window. The constructor for the Frame executes the methods init() and start() required to initialize the applet. The following shows this technique applied to the painting applet described earlier:

```
import java.applet.*;
import java.awt.*;
import java.awt.event.*;

public class PaintApplet extends Applet {

        // executed for applications
        // ignored by applet class
    public static void main (String [ ] args) {
    Frame world = new PaintApplet( ).application( );
    world.show( );
    }

    private Frame application( )
       { return new AppletFrame (this); }

    private class AppletFrame extends Frame {
       public AppletFrame (Applet p) {
          setTitle("Paint Application");
          setSize (400, 300);
          p.init( ); p.start( );
          add("Center", p);
          }
```

```
      }

   . . . // remainder as before
}
```

Trace carefully the sequence of operations being performed here and the order in which objects are created. Since the Frame is nested within the Applet, it is only possible to create the frame (in the method application) after the applet has already been created.

21.6 CHAPTER SUMMARY

An *applet* is a Java application designed to be executed as part of a Web browser. Although much of the code for an applet is similar to that of an application, the two differ in some significant respects. Applets are created by subclassing from the class Applet, rather than from the class Frame. Applets begin execution with the procedure init, rather than main. Finally, applets can be halted and restarted, as the Web browser moves to a new page and returns.

Security over the Web is a major concern, and for this reason applets are restricted in the actions they can perform. For example, applets are not permitted to read or write files from the client system.

The chapter concludes by showing how it is possible to create a program that can be executed both as an application and as an applet.

EXERCISES

1. Convert the pinball game described in Chapter 7 to run as an applet, rather than as an application.

2. Convert the Tetris game described in Chapter 20 to run as an applet rather than as an application.

Glossary

abstract   A keyword applied to either a class or a method. When applied to a class, the keyword indicates that no instances of the class can be created, and the class is used only as a parent class for subclassing. When applied to a method within an abstract class, it indicates that the method must be overridden in subclasses before any instance of the subclass can be created.

abstract class   Syn. *deferred class, abstract superclass.* A class that has been declared using the abstract keyword. Classes can be declared to be abstract even if they do not contain any abstract methods.

abstract method   A method that has been declared using the abstract keyword. Abstract methods can only appear in classes that have themselves been declared abstract.

abstraction   A technique in problem solving in which details are grouped into a single common concept. This concept can then be viewed as a single entity and nonessential information ignored.

access specifier   A keyword (private, protected, or public) that controls access to data members and methods within user-defined classes.

accessor function   A function that is used to access the values of an instance variable. By restricting access through a function, the programmer can ensure that instance variables will be read but not modified. *See also* **mutator**.

ad hoc polymorphism   Syn. *overloading.* A procedure or method identifier that denotes more than one procedure.

agent   Syn. *object, instance.* A nontechnical term sometimes used to describe an object in order to emphasize its independence from other objects and the fact that it is providing a service to other objects.

argument signature   An internal encoding of a list of argument types; the argument signature is used to disambiguate overloaded function invocations, selecting the function body that matches most closely the signature of the function call. *See also* **parametric overloading**.

automatic storage management A policy in which the underlying run-time system is responsible for the detection and reclamation of memory values no longer accessible, and hence of no further use to the computation. *See also* **garbage collection**.

base class Syn. *ancestor type, superclass, parent class*. A class from which another class is derived.

binding The process by which a name or an expression is associated with an attribute such as a variable and the type of value the variable can hold.

binding time The time at which a binding takes place. *Early* or *static binding* generally refers to binding performed at compile time, whereas *late* or *dynamic binding* refers to binding performed at run time.

bytecode The assembly language for an imaginary Java *virtual machine*. So-called because most instructions can be encoded in a form that is one or two bytes in length.

cast A unary expression that converts a value from one type to another.

child class Syn. *subclass, derived class*. A class defined as an extension of another class, which is called the *parent class*.

class Syn. *object type*. An abstract description of the data and behavior of a collection of similar objects. The representatives of the collection are called *instances* of the class.

Class The class that maintains behavior related to class instance and subclass creation. *See also* **metaclass**.

class hierarchy A hierarchy formed by listing classes according to their class-subclass relationship. *See also* **hierarchy**.

client-side computing In a network environment, a program that is executed on the client side rather than on the server side of the network. The Java programming language is intended to perform client-side computing and so is more efficient than programs that must wait for execution on the (generally more overloaded) server machine.

cohesion The degree to which components of a single software system (such as members of a single class) are tied together. Contrast with *coupling*.

collaborator Two classes which depend upon each other for the execution of their behaviors are said to be collaborators.

collection classes Classes used as data structures that can contain a number of elements. Examples include Vector, Stack, Hashtable and arrays.

composition The technique of including user-defined object types as part of a newly defined object, as opposed to using inheritance.

constructor   A method used to create a new object. The constructor handles the dual tasks of allocating memory for the new object and ensuring that this memory is properly initialized. The programmer defines how this initialization is performed. In Java a constructor has the same name as the class in which it appears.

contravariance   A form of overriding in which an argument associated with a method in the child class is restricted to a less general category than the corresponding argument in the parent class. Contrast with *covariance*. Neither covariant nor contravariant overriding is common in object-oriented languages.

coupling   The degree to which separate software components are tied together. Contrast with *cohesion*.

covariance   A form of overriding in which an argument associated with a method in the child class is enlarged to a more general category than the corresponding argument in the parent class. Contrast with *contravariance*. Neither covariant nor contravariant overriding is common in object-oriented languages.

CRC card   An index card that documents the name, responsibilities, and collaborators for a class, used during the process of system analysis and design.

data hiding   An encapsulation technique that seeks to abstract away the implementation details concerning what data values are maintained for an object to provide a particular service.

data member   *See* **instance variable**.

deferred class   *See* **abstract class**.

derived class   Syn. *descendant type, subclass, child class*. A class that is defined as an extension or a subclass of another class, which is called the base class.

descendant type   Syn. *subclass, child class*. *See also* **derived class**.

early binding   *See* **binding time**.

encapsulation   The technique of hiding information within a structure, such as the hiding of instance data within a class.

event-driven execution   A style of programming where the program largely responds to user-generated events, such as a mouse click or a keypress.

exception   An unusual condition that prevents the normal sequence of instructions from going forward. An example would be attempting to use an uninitialized value (a null value) as the target of a message-passing expression.

exception handling   The portion of a Java program devoted to responding to the occurrence of an exception.

extends   A keyword used in forming a new class as a subclass of an existing class, or a new interface as an extension of an existing interface.

final   A keyword used in forming either a final class or a final method within a class.

final class   A class declared using the keyword final. This keyword indicates that the class cannot be used as a base class for inheritance.

final method   A method declared using the keyword final. This keyword indicates that the method cannot be overridden in subclasses.

finalizer   A method with the name finalize, no arguments, and no return type. This method will be invoked automatically by the run-time system prior to the object in which it is declared being recycled by garbage collection.

Frame   A class in the Java library that defines behavior common to all application windows.

framework   A collection of classes that together provide the behavior common to a large variety of applications. The programmer creates a new application by specializing and extending the behavior of the classes contained in the framework, thereby providing the solution to a specific problem.

function member   *See* **method**.

garbage collection   A memory-management technique whereby the run-time system determines which memory values are no longer necessary to the running program and automatically recovers and recycles the memory for different use.

has-a **relation**   The relation that asserts that instances of a class possess fields of a given type. *See is-a* **relation**.

hierarchy   An organizational structure with components ranked into levels of subordination according to some set of rules. In object-oriented programming the most common hierarchy is that formed by the class-subclass relationship.

immediate superclass   The closest parent class from which a class inherits. The superclass relationship is a transitive closure of the immediate superclass relationship.

immutable value   A value that is not permitted to change once it has been set. Variables that hold such values are sometimes called **single-assignment variables**. In Java immutable values can be identified via the keywords final and static.

implements   A keyword used to indicate that a class provides the behavior described by an **interface**.

information hiding   The principle that users of a software component (such as a class) need to know only the essential details of how to initialize and access the component, and do not need to know the details of the implementation. By reducing the degree of interconnectedness between separate elements of a software system, the principle of information hiding helps in the development of reliable software.

inheritance   The property of objects by which instances of a class can have access to data and method definitions contained in a previously defined class, without those definitions being restated. *See* **ancestor class**.

inheritance graph   An abstract structure that illustrates the inheritance relationships with a collection of classes.

inner class   A class definition that appears inside another class. Inner classes are allowed access to both the data fields and methods of the surrounding class. Inner classes are used frequently in building *listener* objects for handling events.

instance   Syn. **object**.

instance variable   An internal variable maintained by an instance. Instance variables represent the state of an object.

interaction diagram   A diagram that documents the sequence of messages that flow between objects participating in a scenario.

interface   A description of behavior. Classes that claim to implement the interface must provide the services described by the interface.

Internet   A world-wide collection of machines that have agreed to communicate with each other using a common protocol.

***is-a* relation**   The relation that asserts that instances of a subclass must be more specialized forms of the superclass. Thus, instances of a subclass can be used where quantities of the superclass type are required. *See **has-a** relation*.

interpreter   A computer program that simulates the actions of the imaginary Java **virtual machine**. The interpreter examines and executes the bytecode representation of a Java program.

iterator   A class that is used mainly to provide access to the values being held in another class, usually a container class. The iterator provides a uniform framework for accessing values, without compromising the encapsulation of the container.

JIT   *See* **just-in-time compiler**.

just-in-time (JIT) compiler   A technique immediately before a program is to execute, the device-independent bytecode representation of a Java program is converted into machine code for a specific platform. The machine code representation will often execute much faster than an interpreter running the bytecode representation.

late binding   *See* **binding time.**

listener   An object that waits for an event to occur, then executes certain actions to respond to the event.

message   Syn. *message selector, method designator, method selector, selector.* The textual string that identifies a requested action is a message-passing expression. During message passing, this string is used to find a matching method as part of the method-lookup process.

message passing   The process of locating and executing a method in response to a message. *See also* **method lookup.**

message selector   Syn. *method designator, method selector, selector.* The textual string that identifies a message in a message-passing expression. During message passing, this string is used to find a matching method as part of the method-lookup process.

method   A procedure or function associated with a class (or object type) and invoked in a message-passing style.

method declaration   The part of a class declaration specific to an individual method.

method designator   Syn. *message selector.* A method name identifier used as a procedure or function name in a message-passing expression. The method designator is used to search for the appropriate method during message sending. In general, you cannot determine from the program text which method a method designator will activate during execution.

method lookup   The process of locating a method matching a particular message, generally performed as part of the message-passing operation. Usually, the run-time system finds the method by examining the class hierarchy for the receiver of the message, searching from bottom to top until a method is found with the same name as the message.

method selector   *See* **message selector.**

mutator   A method that is used to modify the value of an instance variable. By requiring such modifications to be mediated through a function, a class can have greater control over how its internal state is being modified.

native method   A method that is implemented in another language, such as C or assembly language. *See also* **primitive.**

object   A value that can both maintain data fields and perform actions. The behavior of an object is characterized by the object *class*. *See also* **instance**.

object-oriented programming   A style of design that is centered around the delegation of responsibilities to independent interacting agents, and a style of programming characterized by the use of message passing and classes organized into one or more inheritance hierarchies.

overload   Used to describe an identifier that denotes more than one object. Procedures, functions, methods, and operators can all be overloaded. A method that is overridden can also be said to be overloaded. *See* **parametric overloading.**

override   The action that occurs when a method in a subclass with the same name as a method in a superclass takes precedence over the method in the superclass. Normally, during the process of binding a method to a message (see **message passing**), the overriding method will be the method selected.

paradigm   An illustrative model or example, which by extension provides a way of organizing information. The object-oriented paradigm emphasizes organization based on behaviors and responsibilities.

parametric overloading   Overloading of function names in which two or more procedure bodies are known by the same name in a given context, and are disambiguated by the type and number of parameters supplied with the procedure call. (Overloading of functions, methods, and operators can also occur.)

parent class   Syn. *superclass, ancestor class.* An immediate superclass of a class.

Parnas's principles   Principles that describe the proper use of modules, originally developed by the computer scientist David Parnas.

persistent object   An object that continues to exist outside of the execution time of programs that manipulate the object.

polymorphic   Literally, 'many shapes.' A feature of a variable that can take on values of several different types. The term is also used for a function name that denotes serveral different functions. *See* **pure polymorphism**.

polymorphic function   A function that has at least one argument that is a polymorphic variable.

polymorphic variable   A variable that can hold many different types of values. Object-oriented languages often restrict the types of values to being subclasses of the declared type of the variable.

primitive   An operation that cannot be performed in the programming language and must be accomplished with the aid of the underlying run-time system.

private method   A method that is not intended to be invoked from outside an object. More specifically, the receiver for the message that invokes a private method should always be the receiver for the method in which the invocation is taking place (see self). Contrast with *public method*.

procedure call   The transfer of control from the current point in execution to the code associated with a procedure. Procedure calling differs from **message passing** in that the selection of code to be transferred to is decided at compile time (or link time) rather than run time.

protocol   *See* **class description protocol.**

pseudo-variable   A variable that is never declared but can nevertheless be used within a method, although it cannot be directly modified (a pseudo-variable is therefore by definition read-only). The most common pseudo-variable is used to represent the receiver of a method. *See also* this *and* super.

public class   A class that is global and can be accessed from other packages. One public class may be declared in each compilation unit.

public method   A method that can be invoked at any time from outside an object.

pure polymorphism   A feature of a single function that can be executed by arguments of a variety of types. *See also* **ad hoc polymorphism.**

rapid prototyping   A style of software development in which less emphasis is placed on creation of a complete formal specification than on rapid construction of a prototype pilot system, with the understanding that users will experiment with the initial system and suggest modifications or changes, probably leading to a complete redevelopment of a subsequent system.

receiver   The object to which a message is sent. The receiver is the object to the left of the field qualifier (period). Within a method, the current receiver is indicated by the variable this.

redefinition   The process of changing an inherited operation to provide different or extended behavior.

refinement   A style of overriding in which the inherited code is merged with the code defined in the child class.

replacement   A style of overriding in which the inherited code is completely replaced by the code defined in the child class.

responsibility-driven design   A design technique that emphasizes the identification and division of responsibilities within a collection of independent agents.

scope   When applied to a variable identifier, the (textual) portion of a program in which references to the identifier denote the particular variable.

selector   *See* **message selector**.

shadowed name   A name that matches another name in a surrounding scope; the new name effectively makes the surrounding name inaccessible. An example is a local variable with the same name as that of a global or instance variable. Within the procedure, the local variable will be attached to all references of the name, making references to the surrounding name difficult. In Java access to such values can be provided by a fully qualified name.

single-assignment variable   A variable the value of which is assigned once and cannot be redefined. In Java single-assignment variables can be created using the keyword final.

static   A declaration modifier that, when applied to instances variables and functions, means that the variables and functions are shared by all instances of a class and exist even when no instances have yet been created.

static method   A method that is declared static. Since such functions exist even when no instances have been created, they can be invoked using the class name as receiver.

strongly typed language   A language in which the type of any expression can be determined at compile time.

subclass   Syn. *descendant type, derived class, child class.*

subclass coupling   The connection formed between a parent and child class. Subclass coupling is a very weak form of coupling, since instances of the subclass can be treated as though they were simply instances of the parent class. *See also* **coupling** *and* **cohesion**.

substitutability, principle of   The principle that asserts one should be able to substitute an instance of a child class in a situation where an instance of the parent class is expected. The principle is valid if the two classes are subtypes of each other, but not necessarily in general.

subtype   A type A is said to be a subtype of a type B if an instance of type A can be substituted for an instance of type B with no observable effect. For example, a sparse array class might be defined as a subtype of an array type. Subclasses need not be subtypes, nor must subtypes be subclasses.

super   When used inside a method, a synonym for *self*. However, when used as the receiver for a message, the search for an appropriate method will begin with the parent class of the class in which the current method is defined.

superclass   Syn. *ancestor class*, *base class*. A class from which another class inherits attributes.

this   When used inside a method, a reference to the receiver for the message that caused the method to be invoked.

virtual machine   An imaginary Java machine. Java programs are translated into assembly language instructions for this imaginary machine. To execute a Java program, an actual computer must simulate the working of the virtual machine.

void   A type name used to indicate a function returning no value—that is, a procedure.

World Wide Web   A collection of machines on the Internet that have agreed to distribute information according to a common protocol. This information is usually accessed with a *browser*.

yo-yo problem   Repeated movements up and down the class hierarchy that may be required when the execution of a particular method invocation is traced.

Bibliography

Actor Language Manual. 1987. Evanston, IL: The Whitewater Group, Inc.

Beck, Kent and Ward Cunningham. 1989. "A Laboratory for Teaching Object-Oriented Thinking." *Proceedings of the 1989 OOPSLA—Conference on Object-Oriented Programming Systems, Languages and Applications.* Reprinted in *Sigplan Notices* 24(10): 1–6.

Bellin, David and Susan Suchman Simone. 1997. *The CRC Card Book.* Reading, MA: Addison-Wesley.

Budd, Timothy A. 1997. *An Introduction to Object-Oriented Programming.* 2nd ed. Reading, MA: Addison-Wesley.

Cardelli, Luca and Peter Wegner. 1985. "On Understanding Types, Data Abstraction, and Polymorphism." *Computing Surveys* 17(4): 471–523.

Chan, Patrick and Rosanna Lee. 1996. *The Java Class Libraries: An Annotated Reference.* Reading, MA: Addison-Wesley.

Cox, Brad J. 1986. *Object Oriented Programming: An Evolutionary Approach*, Reading, MA: Addison-Wesley.

Cox, Brad J. 1990. "Planning the Software Industrial Revolution." *IEEE Software* 7(6): 25–35, November.

Dahl, Ole-Johan and Kristen Nygaard. 1966. "Simula, An Algol-Based Simulation Language." *Communications of the ACM* 9(9): 671-678, September.

Danforth, Scott and Chris Tomlinson. 1988. "Type Theories and Object-Oriented Programming." *ACM Computing Surveys* 20(1): 29–72.

Gabriel, Richard P. 1996. *Patterns of Software.* New York: Oxford University Press.

Gamma, Erich, Richard Helm, Ralph Johnson, and John Vlissides. 1995. *Design Patterns: Elements of Reusable Object-Oriented Software.* Reading, MA: Addison-Wesley.

Gosling, James, Bill Joy, and Guy Steele. 1996. *The Java Language Specification.* Reading, MA: Addison-Wesley.

Horowitz, Ellis. 1984. *Fundamentals of Programming Languages.* Rockville, MD: Computer Science Press.

Ingalls, Daniel H. H. 1981. "Design Principles Behind Smalltalk." *Byte* 6(8): 286–298.

Kay, Alan. 1977. "Microelectronics and the Personal Computer." *Scientific American.* 237(3): 230–244.

Kay, Alan C. 1993. "The Early History of Smalltalk." The Second ACM SIGPLAN History of Programming Languages Conference (HOPL-II), *ACM SIGPLAN Notices* 28(3): 69–75, March.

Keller, Daniel. 1990. "A Guide to Natural Naming." *Sigplan Notices* 25(5): 95–102, May.

Kim, Won, and Frederick H. Lochovsky (Eds.). 1989. *Object-Oriented Concepts, Databases, and Applications.* Reading, MA: Addison-Wesley.

Lindholm, Tim, and Frank Yellin. 1997. *The Java Virtual Machine Specification.* Reading, MA: Addison-Wesley.

MacLennan, Bruce. J. 1987. *Principles of Programming Languages.* New York: Holt, Rinehart & Winston.

Marcotty, Michael, and Henry Ledgard. 1987. *The World of Programming Languages.* New York: Springer-Verlag.

Meyer, Bertrand. 1988. *Object-Oriented Software Construction.* London: Prentice-Hall International.

Micallef, Josephine. 1988. "Encapsulation, Resuability and Extensibility in Object-Oriented Programming Languages." *Journal of Object-Oriented Programming Languages* 1(1): 12–35.

Milner, Robin, Mads Tofte, and Robert Harper. 1990. *The Definition of Standard ML.* Cambridge, MA: MIT Press.

Morehead, Albert H., and Geoffrey Mott-Smith. 1949. *The Complete Book of Solitaire and Patience Games.* New York: Grosset & Dunlap.

Nygaard, Kristen, and Ole-Johan Dahl. 1981. "The Development of the Simula Languages." In Richard L. Wexelblat (Ed.) *History of Programming Langauges.* New York: Academic Press.

Pinson, Lewis J., and Richard S. Wiener. 1988. *An Introduction to Object-Oriented Programming and Smalltalk.* Reading, MA: Addison-Wesley.

Sethi, Ravi. 1989. *Programming Languages: Concepts and Constructs.* Reading, MA: Addison-Wesley.

Stroustrup, Bjarne. 1982. "Classes: An Abstract Data Type Facility for the C Language." *ACM Sigplan Notices* 17(1):42–51, January.

Stroustrup, Bjarne. 1988. "What is 'Object-Oriented Programming?'" *IEEE Software* 5(3): 10–20, May.

Stroustrup, Bjarne. 1994. *The Design and Evolution of C++.* Reading, MA: Addison-Wesley.

Taenzer, David, Murthy Ganti, and Sunil Podar. 1989. "Object-Oriented Software Reuse: The Yoyo Problem." *Journal of Object-Oriented Programming* 2(3): 30–35.

Wegner, Peter. 1986. "Classification in Object-Oriented Systems." *Sigplan Notices* 21(10): 173–182, October.

Wikström, Åke. 1987. *Functional Programming Using Standard ML*. London: Prentice-Hall International.

Wirfs-Brock, Rebecca, and Brian Wilkerson. 1989. "Object-Oriented Design: A Responsibility-Driven Approach." *Proceedings of the 1989 OOPSLA—Conference on Object-Oriented Programming Systems, Languages and Applications*. Reprinted in *Sigplan Notices* 24(10): 71–76, October.

Wirfs-Brock, Rebecca, Brian Wilkerson, and Lauren Wiener. 1990. *Designing Object-Oriented Software*. Englewood Cliffs, NJ: Prentice-Hall.

Wulf, William A. 1972/1979. "A Case Against the GOTO." *Proceedings of the Twenty-Fifth National ACM Conference*. 1972; Reprinted in Edward Yourdon (Ed.). *Classics in Software Engineering*. Englewood Cliffs, NJ: Prentice-Hall.

Index